THE COMPLETE GUIDE TO
GREENER MEETINGS
AND EVENTS

The Wiley Event Management Series

Series Editor: Dr. Joe Goldblatt, CSEP

THE COMPLETE GUIDE TO
GREENER MEETINGS
AND EVENTS

Samuel deBlanc Goldblatt

FSC

WILEY

John Wiley & Sons, Inc.

Copyright © 2012 by John Wiley & Sons, Inc. All rights reserved.
Published by John Wiley & Sons, Inc., Hoboken, New Jersey.
Published simultaneously in Canada.

All photos not explicitly credited are courtesy of Louise E. Knowles.

This book was printed and bound by Malloy, a Zero Landfill company committed to recycling over 99% of its discarded solid waste. Malloy is also committed to using papers made under the standards of either the Forest Stewardship Council (FSC) or the Sustainable Forestry Initiative (SFI), and Malloy maintains chain-of-custody certification for both FSC and SFI. FSC and SFI are dedicated to ensuring the use of forest management practices that are sustainable and do not deplete the natural resources in our forests, including the protection of endangered species, wildlife, soil quality, and water quality. The papers used in this book are certified by FSC. This book's binders boards are made from 85% pre-consumer recycled fiber, and its inks contain soy content.

Evaluation copies are provided to qualified academics and professionals for review purposes only, for use in their courses during the next academic year. These copies are licensed and may not be sold or transferred to a third party. Upon completion of the review period, please return the evaluation copy to Wiley. Return instructions and a free of charge shipping label are available at www.wiley.com/go/returnlabel. Outside of the United States, please contact your local representative.

For general information on our other products and services, or technical support, please contact our Customer Care Department within the United States at 800-762-2974, outside the United States at 317-572-3993 or fax 317-572-4002.

Wiley also publishes its books in a variety of electronic formats. Some content that appears in print may not be available in electronic books. For more information about Wiley products, visit our Web site at www.wiley.com.

Library of Congress Cataloging-in-Publication Data
Goldblatt, Samuel deBlanc.
  The complete guide to greener meetings and events / Samuel deBlanc Goldblatt.
    p. cm.
  Includes bibliographical references and index.
  ISBN 978-0-470-64010-4 (cloth)
  1. Special events—Planning—Environmental aspects. 2. Green products. 3. Social responsibility of business. I. Title.
  GT3405.G653 2012
  394.2—dc22

                                                            2011010946

Printed in the United States of America

10 9 8 7 6 5 4 3 2 1

CONTENTS

FOREWORD

▇ Why Meetings Matter

The meetings and events industry is a fascinating and vibrant field of study. On the surface, it is the study of logistics, production, hospitality, and customer service, but dig deeper, and you'll find it is so much more. I believe meetings and events reflect the essence of the human experience. So, why do we spend time, energy, and resources to bring a group of people together? Being able to effectively answer this question is the basis of greener meetings.

Whether it is the business need to learn something new, or the desire for social connection, we meet because it is how we as humans get things done in a complex and globally dynamic society. Technology supports our efforts, and virtual meetings are a part of the ever-evolving dialogue. Yet, the compelling necessity to connect with others face to face still exists, as we meet to share ideas, explore solutions, and just be in the same collective space and moment with others; for me, preferably over a locally sourced meal paired with a glass of organically-grown pinot noir for the purpose of making a difference.

What originally attracted me to green meetings (no, not just the organic pinot noir) was being able to witness the power of people in this industry to change and be changed by the deeper purpose of meetings—engagement with people, communities, and natural systems. The more we understand about the economic, environmental, and social impacts of events, the more we want to give back and leave legacies in local host communities. The more we connect with the purpose of our event, the greater desire we have to maximize the onsite experience through innovative learning design. And, the more we understand about the interconnected systems of sustainability and its relationship to events, the better we are able to manage our impact flows and engage our stakeholders to ensure the responsible execution of that event.

The Green Meeting Industry Council (GMIC)—formed in 2003 in my hometown of Portland, OR, USA—is a nonprofit professional organization focusing on sustainability in the global meetings and events industry. In the early years of GMIC's formation, our industry considered green as requiring more work, being more expensive, and having less qualitative value. Fortunately, Amy Spatrisano and Nancy (Wilson) Zavada of MeetGreen, the founders of GMIC, championed the sustainability movement once their outreach to a small group of passionate professionals evolved into a global organization.

What we lacked in the earlier years was a compelling message to engage the naysayers. More than an either-or debate about the economic and environmental aspects of greening the industry, the conversation was about rethinking how we do business and the ethical values that guide our business. By veering the conversation away from greening as a choice, and toward it being just good business practice, the transformation occurred—people saw the need to do the right thing because it was the right thing.

What has since been growing in the last few years is the promotion of global awareness of the importance of sustainable meetings and events through innovation and learning design, as evidenced by Sam Goldblatt's ***The Complete Guide to Greener Meetings and Events***. Through analyzing and solving sustainable event case studies—one of the elements of learning design to boost engagement—the practice of sustainability becomes complex, dynamic, highly relevant, and critical to the business value of our industry. Presenting sustainability issues through innovative formats and design allows for an evolved conversation about grave issues without getting too depressed. Rather, the conversation becomes proactive, a "yes and" conversation rather than a "no but," allowing us to unlock, get excited about, and become creative with our dialogue of the issue.

To create a sustainable future, the industry as a whole must understand green as an integral, value-added aspect of meeting planning. It is the collective power of the industry movement towards adopting sustainable practices that will cause a ripple effect of transformative change to take place. We are not there yet, but we are getting closer thanks to increased awareness, industry standards, great case studies, and books such as ***The Complete Guide to Greener Meetings and Events*** to educate the future of this industry.

Thank you to Sam Goldblatt for pulling together the research and the many dynamic case studies of leading professionals that are modeling how sustainability works in meetings. In elevating the conversation of green meetings from the points of view of innovation, conservation, and education, ***The Complete Guide to Greener Meetings and Events*** carries through the message of greener meetings as "superior experiences through sustainable strategies"—a definition I wholeheartedly agree with.

For the future of this industry, I hope that we can keep in mind that what we love is to bring people together for a purpose to create life-changing experiences. Let's do this in a responsible and forever-engaging manner. Enjoy the learnings in this text, take them seriously, but also remember to unlock from previous patterns, innovate, experiment, engage, and have fun.

TAMARA L. KENNEDY-HILL, CMP
Executive Director
Green Meeting Industry Council

SERIES EDITOR FOREWORD

The World English Dictionary defines the term *environment* as originating from the French word *in vairnment,* which means "external conditions or surroundings, especially those in which people live or work." However, thanks to ***The Complete Guide to Greener Meetings and Events,*** by Sam Goldblatt, the term *environment* as applied to meetings and events has been given even deeper and more profound implications and meanings. Sam has, in fact, expanded our understanding and appreciation of the term in the context of greener meetings and events, and in so doing, has also redefined our industry.

Many years ago, I hosted a conference at the Biosphere in Oracle, Arizona. The Biosphere is an environmental laboratory initially funded by the Bass family of Texas. In the past three decades, it has evolved from a replication of the original biosphere, to a Columbia University research and teaching facility, to a tourism attraction, and finally, to a housing development. However, when I held my conference there in 1998, it was still very much a scientific laboratory.

The 25 persons who joined me for this exploration of the future of special events were all international leaders in the events and meeting industry. They agreed to devote a weekend to exploring future forces and trends and to producing a green paper that would define their aspirations and ambitions for the future of our industry. At the initiation of the conference, we polled them to identify their baseline interests, and the majority stated that economic forces and trends were paramount to the survival of their industry.

However, just two days later, after meeting and discussing with Biospherian scientists and green hospitality industry leaders such as Tedd Saunders, whose family at the time owned the Boston Park Plaza Hotel, a best-practice property for green hospitality, the delegates' focus dramatically shifted to environmental forces and trends. With just a little bit of knowledge and some intense discussion, these 25 leaders reached a strong, unified conclusion that the environmental future of the meetings and events industry took precedent over all other aims and objectives.

Perhaps these men and women were influenced by the Biospherians themselves. During one discussion, I asked one of the scientists how they managed to survive for nearly one year inside the closed environment of the biosphere. One of the female scientists quietly but firmly answered my question by stating, "Science helped us survive, but our meetings, events, and celebrations helped us live."

She went on to state that the scientists looked forward with great pleasure to their regular discussions, celebrations of birthdays, national holidays, the life-cycle events of the biosphere, such as the birth of a new plant or animal, and other iconic symbols of life in all its normalcy and continuity.

Similar to the Biosphere conference, *The Complete Guide to Greener Meetings and Events,* by Sam Goldblatt marks the beginning of a new era for meetings and events. It is the first book of its type to provide strong, scientific evidence, combined with a common-sense approach to creating a sustainable future for meetings and events. Throughout these pages you will find hundreds of examples of how to research, design, plan, coordinate, and evaluate greener meetings and events that will help you grow your business in the future.

More importantly, Sam has interviewed many of the luminaries in the international meetings and events industry to identify the best practices of today and tomorrow to share with you, the reader. This in-depth and practical approach to sustainable development of the meetings and events industry is similar to the seminal work of the United Nations many years ago.

Dr. Gro Harlem Brundtland of Norway chaired the 1983 United Nations World Commission on Environment and Development that historically has been referred to as the Brundtland Commission. The Brundtland Commission drafted the iconic language that served as the catalyst for the Rio Earth Summit in 1992, and later, for Agenda 21. The commission defined *sustainable development:* "Sustainable development is development that meets the needs of the present without compromising the ability of future generations to meet their own needs."

Sam Goldblatt's pioneering work in arguably one of the most important industries in the world is similar to that of Dr. Brundtland and her colleagues in that he has redefined the future mission of meetings and events in an effort to promote sustainability for many generations to come. Many would agree that meetings and events are among the most likely candidates to expand the carbon footprint due to their reliance on travel. Goldblatt recognizes this challenge, but redefines it as an opportunity for creative problem solving through reuse, conservation of resources, waste management, and environmental improvement.

Just as the leaders at the Biosphere recognized the powerful importance of the natural environment in sustaining the future development of meetings and events, thanks to Sam Goldblatt, you now have a similar opportunity. Within these pages you will find not only the tools and techniques to produce greener meetings and events, but also the inspiration to inform and educate others throughout the world. Sam has not just written a book. He has, just as Dr. Brundtland, created a paradigm shift—in fact, a new movement—toward a world in which greener meetings and events are no longer the exception but the norm for doing business. For this, today's and tomorrow's meetings and event planners should be most grateful.

Professor Joe Goldblatt, FRSA
Series Editor
Wiley Event Management Series

PREFACE

On a warm September night in Edinburgh, Scotland, my new home, I found myself pedaling a bicycle while watching a film. I normally wouldn't recommend watching a film while driving, but in this instance, the bicycle was stationary, planted in front of an outdoor cinema screen. Also, I had to keep pedaling, because the bicycle was actually powering the movie.

I was attending a screening of *Mia and the Magoo*, a French children's film with a powerful environmental message, as part of Edinburgh's Take One Action Film Festival (www.takeoneaction.org.uk). The Edinburgh Woodcraft Folk (www.edinburgh-powerpod.org), an organization promoting environmental learning for children, had brought along its latest project, Guerilla Cinema (www.spanthatworld.com/guerilla-cinema). Consisting of two retrofitted stationary bicycles, each connected to a motor, a battery to store the pedal energy, a digital projector, and cinema screen, Guerilla Cinema allows viewers to create electricity for watching a movie completely from their own pedal power.

On this particular evening, over 50 viewers took turns powering the film, which was screened on the patio of the Royal Botanical Gardens of Edinburgh's (www.rbge.org.uk) new building, a state-of-the-art, sustainable venue that hosts greener meetings and events throughout the year. As I pedaled away under the stars while families enjoyed the uplifting film, I reflected on the wonders of sustainability.

When I first arrived at Queen Margaret University (QMU) (www.qmu.ac.uk) to undertake my postgraduate research into greener events, I was astounded by the new sustainable campus, which featured a vast sunroof, solar reflectors, and smart lighting and heating considerations. A central bike station and free shower facilities encouraged me and many other students and faculty to cycle to campus every day. Eco-conscious students at QMU later produced a Green Fashion Event, which featured amazing environmentally friendly clothes made from reused materials.

The Edinburgh International Conference and Convention Centre (EICC) (www.eicc.co.uk) continues to impress me with a growing commitment to sustainable practice. Local startup company Vegware (www.vegware.co.uk) is now expanding internationally with its highly successful, fully compostable cups and food containers made from bioplastic plant matter. Outside Edinburgh, the Kingdom of Fife hosts The Big Tent (www.thebigtentfestival.co.uk), an environmental music festival that features outstanding local cuisine, organic beer, and energy-efficient LED lighting.

If there was ever any doubt that I had found the perfect place to study greener events, that was put to rest when, on January 13, I was invited by VisitScotland (www.visitscotland.com) to an event called Living the Legacy: Sustainable Tourism for Scotland. Held at the majestic Stirling Castle (www.stirlingcastle.gov.uk), this formal reception celebrated a new program of sustainable advice, investment, and accreditation for Scotland's tourist, festival, and events businesses. The event, attended by tourism and event professionals from across Scotland, capped a year-long program of educational workshops and outreach, which was funded by the Scottish government and the European Union. (www.visitscotland.org/business_support/sustainable_tourism.aspx).

As I tasted the organic Scottish hors d'ouevres, mingled with attendees who ranged from organic farmers to managers of green hotels, and listened to experts map out plans for the future of greener events in Scotland, it made me proud to live in a country where sustainability is a core value.

Scotland's venues, vendors, and events are leading the way for sustainable event management, and it is this commitment to sustainability and history of world-class events that lured me here from my work as an arts and events producer in Washington, DC. In DC I served as environmental officer at the Capital Fringe Festival (www.capitalfringe.org), creating a comprehensive sustainability program and marketing campaign that included theater venues constructed from reused building materials and public transportation promotion. My work in DC and in Edinburgh, where I currently serve as Edinburgh producer of the 48 Hour Film Project (www.48hourfilm.com), has inspired this book.

Just one of the inspirations for this book lies in the words and wisdom of over 50 professionals in the meetings and events industries who I interviewed between 2008 and 2010. Kimberly Lewis, vice president of events for the U.S. Green Building Council (USGBC) (www.usgbc.org), phoned me from her office in Washington, DC, to tell me about the extensive sustainability program at Greenbuild, USGBC's annual convention. Frank Supovitz, vice president of events for the National Football League (NFL) (www.nfl.com), e-mailed me information on Super Bowl sustainability from Hawaii, where he was visiting an NFL youth center that uses solar power. Eve McArthur, director of operations at South by Southwest (SXSW) (www.sxsw.com), showed me pictures of the Solar Pump, a solar energy charging station, over burritos in Austin, Texas.

These professionals have embraced the principles of sustainable, environmental, and social responsibility—not as trends, but as integral parts of their work. In producing outstanding greener meetings and events, they discovered something that I discovered on that September night as I was pedaling a bicycle in the Botanics to power a film:

Sustainable events produce superior experiences.

This is the fundamental message of ***The Complete Guide to Greener Meetings and Events.*** Although there are many reasons to incorporate sustainable practices into meetings and events, including saving on costs and resources, protecting the environment, improving social issues, doing business more efficiently and effectively, and attracting new audiences, the number one reason to go green is to do business better.

From Australia's Melbourne Convention and Exhibition Centre (www.mcec.com.au/) to San Francisco's Moscone Center (www.moscone.com), Washington, DC's Capital Fringe Festival to the Edinburgh Festival Fringe (www.edfringe.com), from the NFL Super Bowl (www.superbowl.com) to the London 2012 Olympics (www.london2012.com), sustainable practices are producing fantastic new experiences for attendees of meetings and events.

About This Book

Researching this book has taken me around the world, and now it will take you around the world, too, as you learn about the best practices in sustainable meeting and event management in the United States, United Kingdom, Canada, Australia, Europe, and beyond. The book is divided into three parts, which reflect defining principles of greener meetings and events: *innovation, conservation,* and *education.*

■ Organization

Part One, *Innovation,* begins with an *Introduction to Sustainability* in Chapter 1, showing the forces that have shaped greener meetings and events and greener trends in the hospitality, tourism, meetings, conventions and events industries. Chapter 2 describes event pollution, while Chapters 3 and 4 guide you through a sustainable event plan and provide useful tools for planning, implementing, and measuring sustainable practices strategically.

Part Two, *Conservation,* explains the major topics of greener meeting and event management, including transportation, waste management, energy, and water usage. This section also explores outstanding new developments in sustainable cuisine and decor, as well as greener hotels, convention centers, venues, and vendors that are leading the industry forward.

Part Three, *Education,* shows how meetings and events can support social issues through social sustainability and corporate social responsibility (CSR). Chapter 11 guides you through a complete marketing plan for greener meetings and events, and Chapter 12 closes with inspirational and practical advice from professionals in the field.

■ Learning Aids

At the end of each chapter, you will find a *summary, definitions of key terms, suggested further reading* or *viewing* (Renewable Resources) and an *activity* called "Blue Sky

Thinking," which will help you put your learning into practice. Defined as open-minded and imaginative brainstorming, *blue sky thinking* is your chance to think outside the box. Be creative and find innovative solutions to the challenges that greener meeting and event professionals face every day.

In the Appendices, you'll find not only *references, sample menus, contracts,* and *strategic planning documents* but also *contact information* for important organizations and associations.

Web sites of model greener meetings and events are provided throughout the book. I encourage you to reach out and contact these organizations in your research and career development.

■ Instructor Resources

An **Instructor's Manual** has been developed to help instructors effectively manage their time and to enhance student learning opportunities. The **Instructor's Manual** includes:

> *Learning Objectives* for each chapter
> *Opening Activities* for classroom engagement and discussion
> A summary of *Chapter Key Points* to *Explore*
> *Case Studies* and their suggested answers and talking points pertaining to key chapter topics
> A *Lightning Round* activity to test students on chapter key terms
> Suggested *Homework* assignments
> A *Test Bank* including exam questions and answers

The **Test Bank** has been specifically formatted for Respondus, an easy-to-use software program for creating and managing exams that can be printed to paper or published directly to Blackboard, WebCT, Desire2Learn, eCollege, ANGEL, and other eLearning systems. Instructors who adopt **The Complete Guide to Greener Meetings and Events** can download the **Test Bank** for free. Additional Wiley resources also can be uploaded into your LMS course at no charge.

A password-protected Wiley Instructor Book Companion Web site devoted entirely to this book (www.wiley.com/college/goldblatt) provides access to the **Instructor's Manual** and the text-specific teaching resources. The **Respondus Test Bank** as well as **PowerPoint** lecture slides are also available on the Web site for download.

■ To the Reader

This book broadly explores sustainable management in the hospitality, tourism, conference and exhibition, and meeting and event industries, as well as countless smaller industries that include catering, arts and music festivals, and tour operators. Readers who are studying in, working in, or even just interested in these industries will reap innumerable benefits from the exciting journey ahead of them in **The Complete Guide to Greener Meetings and Events**.

For student readers: Achieve a greater understanding of the modern special events industry, learn how to implement sustainable practices, and acquire useful tools for career development.

For professionals in this exciting industry: Acquire strategic planning tools and inside information on sustainable events to expand your skill sets and give you a competitive advantage in today's marketplace.

For all readers: Experience a rollicking trip around the world as you explore the innovative festivals, events, and conferences that are showing greater environmental and social responsibility through sustainable practices.

Enjoy, engage, and interact with this book, and you will take away valuable skills and knowledge to use in your studies, your work, and your daily life. This book delivers hundreds of practical outcomes, teaching you how to do the following:

- Create a strategic green plan
- Measure your carbon footprint
- Implement a recycling program
- Source renewable energy
- Create delicious sustainable menus
- Make a venue accessible to persons in wheelchairs
- Save money with energy-efficient products
- Write a carbon-free blog
- Use web-based social media to attract new audiences

The Complete Guide to Greener Meetings and Events is also available for purchase as an e-book (www.wiley.com/college/goldblatt). Additionally, there are two ways in which you can directly interact with the book:

1. Visit the *Greener Meetings and Events* blog for exclusive content at greenerevents.wordpress.com.
2. E-mail feedback for future editions at GreenerEvent@gmail.com.

Contact myself or the leaders profiled in this book to progress your journey in sustainable events. We are depending on innovative and enthusiastic greener meeting and event pioneers like you to lead the hospitality, tourism, conference, festival, and event industries forward. Don't just read—engage with this book. The future of greener meetings and events is in your hands.

SAM GOLDBLATT, MA
Edinburgh, Scotland

ACKNOWLEDGMENTS

This book would not be possible without the support of several key people. Mary Cassells, Jenni Lee, and all the good people at John Wiley & Sons have done a tremendous job publishing this material. Thanks also to everyone who reviewed drafts and provided guidance.

Several eco-warriors at the Capital Fringe Festival inspired this book: the staff who built a gypsy cabaret bar from reused doors, the artists who performed in disused buildings, and the audiences who sat on recovered church pews. Zoia Wiseman managed a huge repurposing operation, which included the creation of sandbags from reused burlap. Thanks also to the Board of Trustees for believing in us.

VisitScotland and EventScotland provide the education and resources that continue to make Scotland a world leader in greener meetings and events. Thank you Philip Riddle, Malcolm Roughead, Paul Bush, Leon Thomson, and the entire team.

Great respect to everyone who makes Edinburgh a creative city of ideas, including all the staff of the Edinburgh International Festival, the Edinburgh Festival Fringe, the Edinburgh International Book Festival, the Edinburgh Jazz and Blues Festival, and Edinburgh's Hogmanay. Thanks to Andrew Dixon and Creative Scotland, to Festivals Edinburgh and the Edinburgh City Council. Thanks also to the staff, audiences, and trustees of Edinburgh's Festival City Theatres Trust for their support.

Mark Ruppert, Liz Langston, Christina Ruppert, and Ben Guaraldi do one heck of a job running the 48 Hour Film Project, the world's largest timed film project. Thanks to all the filmmakers who participate in the Edinburgh chapter, and thanks to the audiences, sponsors, and supporters, including Jo Blair of City Screens Ltd, Ian Hoey, and Paul Munro.

Thanks to the staff, actors, audiences, and Trustees of the Shakespeare Theatre Company, one of the world's greatest classical theatre companies and now an international performing arts presenter. Thanks to Nick Goldsborough for his mentorship, and also to Michael Kahn, Chris Jennings, Ed Zakreski, Steven Mazzola, Charles Phaneuf, Dan VanHoozer, Danielle Gordon, Jo Coutts, and the rest of the team.

I am indebted to Douglas Brown, Rachel Blanche, James Waters, and the entire staff of Queen Margaret University's Arts Management Programme, for their support of my master of arts dissertation, which formed the initial research for this book. In addition to all of my wonderful colleagues on the 2008–2009 course, Laura Stevenson, Lynne Russell, Trevor Laffin, and the entire staff of QMU made the journey so special. Through its commitment to lifelong learning and sustainability, QMU remains a pioneering leader in higher education and continues to produce some of the most outstanding students of hospitality, tourism, arts, and event management. I am one of them!

The exceptional staff and students of St. Edward's University in Austin, Texas, provide outstanding support to greener events as part of the International Festival Experience Study Tour (I-FEST), which annually gives students an opportunity to participate in the Edinburgh Festivals. President Martin, Tom Evans, Sheila Gordon, Innes Mitchell, and Erin Ray are inspirations. Go Hilltoppers!

The faculty of The George Washington University, both in the Department of Theatre and Dance and the Department of Tourism and Hospitality Management, annually inspire students and professionals alike to develop their careers in arts and events management. Thank you Maida Withers, Nate Garner, Alan Wade, and Carl Gudenius.

The Communication Arts Program at Montgomery Blair High School instilled in me a lifelong love of reading and writing, and the Humanities Magnet Program at Eastern Middle School set me on my path.

Great respect to the staff and students of Johnson & Wales University, the Australian Centre for Event Management, Temple University, University of Nevada, Las Vegas, Leeds Metropolitan University, and Edinburgh Napier University.

This book is published with great respect for those outstanding universities and places of learning around the world that teach hospitality, tourism, conference and event management, and arts administration, and especially those that include sustainability in the curriculum. Through your commitment to educational excellence and professional development, you are producing tomorrow's greener event pioneers.

I want to thank all of the hard-working professionals in the hospitality, tourism, festival, meeting, and event industries, especially those considering sustainability in their work. I am grateful to the following greener meeting and event leaders from around the world who share their stories, knowledge, and experiences in this book:

Greener Meeting and Event Leaders

- Richard Aaron, CMP, CSEP, president, BizBash Media
- Jenny Baird, green meeting specialist and director of sales, Doubletree Hotel Portland
- Carina Bauer, CEO, IMEX
- Julianne Brienza, executive director and cofounder, Capital Fringe Festival
- Tom Brock, OBE, CEO, Scottish Seabird Centre
- Ronald Brown, project coordinator, Edinburgh Woodcraft Folk
- Arlene Campbell, general manager sales and events, Direct Energy Centre, Allstream Centre
- Ben Challis, cofounder, A Greener Festival

- Jennifer Cleary, head of creative learning, Manchester International Festival
- Chris Coleman, artistic director, Portland Center Stage
- Gene Columbus, executive director, Orlando Repertory Theatre
- Kevin Danaher, president and cofounder, Green Festival
- Sarah Dayboll, manager of environmental affairs, Fairmont
- Thomas Evans, associate vice president for global initiatives, St. Edward's University
- Joe Frankel, CEO and founder, Vegware
- Zoë Furnivall, community fundraising and outreach officer, Friends of the Earth Scotland
- Ian Garrett, executive director, Center for Sustainable Practice in the Arts
- John Graham, president and CEO, American Society of Association Executives
- Patricia Griffin, president and founder, "Green" Hotels Association®
- Reynaldo Guino-o, business excellence advisor, Edinburgh International Conference Centre
- Kevin Hacke, executive director, International Special Events Society
- Jeff Hall, executive chef, Savor . . . San Francisco
- Craig Hamilton, ecotourism scholar
- Monique Hanis, director of communications, Solar Energy Industries Association
- Leigh Harry, CEO, Melbourne Convention and Exhibition Centre
- Kathleen Hennesey, recycling manager, Moscone Center
- Brent Heyning, Crimson Collective lighting team, Ascension
- Lori Hill, president, Lori Hill Event Productions
- Dale Hudson, head of program development, IMEX
- Terre Jones, president and CEO, WolfTrap
- Kimberly Lewis, vice president of conferences and events, U.S. Green Building Council
- Bruce MacMillan, president and CEO, Meeting Professionals International
- Kath Mainland, chief executive, Edinburgh Festival Fringe Society
- Eve McArthur, director of operations, South by Southwest
- Scot McKenzie, festival director, Capital Fringe Festival
- Shawna McKinley, project manager, MeetGreen
- Claire O'Neill, cofounder, A Greener Festival
- Richard Randall, senior account manager, Firefly Solar
- Bryan Raven, managing director, White Light Ltd
- Thomas H. Rawls, vice president, sales and marketing, *Native*Energy, Inc.
- Arlene Rush, producer, Green Fashion Show
- Paul Salinger, vice president of events and marketing, Oracle
- Deborah Sexton, president and CEO, Professional Convention Management Association
- Mike Shea, executive director, South by Southwest
- Martin Sirk, CEO, International Congress and Convention Association
- Lindsay Smith, sustainable programs manager, Colorado Convention Center
- Kathy Speirs, project coordinator, NVA
- David Stubbs, head of sustainability, London 2012 Olympic and Paralympic Games
- Frank Supovitz, vice president of events, National Football League

- Nick Vida, Crimson Collective solar power designer, Ascension
- Andrew Williams, managing director, Seventeen Events
- Nancy (Wilson) Zavada, CMP, principal, MeetGreen
- Matt Wright, creator, Cosy Cosy Gameshow

Book Reviewers

- Elizabeth S. Covino, professor, Johnson & Wales University
- William R. Host, professor, Roosevelt University
- Jill Doederlein, program coordinator, Lansing Community College
- Lindsay Smith, sustainable programs manager, Colorado Convention Center
- Nancy (Wilson) Zavada, CMP, principal, MeetGreen
- Harith Wickrema, president, Harith Productions Ltd
- Elizabeth Valestuk Henderson, CMP, CMM
- Mariela Mcllwraith, CMP, CMM

A personal thanks to the following individuals for their contributions and inspiration: Samantha Lee Cook, Claire Daly, Max Darwin Goldblatt, Sid and Anne Iyer, Carola Jacob, Louise E. Knowles, Leah and Stephen Lahasky, Eileen O'Reilly, Carolyn Peachey, Gabrielle Pointer, Amber Rimmer, David Todd, and Petra Wend, PhD.

I also want to thank the photographers who contributed to this book. Where not otherwise noted, Louise E. Knowles took the beautiful photographs featured within.

I want to thank my mom, Nancy Lynner, the world's best cook of healthy and organic cuisine, and who was recently voted Sales Associate of the Year, Scotland, at a well known organic health food store. Finally, thank you Papa, for giving me the idea in the first place and for believing in me.

Sam Goldblatt

PART ONE

Innovation

San Francisco's Moscone Center is a leading sustainable meeting and conference venue. *Courtesy of The Moscone Center.*

CHAPTER 1

The Theory and Practice of Greener Meetings and Events

"Treat the earth well: it was not given to you by your parents, it was loaned to you by your children. We do not inherit the Earth from our Ancestors, we borrow it from our Children."

—*Native American Proverb*

In this chapter you will learn:

1. Why meetings and events are becoming greener

2. How greener meetings and events have emerged historically

3. The meaning and significance of sustainable development

4. How ecotourism informs and influences greener meetings and events

5. How corporate social responsibility (CSR) and outgreening motivate business

6. How innovation, conservation, and education define greener meetings and events

7. How emerging forces and trends in the conventions, hospitality, tourism, conference, and event industries are driving greener meetings and events

A History of Greener Meetings and Events

In the beginning, all events were green.

Native Americans used every last bit of the animals they hunted in order to make food, clothes, and tools used in ancient ceremonies. Not a single muscle, bone, or skin would go to waste. Similarly, ancient clans of the Scottish Highlands ate sheep intestines rolled with oats in order to avoid wasting this quick-spoiling meat. The dish, haggis, has long been a significant food at Scottish ceremonies, as it is today. Ancient ceremonies not only employed organic, reusable materials with virtually no waste but also strengthened tribal social bonds and boosted local economies.

The Industrial Revolution of the nineteenth century brought immense technological advances such as steam power and electricity, which allowed humans to create meetings on an exponentially larger scale, such as the 1851 London World's Fair, attended by more than six million people. The Industrial Revolution also, however, separated humans from nature, allowing pollution and wastefulness to go unchecked. Like all industries, the meetings and events industry has naturally inherited some of the pollution and waste problems of the Industrial Revolution, which is why many events pioneers today are striving for reform and innovation. We are currently experiencing a new wave of environmental innovation, with more and more businesses opting to "go green" every day.

Today's meeting and event planners are learning that environmentally friendly practices not only minimize waste but also enhance the entire event experience. Green event pioneers look at both preindustrial resourcefulness—such as sourcing local, organic food—and postindustrial technology, using the Internet and renewable energy to reduce transportation and energy usage. Green event pioneers are also inspired by the modern theories of *sustainable development, ecotourism, fair trade, corporate social responsibility (CSR)*, and *outgreening for corporate advantage*.

Sustainable Development

Mainstream environmental practices first emerged in the 1980s, when recycling became a household word for the first time. In 1987, the United Nations took the bold step of writing *Our Common Future*, a new theory for business and society to progress without harming the planet. This important text created the theory of *sustainable development*, or "development that meets the needs of the present without compromising the ability of future generations to meet their own needs" (Brundtland report 1987, ch. 2).

Sustainability means ethical behavior with a long-term perspective, and covers more topics than just environmentalism. Sustainability means thinking not just about tomorrow, or next year, but about 100 or 1,000 years from now, and it remains a critical principle for modern business.

Sustainability comes in many forms, and responsible event leaders will always pursue financial sustainability in their long-term business plans. This book will show you how to pursue environmental and social sustainability alongside financial success. I encourage you to consider the specific ways in which environmental and socially responsible initiatives can sustain and improve your long-term business plans.

Ecotourism

The tourism industry, with its reliance on recreational air travel, is one of the world's largest gas consumers and polluters. Tourist activity can also degrade both the ecological and social life of a native population. University of Edinburgh Scholar Craig M. Hamilton traveled to Mexico to study the effects of tourism on the Cancun region, reporting the following data (Hamilton 2009, p. 3):

> Cancun has developed from a small fishing community in the 1970s into a sprawling tourism site with more than 20,000 hotel rooms and 2.6 million visitors annually. Each day, the local landfill receives 450 tons of waste. Many of the poor among Cancun's 300,000 residents live in shantytowns, and 75 percent of their sewage flows untreated into the lagoon behind the beach.

Hamilton shows that a successful ecotourism resort near Cancun is helping to reverse some of these hazardous trends. The tourism industry predated meetings and events in applying the theories of sustainable development to its field, and we can learn a lot from it. David Fennell defines *ecotourism*, or environmentalist tourism, as follows (Fennell 2007, p. 24):

> a sustainable, non-invasive form of nature-based tourism that focuses primarily on learning about nature first-hand, and which is ethically managed to be low-impact, non-consumptive, and locally oriented (control, benefits and scale). It typically occurs in natural areas, and should contribute to the conservation of such areas.

Green events pioneers can glean much from this definition of ecotourism. Certainly all good meeting planners recognize the value of sustainability in long-term business growth, but is this sustainability "nature-based"? No person is an island, and no event is disconnected from its natural resources and environment. Therefore, think of sustaining not just your business but also your event site, your resources, your energy sources. Similarly, all events impact the culture of their locations, and greener meetings and events must therefore be "locally oriented" to maintain meaningful and beneficial relationships with local culture.

What about "low-impact" and "non-consumptive"? Should not the best events always be high-impact, offering guests a lavish feast to consume? Actually, greener events can deliver a huge, spectacular impact on attendee experience, complete with sights, sounds, and foods to consume—and still maintain a low environmental impact. Japan's Fuji Rock Festival, known anecdotally as the world's cleanest music festival, annually presents major bands like The Red Hot Chili Peppers and The Cure in a huge outdoor environment that encompasses ten different stages for performance, vendors offering outstanding local cuisines, sustainable campgrounds, and other attractions such as a Japanese "onsen" spa and a cable-car ride (www.smash-uk.com). Through rigorous recycling procedures, responsible land maintenance, and consumer education, Fuji Rock Festival gives consumers a high-impact festival experience like none other through sustainable practices that minimize environmental impact.

At Coachella, a spectacular three-day music festival in Indio, California, fliers are not permitted; for every ten empty water bottles returned, you get a free bottle of water; and carpools with more than four people are eligible to enter a contest to win free admission for life. Campgrounds for the event have farmers' markets and recycling stations, and do not allow campfires (www.coachella.com).

If you still doubt that an event can provide a high-impact experience for attendees while retaining a low impact on the environment, consider the National Football League (NFL) Super Bowl. Probably no event has a bigger impact on American culture, but few Americans would have suspected that the 2008 Super Bowl XLII was powered by renewable energy from Arizona's Salt River Project (Salt River Project 2008).

You, too, can make a big impact on your attendees without making a big impact on natural resources. Fennell's definition of ecotourism presents a goal for greener events pioneers to meet, a beacon of sophistication for you to labor toward. Not all events may

Attendees at Coachella relax under the giant solar panels that will provide the energy to light the Ascension sculpture later that night. *Courtesy of Coachella.*

be certified greener events, and very few events will achieve a zero-carbon footprint, but all events may aspire to be a shade greener each time they are created and produced.

Fair Trade

One of the more visible trends to emerge from sustainable development is the *fair trade* movement, created to counteract unfair developing-world labor practices. As defined by the Fairtrade Foundation, a "fair trade" between manager and laborer means the following (Fairtrade Foundation 2011):

- Better prices (prices that do not fall below market price)
- Decent working conditions
- Local sustainability
- Fair terms of trade between farmers and workers that doesn't discriminate against the poorest, weakest producers

Event leaders know firsthand the importance of customer service: A gourmet meal can be tainted by a discourteous waiter. Keep your staff committed to the cause and dedicated to excellence by treating them as partners in your enterprise. Offer them discounts. Keep them informed of company news. Encourage employee culture. Consider an annual employee thank-you event.

The Oxfam charity (www.oxfam.org.uk) runs a hugely popular program for volunteers to serve as stewards at UK music festivals, picking up litter or directing crowds in exchange for free admission to concerts. The music festivals gain a free, enthusiastic workforce and the volunteers gain inspirational work and affordable recreation. Instead of seeing a sharp divide between staff and attendee, try blurring these boundaries to create a festive atmosphere that celebrates fair trade and equality. If the service staff is having fun, chances are, the attendees will, too.

Corporate Social Responsibility (CSR)

In the past ten years, corporate malfeasance at companies such as Enron and Global Crossing, topped by the 2008 financial collapse, have tainted the world's view of the corporate sector. In an effort to emphasize ethical behavior within a company's mission statement and to regain the public trust, many major corporations have embraced *corporate social responsibility* (CSR), a policy promoting ethical and charitable corporate behavior. One major part of a company's commitment to CSR is often charity or fundraising events, planned by greener event professionals. As Gene Columbus notes in *Careers in Special Events*, Walt Disney World shares its tremendous wealth by donating resources to charity fundraisers such as races. Disney also engages staff in CSR by encouraging employees to participate in and volunteer at these local charity events (Columbus 2010, p. 28).

You probably know the Super Bowl, the National Football League's (NFL) annual competition, watched all across the United States, but did you know that the NFL carries out a robust CSR commitment? When I spoke with him in May 2010, Frank Supovitz, senior vice president of events for the NFL, described an industry-leading set of environmental strategies implemented at every Super Bowl, which include:

- Recovering and recycling plywood, cardboard, fabric, and other used materials
- Recycling plastic, paper, and office supplies
- Recovering and donating over 90,000 pounds of unserved food to food banks in the host community
- Operating a sports equipment and book redistribution project, which donates several tractor-trailers of resources for area schools
- Planting between 1,000 and 3,000 tree seedlings annually in the host region to sequester carbon

After describing this strong commitment to environmental sustainability, Supovitz stated, "We do these things to be good corporate citizens, and yes, there is an economic benefit to consuming less, but we spend more on our Super Bowl and Pro Bowl environmental programs than we receive in financial benefits." Supovitz and his team at the NFL practice these sustainable initiatives simply because they are the right thing to do, and that is the true meaning of CSR.

Since 2007, Meeting Professionals International (MPI, www.mpiweb.org), an association for the meetings industry, has produced an annual CSR Survey of meeting professionals. The 2008 survey found that newcomers to the industry valued CSR more than older industry veterans, and that Canada and Europe both top the United States in terms of awareness of and commitment to CSR. Overall CSR awareness in the meetings industry rose from 2007 to 2008 and was predicted to continue increasing (MPI 2008 CSR Survey Summary).

Outgreening for Corporate Advantage

Corporations are increasingly demanding environmental events that reduce egregious corporate waste, to show their commitment to CSR. However, a growing number of forward-thinking companies are environmentally motivated by sheer profit incentive and competitive advantage. In *Hot, Flat, and Crowded,* Thomas L. Friedman describes how green initiatives saved money and improved the performance of New York City taxicabs, and how solar power gave the U.S. Army a tactical advantage in the Iraq War. He calls these strategies *outgreening*, and calls for companies to not just settle for being carbon neutral, but to seek a carbon advantage for increased profitability and heightened performance. *Outgreening,* as Friedman defines it, is outperforming your competition based on making the best, most efficient use of resources (Friedman 2008, p. 322). He explains outgreening in a political context when he quotes energy expert David Rothkopf: "Green is not simply a new form of generating electric power. It is a new form of generating national power—period" (Friedman 2008, p. 23).

Similarly, green is a new form of generating business power—period. Live Earth's Green Event Guidelines lists "Business Advantage" as a key motivation for sustainable practice, saying, "By 'going green' you are also giving the audience what it wants, possibly stepping ahead of your competition, and the likelihood of attracting sponsors and media attention. You may also find some financial savings through reduced waste and energy costs" (Green Event Guidelines 2009).

Financial savings come not just from fewer expenses but also from government grants, which green companies are increasingly eligible for. As an event leader, you will know the iconic value of a Steinway piano, but did you know that Steinway & Sons runs on solar?

Steinway's New York factory has the largest solar rooftop of its kind in the world, for which it received a $588,000 grant from the New York State Energy Research and Development Authority, and for which it expects to claim $266,000 in federal solar-energy tax credits. As Steinway's vice president for manufacturing Andrew Horbachevsky explains, "We kind of backed into the ecological thing. Green is also the color of money" (Barron 2008).

Green is certainly the color of money for billionaire media mogul Ted Turner, America's largest land owner, a committed environmentalist, and creator of the cartoon show "Captain Planet," about an environmental superhero. At a fundraiser for the Captain Planet Foundation, the *New Yorker* quotes a conversation that Turner's daughter recalls having with her environmental father:

"He reminds me constantly, 'Do you know who Captain Planet is?' I'm like, 'No, Dad, who is he?' And he's like, 'It's me!'" (Widdicombe 2008, p. 31).

Friedman predicts that tomorrow's captains of industry may all be Captain Planets.

A Theory of Greener Events: Innovation, Conservation, and Education

The green business strategies of CSR and outgreening are two important aspects of emerging greener meetings and events. Figure 1.1 shows that these strategies, along with eco-tourism, sustainable development, and fair trade, help to define the principles of greener

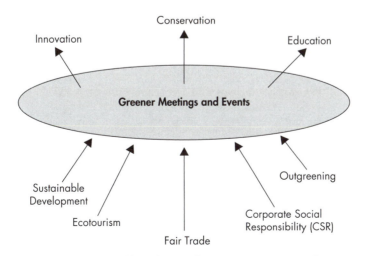

Figure 1.1 S. Goldblatt Theory of Greener Meetings and Events

meetings and events. These diverse inputs form the modern definition of greener events and generate the three core outputs of innovation, conservation, and education.

These three key outputs should define outstanding greener meetings and events. Tomorrow's meeting planners and event producers will find innovative ways to produce outstanding, sustainable events. They will intelligently conserve their resources so as to curb waste. And they will educate their guests and their colleagues on sustainability as part of a continual quest for improvement.

These three concepts in Figure 1.2 appear throughout this book, as aspects of exceptional environmental strategies, and as design elements of model greener meetings and events. They also divide this book into three parts. The first part of this book, Innovation, shows you how greener meetings and events have evolved as a new and cutting-edge approach to event management. The second part, Conservation, outlines key strategies for minimizing waste, maximizing resources, and protecting the environment. The third part, Education, deals with social impact, the audience/guest/delegate/traveler experience, and greener event marketing opportunities.

One critical thing to remember: Sustainable strategies do not just improve the planet, *they actually improve the event experience.* Just as waste can degrade the event atmosphere, effective waste minimization offers your guests a superior event atmosphere. The word *event* comes from the Latin *e venire*, which means outcome; greener meetings and events have two core outcomes, each equally important:

1. Superior experiences
2. Sustainable strategies

These two core outcomes, each reliant on the other for success, make up the definition of greener meetings and events.

Sustainability is a journey, not a destination, and so greener meeting planners and event producers will continually search for new, innovative ways to improve on sustainable strategies and superior experiences.

By the end of this chapter, you should be able to create your own image of a greener event. Your definition should include environmental strategies and technologies, harnessed

Don't forget the ICE! Greener meetings and events employ the following three core strategies.

Innovation	Creatively harnessing emerging strategies and green technology for increased energy efficiency and environmentalism
Conservation	Responsible use of the earth's natural resources and waste minimization
Education	Promoting ethical behavior toward energy and the environment by creating memorable event experiences

Figure 1.2 ICE for Greener Meetings and Events

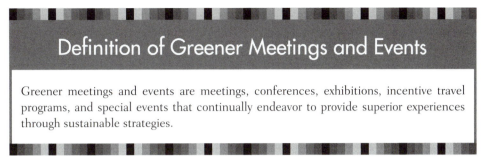

Definition of Greener Meetings and Events

Greener meetings and events are meetings, conferences, exhibitions, incentive travel programs, and special events that continually endeavor to provide superior experiences through sustainable strategies.

to provide unique experiences. It should imply a symbiotic, mutually beneficial relationship between event experience and the natural biosphere. It should include the three core values of innovation, conservation, and education. Above all, it must describe and aspire to sustainability.

Emerging Trends in the Meetings and Events Industry

The 2007 *Event Solutions* magazine forecast of the events industry found that, of the over 1,350 events professionals surveyed, "green meetings" was rated the third-most-anticipated trend (Baragona 2007, p. 4). In 2011, greener meetings and events are no longer anticipated—they have arrived!

Meeting Professionals International's (MPI) *EventView 2009: North America* survey of the industry reports that 68 percent of all respondents plan on implementing or have already implemented greener event initiatives, and that environmental strategies make up 12 percent of the average event budget. What's more, 73 percent of event marketers and 68 percent of sales and marketing executives plan on implementing or have already implemented greener event initiatives. Moreover, 43 percent of respondents are going green as part of their CSR commitment, but 36 percent are doing so to win or maintain customer loyalty, to gain a competitive advantage, and to cut costs (MPI 2009, p. 9).

The *meetings and events industry* is a broad term that encompasses several different sectors, each full of dedicated professionals working hard to produce outstanding events. It is sometimes referred to as the MICE industry, short for meetings, incentives, conventions, and exhibitions. Groundbreaking environmental initiatives are currently taking root in the various fields of conventions and exhibitions, hospitality, incentive travel and meetings, and events.

Conventions and Exhibitions

Perhaps the most significant indication of the rise of greener meetings and events has been the formation of several associations within the conventions industry, which include Convene Green Alliance (www.convenegreen.com) and the Green Meeting Industry

Council (GMIC) (www.greenmeetings.info). With twelve chapters and another eight in development, GMIC offers many benefits to the green meetings industry, including an annual Sustainable Meetings Conference, an excellent Web resource (www.sustainable meetingsportal.com), and the International Green Awards, the only official awards program for greener meetings and events. The Green Meetings Award "recognizes environmental awareness amongst meeting organizers, highlighting the opportunities that now exist to stage business tourism events in 'green-minded' venues, whilst also planning an agenda in which sustainability issues have been taken fully into account." Previous winners include the U.S. Green Building Council's GreenBuild conference and Oracle OpenWorld (www .imex-frankfurt.com/envaward.html).

The Convention Industry Council (www.conventionindustry.org) is making its own contributions to the field of greener meetings and events by assisting in the creation of the new APEX/ASTM Green Meetings and Events Standard. As local convention, conference, and meeting planners in your area continue to invest in environmental strategies, associations such as GMIC will continue to expand and promote greener meetings and events worldwide.

Hospitality

As the meetings industry continues to lead in environmental innovation, the hospitality industry is also working hard to define greener hospitality and to promote environmentalism. The American Hotel and Lodging Association (AH&LA) (www.ahla.com) has installed a thorough Green Resource Center for hospitality professionals on its website. On Earth Day 2009, AH&LA encouraged more than 200 properties to take the AH&LA Green Guidelines Challenge. These 11 Minimum Green Guidelines range from forming an environmental committee on staff to installing 1.6-gallon toilets in all guest rooms.

Because of guests' expectations for constantly washed towels and sheets, as well as small, one-use containers of shampoo, many hotels have a high amount of waste. Green hospitality pioneers are working to reform this. In the January 2010 issue of *one+*, the official magazine of Meeting Professionals International (MPI) (www.mpiweb.org/ Magazine), Kathy Manfredi explains how she got her local conference to collect 1,100 bars of partially used soap from hotels, to be donated to those who need it through non-profit group Clean the World (www.cleantheworld.org) (Manfredi 2010).

AH&LA celebrates its one-hundredth birthday this year, showing that it's never too late to go green. At about the same age, the famous Ritz-Carlton hotel chain (www .ritzcarlton.com) has recently unveiled a green wedding package at its San Francisco location, which features local foods, organic flowers, recycled glass centerpieces, and tablecloths made from natural fibers (Crail 2009). The Ritz-Carlton is picking up on a service that Fairmont Hotels have been providing for several years now. Through their unique Eco-Meet program, Fairmont Hotels offers a four-pronged approach to greener meetings: eco-accommodation, eco-cuisine, eco-service, and eco-programming (www .fairmont.com).

Incentive Travel

Incentive travel means travel or tourism packages marketed to consumers or employees as a motivational tool. As the incentive travel industry grows conscious of the negative environmental impacts of long-distance flight, they are increasingly seeking green alternatives, creating opportunities for travel and meeting planners with environmental experience. In January 2010, the Institute of Travel & Meetings (ITM) (www.itm.org.uk) announced its recruitment for a head of sustainability for the United Kingdom.

In August of 2009, Green Globe Productions (www.greenglobeproductions.net) created an environmentally friendly annual conference for the National Business Travel Association (NBTA) (www.nbta.org) at the San Diego Convention Center. All event vendors signed individually tailored green contracts that included environmentally friendly requirements. NBTA had Green Globe identify key areas for conservation and create a plan for continual improvement in future meetings, toward a goal of being carbon neutral. According to Green Globe, the plan is based on "certifiable, quantifiable, realistic objectives based on the assets and resources available" (Hayes 2009).

IMEX 2010 Green Initiatives

- The badge lanyards are supplied by IF Solutions (www.ifsol.co.uk) and are made from plant silk, an organic material manufactured from the waste stems of grain crops. No chemicals are used in the process and the fabric is biodegradable.
- Hydroelectricity is used for all power during the exhibition including build-up and breakdown. In 2009, IMEX was the first trade show in the meetings industry to offer green energy—hydroelectric power—to its exhibitors.
- Recycled and recyclable paper badges are coated in cornstarch laminate.
- Recycled and recyclable luggage tags are coated in cornstarch laminate.
- IMEX buses have an anti-idling policy.
- Biodiesel buses are used for 20 percent of the hosted buyer transfers.
- Reusable recyclable polypropylene visitor bags and jute bags are available for Association Day.

- Hosted buyers travel by train where possible.
- The IMEX Green Awards—including the Green Supplier Award—are presented at the IMEX Gala Dinner.
- A waste reduction program resulted in a saving of 34 tons during the 2008 show, a reduction of 20 percent on the output in 2007. The program continues to show gains, as IMEX 2010 reduced waste by 30 tons over 2009. Follow this link for more information on IMEX recycling: www.imex-frankfurt.com.
- 95 percent polypropylene carpets are used in the exhibition hall. Polypropylene is a derivative of oil and is recyclable. The IMEX carpets are recycled following the show and made into either carpet again or other polypropylene products.
- All coffee and tea provided in seminar rooms will be fair trade and sugar will be provided in sugar bowls instead of in individual packaging.

The environmental movement in the Incentive Travel Industry was spearheaded by the preeminent conference, IMEX, the worldwide exhibition for incentive travel, meetings, and events. IMEX has made environmentalism a core value of its annual conference, as illustrated by the following list of initiatives for IMEX 2010.

With its extensive, groundbreaking strategies for environmental meeting, IMEX stands as a world leader in the new field of greener meetings and events, and we will profile IMEX at the end of this chapter. Importantly, IMEX not only looks inward with its green policies but also outward, striving to influence industry policy and rewarding greener event pioneers through their awards program.

Meetings and Events

Environmental meeting planners and advocates on the MeetGreen team (www.meetgreen.com) continue to lead the U.S. meetings industry with its landmark environmental practices. Not only has MeetGreen developed some of America's leading greener meetings and events practices, it is also the nation's foremost educator on the subject. Through its popular seminars at meetings industry conferences, its development of a green event carbon calculator, its online directory of certified greener meetings venues, and its book *Simple Steps to Green Meetings*, MeetGreen continues to lead the industry in greener meetings and events. In the United Kingdom, December 2009 saw the publication of the breakthrough book *Sustainable Event Management* by Meegan Jones, famous for having reformed major UK music festivals with environmental practices.

Industry flagship magazine *Special Events*, which in 2007 installed a permanent online section on greener events (specialevents.com/green_events), published an article in November 2009 titled "Go Green to Keep Going," suggesting that greener events are the wave of the future (Hurley 2009). Those listed among their twelfth annual "30 Top Event Rental Companies" consistently cite environmental strategies as a key to their continued success. Greener meetings and events are no longer a trend—they are the future.

Figure 1.3 summarizes the trends emerging across the meetings and events industry and shows some of the forces behind these trends.

Standards and Certifications

Although the emergence of greener meetings and events may be observed through publications such as *Simple Steps to Green Meetings*, associations such as GMIC, and statistics from surveys such as *EventView*, it is the process of standardization that will propel the green movement from a nice idea to a critical component of all meeting and event planning.

■ British Standard 8901

In 2007, the British Standards Institute (BSI) (www.bsi-group.com), a world leader in setting industrial standards based on empirical data, created a standard titled "Specification for a Sustainable Event Management System with Guidance for Use," or BS 8901 for short.

Sector	Forces	Trends
Conventions and exhibitions	Industry recognizes demand and opportunities for sustainable practices.	Major associations are formed.
Hospitality	Hotels show increased attention to reducing waste.	Individual chains outgreen the competition. Industry associations advocate for greener hotels.
Incentive travel	Negative environmental impacts of travel, including carbon debt of air travel, factor into some travel decisions. Ecotourism becomes more prominent.	There is increased demand for greener, more ecotouristic incentive travel events.
Meetings and events	Clients demand ethical and environmental events. Industry recognizes opportunities of greener events.	Outstanding greener events gain public eye. Certifications and standards emerge.
All sectors	There is increased awareness of global warming and climate change. Public becomes more interested in green business strategies. Global recession beginning in 2008 affects events industry.	Increased demand for greener events. Opportunities emerge for early adopters. Emerging associations, certifications, and industrial standards gain more prominence.

Figure 1.3 Emerging Forces and Trends Across the Meetings and Events Industry

As its title suggests, BS 8901 does not dictate specific environmentally friendly practices (EFPs) but, rather, provides the specification and methodology for creating one's own sustainable event management system. Although unique EFPs are highlighted in areas including biodiversity, archaeology, equal opportunity, and supply chain management, BS 8901 focuses on managerial tools such as defining objectives in terms of scope, performance level, criteria, and consistency, using key performance indicators (KPI) to measure progress, and documenting results. Charts are provided, including an "Outline structure for a sustainable development maturity matrix—guidelines for continual improvement," which shows how progress in areas of inclusivity, integrity, stewardship and transparency can be measured from "minimum involvement" to "full engagement." Most importantly, although it encourages gradually increasing EFPs, BS 8901 firmly states that sustainability "should be an integral part of the event management process, and not regarded as an 'add-on' component," and that "its influence should extend throughout the entire supply chain" (BS 8901, pp. 1, 8-9, 10, 13, 19, 24).

Rather than provide baseline advice, available elsewhere, BS 8901 targets the higher goal of redefining event management altogether with a new system and a new ethos. The standard, at £120 per copy, attracts high-profile companies such as Live Nation that seek industry prestige and competitive advantage. In presenting Live Earth at London's Wembley Stadium in 2007, Live Nation, the world's biggest concert producer, became an early adopter of BS 8901. Live Nation Production Manager Andy Pearson frames the decision in terms of savvy business advantage (BS 8901 Case Studies 2009):

> Sustainability might not be a massive issue now but I think in the next few years it will become one. If you fail to do something now, you will find yourself in a position of scrambling to catch up, or simply out of business.

Pearson reflects a desire to stay at the forefront of his industry and in good standing with government policy, values shared by the other high-profile implementers of BS 8901 thus far, which include professional conference organizers EC&O, sports venue the Lord's Cricket Ground, and major arts event the Manchester International Festival. In the U.S., Meeting Professionals International (MPI), Microsoft, and MeetGreen are all BS 8901-certified.

■ APEX/ASTM Green Meetings and Events Standard

As one of the first U.S. companies to be certified by BS 8901, MeetGreen is working hard to bring the rest of the industry up to speed. Since 2007, Shawna McKinley, project manager at MeetGreen and the first executive director of the Green Meetings Industry Council (GMIC), has been working with Accepted Practices Exchange (APEX), ASTM, another international standards agency, and the U.S. Environmental Protection Agency (EPA) to create a U.S. greener event standard, inspired by BS 8901 but tailored for U.S. meetings and events.

Taking a collaborative approach, APEX organized several city discussion groups in major U.S. cities, gathering meeting planners around the nation to discuss the details of the proposed green meetings and events standards. It has also created a blog that enables industry professionals to share an online dialogue about the guidelines. Based on all input, APEX proposed nine categories for the APEX Standard for Green Meetings and Events:

1. Audiovisual
2. Accommodation

3. Communication
4. Destination
5. Exhibits
6. Food and beverage
7. Meeting venue
8. On-site office
9. Transportation

McKinley discussed this collaborative process with me in May 2010:

The U.S. Environmental Protection Agency (EPA) had contacted ASTM, the federal standards development agency in the U.S., to create a standard for its own procurement of meetings. At the same time, the GMIC had been speaking with APEX about revisiting the Convention Industry Council (CIC) Best Practices Framework, to reflect the emerging trends in green meetings. The two organizations sat down together and said, "Let's work together on this, because we don't want multiple standards, we want one for everyone."

Nine subcommittees emerged, working under an APEX panel to create standards in nine different areas of meeting management. It is a performance-based standard, so in each of those nine areas, which include everything from transportation, accommodation, technology, hotels, etc, there are clear practices that need to be implemented and performance standards that need to be met in order to claim compliance with the standard.

Level One is the minimum requirement for compliance with the APEX Standard, but there are three voluntary levels above that. Once the standard is launched, in order to claim compliance, you will have to achieve Level One for each category, but you can choose to go beyond that and claim compliance up to Level Four.

This is just a hypothetical example, but if you look at the performance requirement of recycling at your meeting venue, if you have a program that captures a minimum of three streams and achieves the minimum recommended diversion rate, that might be Level One. If you can claim a higher level of recycling diversion or divert more materials, then you may be able to claim the higher levels.

Green Is the New Black

Because of cost cuts sparked by the 2008 recession, interest in CSR, and increased awareness of climate change and the energy crisis, greener meetings and events are more popular now than ever before, and, where clients would once demand luxury and extravagance, they now seek ethical and environmental events. As Figure 1.4 shows, green is the new black (and it can keep your business in the black)!

Old Trends		New Trends
Luxury	→	Responsibility
Extravagant events	→	Ethical events
Very important person (VIP)	→	Environmentally friendly practice (EFP)
Black tie	→	Vintage tie
Red carpet	→	Recycled carpet
Elaborate invitations	→	Recycled paper or e-vites
Caviar and lobster	→	Sustainably harvested seafood
Expensive giveaways	→	Charitable giveaways such as carbon offsets

Figure 1.4 Green Is the New Black

Model Greener Event: IMEX

IMEX is a worldwide exhibition for meeting and incentive travel organizations. Held annually in Frankfurt, Germany, the 2009 IMEX hosted 3,500 exhibitors from 157 countries, including national tourist organizations and major hotel, airline, and destination management companies. For those in the meeting and event tourism industries, IMEX is the place to be. It is also a trailblazer in the greener event movement, and I spoke with CEO Carina Bauer and head of project development Dale Hudson in March 2010 to find out more.

Bauer recalls how environmentalism has been at the heart of IMEX since its inception:

Chairman Ray Bloom launched IMEX with a number of New Vision Initiatives, each one dedicated to promoting an issue of importance in the meetings industry. One of those, from the beginning in 2001, was sustainable meetings. For us, sustainability integrates into what we do as a company and how we are set up.

Hudson, says that for IMEX, greener meetings and events means "trying to incorporate sustainable activities into each part of an event and also to educate and inform delegates attending the event on how better practice can make a difference within the industry."

IMEX's world-leading environmental policies have grown over the years, and now include recycled and recyclable badges and luggage tags, badge lanyards made from organic plant silk, recyclable carpets, USB sticks made from 100 percent eco-friendly plastic, biodiesel buses and an anti-idling policy, hydroelectric-powered venues, and a waste reduction program that saved 34 tons of waste in 2008. "We did not try and do everything overnight," Hudson says, "and what we have now is a nine year program—incorporating three or four initiatives per year."

Bauer agrees that greening is a process rather than a switch you flick on, saying, "We try to do it in incremental stages. You can build each year on some good practice rather than try to do it all at once. There's still a lot for us to do."

It is critical to recognize that greener meetings and events are *not* just a passing fad or a business trend. All major associations within the various convention, hospitality, incentive travel, meetings, and events industries are making significant, long-term changes: developing certifications, publishing reports and books, organizing conferences, and altering mission statements to reflect the principles of greener meetings and events. Even the U.S. government recognizes the long-term importance of environmental strategies for events: The EPA has created an official guide to greener meetings and events at www.epa .gov/oppt/greenmeetings/. Perhaps the *Special Events* magazine headline says it best: Go Green to Keep Going!

Hudson lists good venue and vendor relations as one of the keys to green meeting success:

Always talk to your venue and suppliers to find out what sustainable alternatives are on offer. If you have a strong buying power, go as far as to implement these requests into your contracts. Remember that you can't always make all the changes at once—go for a step-by-step approach to implement the changes successfully.

Green pioneers can seek out stakeholders with outstanding environmental policies. Hudson notes, "We were very lucky to be holding our exhibition in Germany, where many green practices such as recycling were common practice." Bauer emphasizes the value of a green venue, such as Messe Frankfurt, where IMEX is held:

We are lucky to be at Messe Frankfurt. On an environmental side, they are outstanding. Part of that is what the government of Germany requires in a way we are not required in the UK. That's legislation. Another part is what they've done

themselves. When we started and were asking them about their environmental initiatives, they didn't understand what we were talking about. At first we thought they didn't have environmental initiatives, but then we realized that they just didn't call them that, because they were fundamental. They didn't see policies such as recycling as special initiatives, but rather part of their standard operation.

One of IMEX's most pioneering efforts is the Green Awards, run in conjunction with the Green Meeting Industry Council (GMIC) (www.greenmeetings.info) and sponsored by Rivanna Natural Designs (www.rivannade-signs.com). The IMEX Green Awards recognize those in the meeting and incentive travel industries with outstanding environmental initiatives. "The first IMEX was in 2003, and we have been running the green awards since that time," says Bauer. "It was not big news at that time. We had to convince people that green meetings were a trend, and people have jumped on it since that time. For very long time they were the only awards of that kind in the industry. I am proud to have seen such an

(continued)

(continued)

increase in the number and quality of entries for these awards since their launch."

Categories for the IMEX Green Awards include Commitment to the Community, Green Meetings, and Green Exhibitor and Green Supplier. Past winners include The U.S. Green Building Council (USGBC) (www.usgbc.org) for its Greenbuild Convention and the Melbourne Convention and Exhibition Centre (www.mcec.com.au), which features a solar hot water system that offsets over 40 percent of general hot water and can provide 100 percent of public hot water. UK firm World Events (www.worldevents.com) has won Commitment to the Community two years in a row for its outstanding conferences for major pharmaceutical companies.

"Some of the winners have done amazing things, and quite simple things as well," Bauer says, "by showing how much money and carbon can be saved by using jugs of water instead of bottled water, or by using proper cutlery instead of throw-away cutlery, which the delegates prefer anyway." Bauer views the Green Award recipients as inspirations to those in the meetings and events industry. She says that the message is, "Take things one step at a time and look at the little things first, just to make a start. Don't be scared of it, do it incrementally year on year, and after a few years you'll find you have quite a distinguished program of initiatives."

Bauer says that this message is really taking off now. "People weren't really that interested in 2003. Slowly we started to get more calls from exhibitors and planners who wanted to apply for the Green Awards, wanted more info, wanted advice," she says. "We have noticed an increase of interest within the industry as a whole. That's the best thing, really."

Through its sustainable initiatives, IMEX has shown that green meetings and events truly can provide superior experiences through sustainable strategies. Bauer says, "It's true that you wouldn't take a step toward sustainability if it reduced the experience of delegates, and that's quite important. A lot of people think that doing green initiatives will cost more money or be a worse experience, which doesn't need to be the case."

Indeed, Bauer is working hard to advance greener policies in the meetings and events sector, saying, "We strive to improve our environmental footprint on a year on year basis, as well as being committed to promoting the concept of sustainable meetings and events throughout the industry. Those are our dual strategies."

For Carina Bauer and the staff of IMEX, sustainable strategies are not additional, but rather core values of their work. Thanks to the advances they are making in greener meetings and events, the industry is progressing by leaps and bounds toward sustainability.

Summary

Greener meetings and events are meetings, conferences, exhibitions, incentive travel programs, and special events that continually endeavor to provide superior experiences through sustainable strategies. Theories of sustainable development, ecotourism, fair trade, corporate social responsibility, and outgreening have contributed to the emergence of greener events. Greener meetings and events exhibit three core strategies: innovation, conservation, and education. More than just a passing fad, principles of greener meetings and events are increasingly pervading industry doctrine. Organizations and associations within the conventions, meetings, hospitality, incentive travel, and events industries are adopting environmental policies and implementing standards and certifications.

Key Terms and Definitions

- **Greener meetings and events**: meetings, conferences, exhibitions, incentive travel programs and special events that continually endeavor to provide superior experiences through sustainable strategies.
- **Sustainable development**: development that meets the needs of the present without compromising the ability of future generations to meet their own needs.
- **Ecotourism**: a sustainable, noninvasive form of nature-based tourism, ethically managed to be low-impact, nonconsumptive, and locally oriented.
- **Fair trade**: an ethical standard of labor agreement that includes better prices (prices that do not fall below market price), decent working conditions, local sustainability, and fair terms of trade between farmers and workers that doesn't discriminate against the poorest, weakest producers.
- **Corporate social responsibility (CSR)**: commitment to ethical and/or charitable behavior by a corporation, often involving green or ethical events.
- **Outgreening**: environmental strategies used for competitive corporate advantage, such as leading the market in innovation and cutting costs.
- **Incentive travel**: tourism packages marketed to consumers or employees as a motivational tool.

Blue Sky Thinking

Staying abreast of current events can help you get ahead in business. I get the *New York Times* headlines e-mailed to me every morning. Based on your knowledge of current events, why has there been such an increased interest in greener meetings and events recently? What combined current events or social trends have created this enthusiasm for environmental responsibility? Why are greener meetings and events more important and more popular now than ever before, and what can they do to solve specific social and business issues today?

Apart from those mentioned in this chapter, what other environmental trends might influence and inspire greener meetings and events?

Renewable Resources

Fennell, David A. (2007). *Ecotourism*. London: Routledge.

Green Events section of *Special Events* magazine: SpecialEvents.com/green_events.

Report of the World Commission on Environment and Development: Our Common Future: www.un-documents.net/wced-ocf.htm.

This sign, written in Scots dialect, stops festivalgoers from polluting the streams of the Falkland Estate during The Big Tent.

CHAPTER 2

Event Pollution

"Oh Beautiful for smoggy skies, insecticided grain,
For strip-mined mountain's majesty above the asphalt plain.
America, America, man sheds his waste on thee,
And hides the pines with billboard signs, from sea to oily sea."

—*George Carlin, Comedian (1937–2008)*

In this chapter, you will learn:

1. How to create a healthy and successful event ecology

2. How pollution can degrade both the environment and the event experience

3. How outdoor and indoor events impact their environments

4. Common instances of land, air, and water pollution

5. How noise pollution can disrupt the environment

6. How to reverse pollution and create a positive environmental legacy

Humans have polluted since the dawn of time. During the middle ages, citizens of Edinburgh, Scotland, would nightly empty their waste buckets from their windows and onto the street, where it would roll down the Castle Hill and into the Nor Loch, which was not a loch at all but an unregulated cesspool of human waste. It was no wonder that Edinburgh earned the nickname "Auld Reekie," or old stinky. Before deciding that the human species has evolved greatly since these days, one might visit a modern landfill.

This book contains a positive message, and seeks to encourage, not discourage, the events industry. However, before learning the key strategies for greening any meeting or event, we need to face the challenges ahead. This chapter reveals the number one challenge for greener events: pollution.

Event Ecology

Andrew Williams, director of the London events firm Seventeen Events (www .seventeenevents.co.uk), is working to change the perception of events from liabilities for waste into opportunities for sustainability. When I spoke to him in May of 2010, he said, "The events industry has traditionally been an extremely wasteful place to run a business." Williams said, "The fixation on the latest fads and fashions, as well as a conservative approach to environmental and social issues, has meant that there have been a lot of easy wins. The challenge is to change that perception and allow clients to see events not just as a great way of communicating, but also a way in which they can demonstrate their commitment to sustainability."

Williams believes that sustainability should be a core value, not an additional service, for any event producer:

> Clients and sponsors see our sustainable approach as a great extra benefit, but not a must-have. We hope to persuade them, as sustainable issues continue to dominate the world business market, to prioritize a sustainable approach at all levels of their business. We aim to turn positive attitudes into commercial decisions over the months and years ahead. We want to show that planning your event in a sustainable manner is just a better way of doing it. We want initiatives to be known not necessarily as green, but as simply the right way of doing them.
>
> —*Andrew Williams, Seventeen Events, interview, May 2010*

Dale Hudson, head of program management at IMEX (www.imex-frankfurt.com), echoes Williams' sentiments, saying, "My perception of events has always been that there is a huge amount of waste within this industry. However, I am realistic enough to realize that this industry is crucial for business and very important. We have all experienced conference calls with more than three people, and know the difficulties that arise from this type of meeting." She continues:

> Fundamentally, meetings are still very important. Issues such as trust and spending time getting to know people cannot be achieved any other way. Therefore, as an industry which is crucial to underpinning business needs across all sectors, it is important that we become more sustainable and prove that events can be conducted with a reduced impact to the environment.
>
> —*Dale Hudson, IMEX, interview, March 2010*

Before the mainstream emergence of greener events, some special events were thought of as "special" not just because they were out of the ordinary, but also because they were thought to be exempt from environmental responsibility. In this way, festivals such as Woodstock were valued as exceptional arts experiences, and waste and pollution went unchecked. These previously invisible event outcomes are now highly scrutinized, and modern meeting and event planners must be acutely aware of their pollution, waste, and carbon footprints.

We no longer think of an event as a movable feast, using the resources of one event site and then moving on to another. Instead, we now focus on *environmental impact*, or the effects, both immediate and long-term, that an event has on its surroundings. Modern events must exist on their premises as part of an *event ecology*, the temporal event and the permanent environment existing as part of a symbiotic, mutually beneficial relationship.

Outdoor events have an obvious impact on their environments, as crowds trample on plants and pollute grounds with litter. Indoor meetings and events have a direct impact on the cleanliness of their venues, but the venues themselves typically have a larger impact on the outside world, namely the carbon footprint generated by energy use. These are examples of direct and indirect pollution.

Direct and Indirect Pollution

Direct pollution has an immediate effect on the event environment, such as a cigarette butt littered on the ground, or a grassy field trampled and turned to mud. Outdoor events have the potential to cause much direct pollution. Classic categories of direct pollution, shown in Figure 2.1, include land, air, and water.

Indirect pollution describes an action that does not immediately degrade the event environment but that still causes negative environmental impacts. Indirect pollution is less visible but can be more harmful, as is the case with excessive amounts of waste being sent to landfill. Indoor events tend to cause indirect pollution, depending on their venue. A venue that is not energy efficient and that relies on coal power causes much indirect pollution, because the factory supplying the energy releases excessive carbon emissions into the atmosphere. Examples of indirect pollution include landfill deposit and carbon emissions, as shown in Figure 2.2. Chapter 6 will show how to reduce landfill deposit. Chapters 5 and 7 will address how to lower carbon emissions in transportation and energy use, respectively.

Land	Air	Water
Litter	On-site, gas-powered electrical generators	Contamination of local streams
Turf destruction	Idling gas-powered vehicles	Cruise ship waste dumping
Deforestation	Smoky gas-powered barbecue grills	Disruption of underwater ecologies, such as coral reefs

Figure 2.1 Direct Event Pollution

Land	Air	Water
Landfill deposit of garbage	Gas-powered vehicles traveling to/from event	Pesticides in grass runoff into streams
Use of nonorganic foods	Coal-powered electricity	Purchasing endangered or unsustainably harvested seafood
Contracting companies with high waste margins	Shipping in goods from long distances	Excess purchase and waste of bottled water

Figure 2.2   Indirect Event Pollution

Pollution: Direct and Indirect

Direct pollution can be summarized as degradation of the event site itself, whereas indirect pollution describes a negative environmental impact on the world at large.

- Direct pollution is a Styrofoam cup littered on the ground.

- Indirect pollution is the same Styrofoam cup placed neatly in a trash container and then sent to landfill.

Greener event pioneers can combat all pollution by ceasing to purchase Styrofoam cups, and instead purchasing recyclable, biodegradable, or reusable cups!

Land Pollution

The most basic aspect of an outdoor event ecology is the land, including the grounds and plant life on the site. UK advocates for environmental arts festivals, A Greener Festival (http://www.agreenerfestival.com/land.html), recommend the following strategies to minimize land damage:

- Use portable tracking and roadway to keep cars off the grass and out of the mud.
- Where possible, enhance the environment by planting trees and preserving nature.
- Research the local wildlife and consider ways to support it.
- Liaise with local environmental and wildlife charities and organizations to create a plan for sustaining the event site ecology.
- A percentage of income could be donated or invested into local environmental/ wildlife projects.

The major ways that meetings and events disrupt their grounds are through litter, turf destruction, and deforestation.

Litter

According to Keep America Beautiful (www.kab.org), America's premier waste-prevention association, over 51 billion pieces of litter land on U.S. roadways each year, or 6,729 pieces of litter per mile. Not only does this degrade the environment and lower property values, but litter cleanup costs the U.S. almost $11.5 billion each year (Keep America Beautiful 2010).

Outdoor events have the potential to generate a lot of trash. Between water bottles, paper plates, napkins, cigarettes, disposable diapers, leftover hot dogs and other food, paper, and plastic products, attendees can leave an event site looking like a windstorm scattered the local landfill across the grounds. But today, modern event planners have a responsibility to leave their grounds in the same or better shape than they received them in. Remember the U.S. Boy Scout pledge to "Leave No Trace." Earthfest 2011 in Knoxville, Tennessee, for example, is shooting for a zero-waste festival, after an Earthfest 2010 in which only 6.25 pounds of litter had to be sent to a landfill and 880 pounds were either recycled or composted (see www.knox-earthfest.org/).

Chapter 5 will show you how to deny your attendees the opportunity to litter. Place waste bins in every conceivable location that they may be required, and reduce excess waste, such as brochures and food packaging. Employ stewards to patrol the grounds and to help attendees dispose of their waste correctly.

Turf Destruction

The most obvious environmental impact is the one that your foot makes with the ground. Outdoor events often struggle to keep their fields from turning into mudslides after guests trample the grass. One solution is to completely protect the grass by placing a raised walkway on top of it. For many years at the Edinburgh Festival Fringe (www.edfringe.com), Spiegelworld Productions (www.spiegelworld.com) transformed Edinburgh's George Square into a magical, albeit muddy, cabaret venue. The grass in George Square never fully recovered from the trampling of festival feet. When Underbelly Productions (www.underbelly.co.uk) took over the location in 2009, it put down a giant, reusable artificial-turf covered floor, which protected the grass below and allowed patrons cleaner feet, thus delivering a superior experience through a sustainable strategy. This strategy could be improved by replacing the artificial turf with a used or recycled floor covering. Rather than covering the entire grounds, the Edinburgh International Book Festival (EIBF) (www.edbookfest.org.uk), in comparison, installs pedestrian walkways over their grassy location, reducing foot traffic on grass without restricting it completely.

Another solution is postevent turf restoration, which is not as easy as simply throwing grass seeds at a muddy field. Grass beds will likely need to be purchased and installed, and the entire field will probably need to be cordoned off from any traffic for several months to allow the new grass to grow. Turf restoration is common at outdoor sports grounds, and groundskeeping companies such as Dol Turf can provide turf restoration services such as aeration, seeding, fertilizing, or irrigation (www.dolturf.com).

Deforestation

Deforestation typically refers to the mass clearing of forests, but events can damage trees on a smaller scale as well. Trees often feature in an outdoor event site, tempting event planners to use them as set pieces, decorations, or meeting points. Geoff Monck reports for A Greener Festival (www.agreenerfestival.com) that most tree roots grow out, rather than straight down, so that extensive foot traffic around tree roots can severely endanger the trees, making them unhealthy. Unhealthy trees have a higher potential for collapse, and are therefore unsafe. Monck recommends that patrons at major outdoor events be kept away from trees at a distance of roughly 12 times the diameter of the tree trunk (Monck 2010).

Air Pollution

A new event rental business has emerged recently. Such businesses bring a fancy mobile bar to conventions and events, but they don't serve drinks—they serve oxygen. As air pollution steadily increases, event suppliers such as Oasis Oxygen Bars (oxygenbars.com) can attribute their success to the increasing demand for a simple breath of fresh air. It's no wonder that this trend began in Los Angeles, notorious for its intense *smog* (a contraction of smoke and fog, describing low-hanging air pollution) caused by excessive gas-burning vehicles. In *A Brief History of Pollution*, Adam Markham notes that Los Angeles, the world's largest market for automobiles, experiences between 60 and 80 stage 1 alerts every year, in which the public is advised to stay indoors because of air pollution (Markham 1994).

The negative environmental impacts of greenhouse gases such as carbon dioxide, methane, and ozone are no longer invisible concepts; this air pollution can now be seen, and breathed, all around us. Meetings and events can contribute to both local and global air pollution.

On Site

Transportation is the number-one polluter of meetings and events today. Not only do gas-powered vehicles pollute the atmosphere before they have even arrived at the meeting or event, but they bring this pollution to the event site. Massive parking lots, slow-moving traffic, and idling vehicles generate inordinate amounts of vehicle exhaust at the event site. By encouraging public and group transportation, preventing traffic jams, and discouraging vehicle idling, greener event pioneers can drastically cut the amount of vehicle exhaust polluting the event site. In most cases, this will create a noticeable difference in air quality, leading to happier, healthier attendees.

Portable gas-powered electrical generators are another culprit for on-site air pollution. Not only do these generators pollute the event atmosphere, but they are also typically unattractive, large industrial machines, needing to be carefully hidden. Instead of hiding your air pollution, why not publicly celebrate your clean event air energy? Wind turbines make a striking, powerful statement and generate energy that can power your event. Celebrate the event atmosphere, and show your attendees that clean energy is all around them.

The intoxicating smell of an open-air barbecue may be appropriate, even demanded, at events such as a company picnic or a Fourth of July parade, but not every event attendee wants barbecue smoke in their nose, clothes, and hair. You can avoid carbon emissions from gas grills by using electric grills powered by renewable energy. In order to cut down on wandering cooking fumes, remind your food vendors to "Keep a Lid on It": Close the lids of portable barbecue units or grills, and use lids when cooking in pots and pans. Not only does this cut down on air pollution, but it conserves energy, providing greater heat for food to cook. This is something you can do at home as well.

Global

If automobiles generate a significant amount of gas exhaust at the event site, imagine the exhaust emitted on the journeys there and back. Greener meeting and event pioneers consider the indirect pollution generated from travel to and from the site as a major percentage of the meeting or event's total carbon footprint. Chapter 5 offers many ways in which to cut down on this indirect air pollution. Similarly, any event at a venue relying on coal energy carries a significant negative environmental impact on the atmosphere. As Chapter 7 will demonstrate, choosing renewable energy is easier than you think, and can significantly lower your indirect pollution of the Earth's atmosphere.

Water Pollution

The tourism industry, with its penchant for water sports, cruise lines, and fishing trips, makes extensive use of the Earth's natural bodies of water with activities that often carry a negative environmental impact. Unregulated water sports can disrupt underwater ecologies such as coral reefs. According to Oceana North America, cruise ships generate up to 25,000 gallons of sewage from toilets, and 143,000 gallons of sewage from sinks, galleys, and showers every day. Oceana also reports that overfishing has depleted the tuna, swordfish, and marlin population by an astonishing 90 percent (Oceana 2010). Water-based meetings and events must partner with responsible ecotourism agencies to ensure that cruise ship waste is minimized, underwater ecologies are undisturbed, and fish populations are managed responsibly.

Land-based meetings and events, however, like the endangered bluefin tuna, are not yet off the hook. Pollution that begins on land but finds its way to water accounts for 77 percent of all ocean pollution (Markham 1994). Half of this land-based water pollution travels via the atmosphere, showing that air pollution damages not just the air but everything the air touches, including water.

Another major contributor to water pollution is *runoff*, or ground sediment carried to water by heavy rain or snow melt. Outdoor events using pesticides or chemicals on the grounds risk causing indirect pollution when rain carries the runoff pesticides into nearby water. Greener meeting and event pioneers should use organic fertilizers, such as manure, and organic weed-killers, such as vinegar.

Markham notes that the earliest form of pollution was no doubt prehistoric cave men urinating in a river stream. Some things never change: One of the main duties of Glastonbury's Green Police (Save the World Club 2011), volunteers dedicated to spreading environmental awareness at the iconic UK music festival, is to keep festival-goers from urinating in the nearby stream. From this basic form of pollution to the more complex issues of overfishing and runoff, water pollution presents several areas for greener meeting and event pioneers to investigate.

Noise Pollution

It may not produce carbon emissions or waste natural resources, but excessive noise pollution certainly disrupts the event ecology. The word *noise* derives from the Latin word *nausea*, and studies by the World Health Organization (WHO) have found that excessive, unwanted noise can actually make you sick, affecting your cardiovascular system and

Top Ten Strategies for Event Noise Reduction

1. Always do a preevent sound check with the talent/musicians/speakers performing at their normal volume.
2. Gather a diverse group of staff and stakeholders to assess appropriate volume levels.
3. Consult government or industry experts. The U.S. Environmental Protection Agency (EPA) has established 70 decibels as the threshold volume at which constant sound becomes harmful noise (U.S. EPA 2010).
4. Listen to the sound check from various locations around the event site.
5. Consult with neighboring residents and notify them of the potential event sounds.
6. Adjust speakers and sound equipment to minimize any unwanted feedback or buzzing sounds.
7. Always turn volume all the way down before turning on or off equipment.
8. Monitor sound during event, asking attendees and staff if volumes are satisfactory.
9. Assess white noise generated by non-sound equipment, such as computers, heaters and air conditioners, and vehicles. Consider turning off these devices during the event.
10. Consider providing ear plugs for staff and patrons.

your metabolism (WHO 2011). Outdoor noise can also disturb wildlife, disrupting animal communication. Consider the impact your event has on the eardrums of your patrons, your neighbors, and the animals around you.

Minimize amplified feedback from speakers, and consider sound levels when renting or purchasing vehicles or generators. Always do a preshow sound check before using any kind of amplified sound, and consider the effects of your various volume levels on the staff, guests, stakeholders, and the environment. Washington, D.C.'s Fort Reno Concert Series, which features loud punk bands such as Fugazi, enforces a strict 9:30 P.M. curfew in order to maintain a healthy relationship with local residents (www .fortreno.com). Even major venues enforce curfews to appease local residents. When the Santa Barbara Bowl presented Radiohead, it was legally bound to end the concert by 10 P.M. (sbbowl.com).

Legacy

One way you might think about their long-term impact on the environment is through your event's *legacy.* As with the performing arts, meetings and events are temporal experiences, here one moment and gone the next, but they have the power to affect people and places for generations to come. Although produced with good intention, the Woodstock 1999 concerts had a sadly negative legacy, criticized not only for extensive waste and pollution but also for several unfortunate acts of violence and rioting. The 2007 Live Earth concert series (liveearth.org), by contrast, provided a free concert to over two million people around the world, spreading awareness on climate change and global warming like never before. If that wasn't legacy enough, Live Earth also wrote the rulebook on greener events by creating an extensive *Environmental Guidelines* document that it followed for its concerts on seven continents.

An old saying in the catering business is that guests won't notice a perfectly set table, but they sure will notice if one spoon is out of place. The same goes for pollution control at events. Attendees may never notice the complex environmental strategies behind an event, but they sure will be quick to criticize any direct or indirect pollution generated by that event.

Every year, Eve McArthur, director of operations at the South by Southwest Music and Media Conference in Austin, Texas (www.sxsw.com), hears complaints about litter in a downtown area that SXSW has limited control over. I met McArthur at Polvos, a neighborhood restaurant in Austin in September 2009, and, over burritos, she explained the typical public reaction to waste control. McArthur said, "People complain every year when 6th Street has trash on it," she says, "but they don't, to my knowledge, ever have feedback on the improved trash control from year to year. It's unfortunate. But we know." McArthur knows that her trash control efforts are improving the event ecology, and that, while they may not attract notice, they certainly reduce complaints and heighten the experience.

Greener Events Company: Lori Hill Event Productions

After graduating from the Robert H. Smith School of Business at the University of Maryland and The Event Management Program at The George Washington University, Lori Hill founded her own highly successful event management company in the Washington, DC, area, Lori Hill Event Productions (http://lorihillevents.com).

She has produced high-profile events for the Clarice Smith Performing Arts Center, Freedom House, the Mexico Tourism Board, and the United States Green Building Council (USGBC), and is also a proud 14-year member of the International Special Events Society (ISES) (www.ises.com). When Hill served as president of the Greater Washington, DC, chapter of ISES, it won chapter of the year.

An industrious entrepreneur, Hill is also an environmentalist. It was not until she watched Al Gore's 2006 documentary *An Inconvenient Truth*, though, that she realized that she could apply environmentalism to her burgeoning event management business. She recalls, "I was inspired by *An Inconvenient Truth* and realized that I needed to practice sustainability, because events can be so wasteful. I realized how much excess there was in the world and asked, 'Do we really need all this stuff to make our point?' We really need to change our priorities."

Initially, Hill offered her clients environmental services as add-ons to the basic event management package, but it wasn't long before she dedicated her entire company full-time to producing greener meetings and events. "About a year after I started offering green alternatives, I realize that protecting the planet is not an "a la carte" item or a part-time job," Hill says. "Protecting the planet is a full-time job and we need to do it with our every action.

For Hill, sustainable event management means "looking at every single component of the event, including the invitation, venue, floral, menu, entertainment, waste disposal, guest gifts, name badges, signage and lighting, and ensuring that you are choosing the most sustainable options possible."

Hill's beautifully designed greener events feature beeswax (rather than petroleum) candles, locally grown organic food, and organic cotton t-shirts. Disposable tableware and bottled water are banned, and in their place are china and silverware, ceramic mugs, cloth napkins and linens, and filtered tap water. Condiments are purchased in bulk rather than individual packages, and excess food is distributed to client, staff, or a local soup kitchen. Linen and floral containers are returned to vendors for reuse, and soiled linens are stored in canvas, rather than plastic, bags.

Hill has a similarly ambitious agenda for greener meetings. She uses flash drives instead of three-ring binders and 100 percent post-consumer recycled paper with vegetable or soy-based ink. Signage, badges, and lanyards are reused, and all paper is recycled. "For events with exhibitors, we encourage them to bring only the quantities they need and to print on both sides with recycled paper. We also to encourage them to provide Earth-friendly giveaways."

Hill laments the number of disposable giveaways distributed at meetings and events, and works with clients to reform this practice. "If a client wants to provide a guest gift, we ask them if it is absolutely necessary to provide a gift," she says. "If it is a must, we encourage them to provide a gift that is useful, such as a flash drive or notepad made of recycled paper. We also try to support manufacturers in the U.S. versus overseas manufacturers that ship their products thousands of miles."

A commitment to the triple bottom line of people, planet, and profit is one key to Lori Hill's success. She believes in being good to people, saying, "I mostly work with independent contractors and pay them a fair wage. I believe in paying people for their work. I don't have unpaid internships." Hill's environmental policies show that she believes in being good to the planet, and all of this is good for her profits. "My company is becoming known as a green event producer, one of a few in the area," she says, "and clients often choose to work with us because we produce green events. We also work with other green vendors to help improve the green economy."

Hill has produced sustainable events for clients of widely differing backgrounds. "Some clients choose us because we are green and some clients have been with us before we went green," she says. "Then there are clients who hear about us without knowing that we are green, but who are really excited when they hear about all the things we do. That is very encouraging."

Indeed, Hill has received tremendous feedback from clients since going green. "They love it! I can't begin to tell you how many people tell me that I have inspired them to go green," she says, naming a caterer and event professionals, as well as regular citizens. "Just the other day, I had a fellow event planner tell me that she picked a plastic water bottle out of a trash can so that she could take it home to recycle it. She saw me do this two months ago. I've been doing my best to spread the gospel of green and it is so wonderful to know that I am getting through to people! It makes my day."

"When we co-produced the Mid-Atlantic Green Wedding Showcase, we received lots of positive feedback about what we were doing," Hill says. "People said, 'You are doing a great service.' It is a no-brainer to us."

Hill suggests that those event planners interested in going green, "start out by aiming for the low-hanging fruit (the easy things) and move on from there. Your clients will be impressed by what you are doing." She also cautions, "You need to hop of this bandwagon now or you'll get run over. As the Great Law of the Iroquois Confederacy says, 'In our every deliberation, we must consider the impact of our decisions on the next seven generations.' Enough said" (Hill, interview, March 2010).

Frank Supovitz, senior vice president of events for the National Football League (NFL), and his colleagues work around the clock to minimize waste at large-scale events such as the Super Bowl:

> Events can be inherently wasteful. If you ascribe to the philosophy that a special event is a unique moment in time, then by its nature, it will generate a lot of materials that are used only once and for a short period of time. That includes documents, lumber, office supplies, disposable catering goods, banner fabric, posters, ticket stock, signage, food waste, you name it. Events also consume a great deal of extra electrical power, fuel consumption and traffic that generates carbon emissions, wastewater, unconsumed food and trash.
>
> —*Frank Supovitz, NFL, interview, May 2010*

It is this awareness of any event's potential for pollution that inspires the NFL to pursue set rigorous environmental policies, reusing materials and supporting environmental causes. "Cities that host our major events do it for the economic impact, but also for the improved quality of life that events bring," says Supovitz. "Leaving behind waste and trash would detract from the benefits of hosting these events, and to us, that's self-defeating."

Instead of leaving behind waste, the NFL tends to leave behind newly planted trees, ensuring that it leaves its host site in better shape than it received it in. At Super Bowl XLII in Arizona, the NFL helped repopulate an area of the Chadeski-Rodeo Forest that had been hit with a forest fire, and in South Florida, trees were added to Keys that had lost foliage due to hurricanes. When assessing the potential direct and indirect pollution for your event, think of your legacy. Will you leave your event site in the same, or better, shape than you received it in? What about your effect on the planet? Will you create a happy event ecology, where the temporary event experience exists in harmony with the permanent surrounding environment? Greener meetings and events pioneers will not only protect the environment, they will use their events to actually improve it.

Don't let your legacy be a landfill. Let it be a garden.

Summary

Unlike in the past, event pollution is now heavily scrutinized by media, individuals, and government. Event ecology describes the relationship between a temporary event experience and the permanent environment surrounding it. An event that improves, rather than degrades, the event site will lead to a positive event ecology. Direct pollution, such as land, air, and water pollution, has an immediate impact on the event site. Indirect pollution, such as landfill deposit and carbon emissions, has a delayed impact on the global environment. Understanding the potential for meeting and event pollution will help you to minimize it in the future.

Key Terms and Definitions

- **Environmental impact**: the effects, both immediate and long-term, an event has on its surroundings.
- **Event ecology**: the symbiotic relationship between the temporal event and the permanent environment. In a positive event ecology, this is a mutually beneficial relationship.
- **Direct pollution**: immediate denigration of the environment. Litter is an example.
- **Indirect pollution**: actions causing long-term, distant, or global environmental damage, without immediate impact on the event site. Landfill deposits are an example.
- **Turf preservation**: conservation and protection of the grounds being walked on at an outdoor event.
- **Deforestation**: removal or damage to trees.
- **Smog**: a contraction of smoke and fog, describing low-hanging air pollution.
- **Runoff**: ground sediment carried to water by heavy rain or snowmelt.

Blue Sky Thinking

Tom and Linda get married under an outdoor gazebo on Lake Michigan. Over 200 guests arrive individually in cars and enjoy a delicious barbecue meal on paper plates under a tent. Later, they all dance in the grass to a band, with sound and light powered by a gas generator. As the sun sets, the trash containers are increasingly difficult to see.

What are the potential pollutants in this event? How could the wedding planner avoid pollutants here?

Renewable Resources

America Beautiful, Inc. (January). Accessible at kab.org/research09.

Carson, Rachel (2002). *Silent Spring*. New York: Mariner Books.

Keep America Beautiful, Litter Prevention, Waste Reduction, Beautification: www.kab.org.

Keep America Beautiful (2010). "Litter in America: Results from the Nation's Largest Litter Study." Prepared by the MidAtlantic Solid Waste Consultants for Keep

Live Earth: liveearth.org.

Oceana, Protecting the World's Oceans (2010). Cruise Ship Overview. na.oceana .org/en/our-work/stop-ocean-pollution/cruise-ship-pollution/overview.

Save the World Club (2011). Green Police. savetheworldclub.org/greenpolice.htm.

World Health Organization (WHO) (2011). Noise. www.euro.who.int/Noise.

At The Big Tent, EventScotland provided reusable wooden signs that used actual plants to spell out "Scotland."

CHAPTER 3

Planning the Greener Event

"There are no passengers on Spaceship Earth. We are all crew."

—*Marshall McLuhan, Philosopher (1911–1980)*

In this chapter, you will learn:

1. How to use research to form a green team of staff and stakeholders

2. How to conduct a green SWOT analysis

3. How to design an event that defines your triple bottom line commitment to people, planet, and profit

4. How to design an event that prioritizes your strategies, creates a green mission statement, and creates a strategic green plan

5. How to use consulting, hotel, and vendor contracts to plan for a greener event

6. How to create a sustainability rider

7. How to conduct a risk assessment

8. How to coordinate a successful event, engaging attendees and solving problems ethically during the meeting or event

9. How to conduct a survey to evaluate success

In *Special Events*, Dr. Joe Goldblatt, CSEP, outlines the basic process for planning an event: research, design, planning, coordination, and evaluation—a final stage that feeds information back into research for a future event. These same tried and tested stages of management can be applied to greener meetings and events.

Shawna McKinley, project manager at MeetGreen (www.meetgreen.com), told me in May 2010 that she is concerned when sustainability is not inserted into the business and economic curriculum around tourism, travel, and meetings. Her advice to meeting planners is, "Don't separate them into two separate things, as in, 'I do meetings, and then I do green.' This is where educators have a role to play."

> Sustainability needs to be considered from the outset, so that when you are creating your event plan, you don't really have a separate sustainability plan—your event plan includes sustainability in each and every part, in the program content, in the site selection, in the objective setting, fundamentally and early on.
> —*Shawna McKinley, MeetGreen, interview, May 2010*

All meetings and events have the ability to become greener. This chapter will show how to incorporate sustainability into every stage of the planning process. Every meeting or event follows basic management stages: research, design, planning, coordination, and evaluation. Greener events follow these stages as well.

Research

Often overlooked, the research stage is the critical foundation upon which any greener meeting or event is built. Many planners say that it is never too early to begin preliminary research for a future event.

When I spoke to Kimberly Lewis, vice president of conferences and events for the U.S. Green Building Council (USGBC) (www.usgbc.org) in May 2010, she said, "You need to give yourself time to plan how you will do it. Sit down and say, 'Here are the two or three things I really need to make happen.' That can't happen less than three months before the event. You can't tack it on the end and create true performance."

Green Teams

The key to good research is diversity of sources, and you will need to assemble a diverse team of staff and stakeholders to begin the brainstorming process of the research stage. In looking for candidates for your green team, look for individuals who are passionate about environmental, social, political, or ethical issues. Creative people interested in emerging trends also tend to be well suited for the innovative side of environmental initiatives. Most importantly, gather a diverse group of people from different backgrounds and different departments.

Innovative meeting planner

Experienced event manager

Skilled member of technical crew

Enthusiastic intern

Creative decorator

Chef or catering manager interested in green cuisine

Member of board of directors interested in corporate social responsibility (CSR)

Trusted client interested in greening his or her next event

Figure 3.1 Green Team Players

Lewis suggests opening the invitation to all staff, saying, "Look at your entire organization and share with your staff what you are trying to accomplish." She also recommends younger interns as ideal candidates for a green team, saying, "The biggest opportunity for your internship program is to give that generation an opportunity to participate in your sustainability goals. The new generation is passionate about it, because they know they're going to be left holding the reins for what we've done." Figure 3.1 suggests some potential candidates to guarantee a diverse and skilled green team.

Once you have assembled a green team, schedule a meeting to brainstorm potential environmental and sustainability issues relating to your meeting or event. Remember to emphasize *blue sky thinking*, which means allowing for open-minded and imaginative discussion, unhampered by realistic constraints. Andrew Williams, of Seventeen Events (www.seventeenevents.co.uk), told me he uses the following brainstorming questions to stimulate discussion.

> These criteria reflect the measurements set out in the original 2007 version of BS 8901. However they are—on the face of it—fairly theoretical in practice. We aim to take these guidelines and use them to ensure that our practical operations are as sustainable as possible.
> —*Andrew Williams, Seventeen Events, interview, May 2010*

The simple answer to most of these questions will typically be yes, but what matters more is the way in which you deal with these issues. For instance, in answer to the first question, most events require energy. How can you source renewable energy, or at least minimize coal energy? Your green team may not have immediate solutions to complex issues such as energy usage, but the important thing is to define these issues so that solutions can be researched and developed.

Depending on the size of your organization, you may have different answers for different departments of your operation. For instance, perhaps your office is solar-powered, but your event venue is not. Divide your answers into categories, such as office, marketing, event operation, event production, catering or vendor relations. Assign different members

Green Team Brainstorming Questions

- Will the activity generate energy demands?
- Will the activity generate a greater need for travel?
- Will the technologies employed for the activity's energy supply and transport generate air emissions?
- Will the activity require water?
- Will the activity require previously developed land (not greenfield) to be used?
- Will the activity affect its surroundings?
- Will the activity affect existing biodiversity resources?
- Will the activity affect sites of archaeological or cultural interest?

- Will the activity affect the water quality?
- Will the activity affect the watercourses?
- Will the activity give rise to risks of ground contamination at the site?
- Will the activity generally waste materials?
- Will recyclable or reusable waste be generated by the activity?
- Will the activity give rise to ethical or environmental issues from the procurement of products?
- Will the activity give rise to ethical or environmental issues from the supply chain?

of the green team to research the various issues that arise from this initial brainstorming session. Have each team member report back with several potential solutions to each problem, which can be further investigated.

Strengths, Weaknesses, Opportunities, and Threats (SWOT Analysis)

The initial brainstorming session may raise issues that might intimidate your green team. McKinley recalls a client situation: "It was clear that there was interest and enthusiasm, but one of the challenges was, 'Where do you start to bite off the huge task that is event sustainability?'"

One way to motivate the research process is to engage your green team in a *SWOT analysis*, where they list the current strengths, weaknesses, opportunities, and threats of the organization, meeting, or event. The strengths and weaknesses refer to the current state of affairs, while opportunities and threats look to the future. Strengths and weaknesses describe internal forces, while opportunities and threats refer to external forces. Figure 3.2 shows a sample SWOT analysis with examples for greener meetings and events. If needed, make a separate SWOT analysis for each department of your business.

A SWOT analysis should help to define the major issues raised in the research process, and to reveal your potential to tackle these issues. According to Figure 3.1, the company is well positioned to get staff and clients on board with environmental initiatives. They also have the potential to create new relationships with public transportation authorities and local food providers. However, finding sources for renewable energy and clean tap water could prove more difficult.

STRENGTHS	WEAKNESSES
• Eco-aware staff • Clients with corporate social responsibility (CSR) mandates	• Coal energy provider • Reliance on staff car travel
OPPORTUNITIES	THREATS
• Venue accessible by public transportation • Potential local food providers	• Lack of clean tap drinking water • Lack of environmental experience among venue staff

Figure 3.2 SWOT Analysis of a Greener Meeting or Event

Design

Once background research has been assembled on the potential environmental issues arising from your meeting or event, the design phase can focus this research into a strategic plan for action. McKinley describes this process of focusing event goals by saying, "The team needs to know what the direction of the company is, what is within their power and what the priorities and intentions for event sustainability are. That gives them the direction to know which part of the beast to tackle."

> There are a myriad of impacts, some within, some outside of your control, so you need to have a framework to act within. With a large-scale event there are so many environmental things that can be done, so that processing and prioritizing and giving clear policies are important.
>
> —*Shawna McKinley, MeetGreen, interview, May 2010*

Greener meeting and event pioneers can prioritize their goals during the design process with organizational tools such as a triple bottom line and a strategic green plan.

Triple Bottom Line (TBL)

One way to focus the research and motivate your team is by defining your *triple bottom line*, or your commitment to people, planet, and profit. First conceived by John Elkington, the triple bottom line concept is now used many corporations seeking to establish values beyond sheer profit incentive (Elkington 1998). Figure 3.3 shows how greener meetings and events may define their commitment to people, planet, and profit.

Ask your green team to research how your meeting or event might impact specific groups of people and the environment. How can you create a positive impact for these people and the planet, while making a healthy profit?

People (Social): Your guests, your staff, your vendors, your stakeholders, the local population, and the global population. How does your event impact these people? Could your event actually improve their way of life? You can educate your guests, train your staff, reward your vendors and stakeholders for ethical initiatives, and leave the local and global population with an improved environment.

Planet (Environmental): The plants and animals in your local ecosystem, and the global environment at large. How does your event impact the local, and global environment? Could your event actually improve the environment? Your event could bring awareness to local or global environmental issues, and inspire guests to take action either at the event or afterward.

Profit (Financial): Income, productivity, capital, market share. How can your event maximize profit through sustainable initiatives? Could greener strategies actually increase your event's profitability? By conserving resources and energy, you can cut costs, outgreening the competition and attracting a wider market.

Figure 3.3 Triple Bottom Line for Greener Meetings and Events

Strategic Green Plan

Using your blue sky thinking, SWOT analysis, and triple bottom line, construct a list of strategic goals for your meeting or event. Based on Figure 3.2, your goals might look like the following list.

Continue to develop a longer list of strategic goals by engaging your green team in blue sky thinking. Chapter 4 will discuss in detail how to turn these ordinary goals into key performance indicators (KPIs), or outcomes that are specific, measurable, achievable, realistic, and timely (SMART). It will also take you through a process of prioritizing these strategic goals according to those that are most needed, most achievable, and most likely to be effective. Make sure that your prioritized strategic goals reflect the values of your triple bottom line.

Once you have prioritized your list of strategic goals, highlighting the major initiatives and eliminating those that are extraneous or unrealistic, assign timelines for completion to each goal. Then delegate responsibility for each major strategic goal to a person or group on the green team. It might be the person who suggested the strategic goal, or the person best suited to achieve the ambitious result. Figure 3.4 demonstrates how strategic goals may be prioritized and assigned to members of the green team.

Greener Strategic Goals

- Delegate green responsibility among staff.
- Convert to renewable energy.
- Maximize public transportation use.
- Reduce staff car travel.
- Develop water filtration system.
- Engage venue staff in environmental initiatives.
- Partner with local food providers.

Strategic Goal	Timeline for Completion	Staff Assignment
Maximize public transportation use.	Today: Seek out partnership with public transit authorities to begin promoting public transit immediately. Over the next month: Consider locating future meetings and events near public transit stops.	Innovative meeting planner
Partner with local food producers.	Today: Research potential local food providers. Over the next month: Send out requests for proposals (RFPs) to top providers.	Experienced event manager Chef or catering manager interested in green cuisine
Delegate green responsibility among staff.	Over the next month: Communicate green office practices such as turning off lights to all staff. Over the next six months: Ban disposable cups, silverware, and plastic bags in the office, and provide reusable alternatives.	Enthusiastic intern
Engage venue staff in environmental initiatives.	Over the next month: Build environmental training (recycling policies, etc.) into venue staff orientation.	Creative decorator
Reduce staff car travel.	Over the next six months: Encourage staff to carpool and use public transit when possible, perhaps creating an incentive scheme.	Enthusiastic intern
Develop water filtration system.	Over the next six months: Research feasibility.	Trusted client interested in greening his or her next event Skilled member of technical crew
Convert to renewable energy.	Over the next six months: Research feasibility.	Member of board of directors interested in corporate social responsibility (CSR) Skilled member of technical crew

In addition to the staff assignments suggested here, each task needs to be supervised by an experienced manager.

Figure 3.4   Prioritized and Assigned Strategic Goals

EcoEvents is a meetings, events, and exhibitions management company specializing in environmentally friendly practices. We provide superior experiences through sustainable strategies.

By encouraging group travel and public transit use, we help our clients to decrease their carbon footprints. We also specialize in locally sourced foods, supporting local economies while presenting outstanding catering options. Our entire staff is engaged in the sustainable agenda, and we provide free training for venue staff and clients.

Our comprehensive portfolio of sustainable meeting strategies helps our clients to improve not only the environmental and social aspects of their events but also the financial aspects as well, as attendees return again and again.

Figure 3.5   Green Mission Statement

Look at your new prioritized list of strategic goals and summarize some of the major values suggested there. These values should also be reflected in your triple bottom line and might include conservation of resources, minimization of waste, or education. Create a *green mission statement*, a prose summary of your ongoing commitment to these values. Figure 3.5 provides an example of a green mission statement that could be derived from the strategic goals listed in Figure 3.4. This green mission statement and your prioritized strategic goals, supported by planning documents such as your SWOT analysis and triple bottom line, constitute your new *strategic green plan*.

The company described in Figure 3.5 is quite accomplished. If you are in the early stages of planning greener events, your green mission statement may be more of a series of goals to aspire to. Over time, you will turn these goals into achievements.

Planning

It is now time to turn all of your research and designs into concrete plans for managing a successful meeting or event. In the planning stage, turn the strategies listed in your strategic green plan into specific tasks, and make them happen through contracting and staff engagement.

Greener Contracts

The best way to be clear and transparent about your sustainable policies from the start is to build them into all of your standard contracts. Dr. Goldblatt explains most standard event management contracts in his book *Special Events*, and provides attorney-reviewed examples (Goldblatt 2009). Rather than create new contracts, greener meeting and event pioneers insert the language of environmentalism and sustainability into existing ones.

Reputation

Both parties agree to use their best efforts to preserve and protect each other's reputation during the conduct of this event. The purchaser recognizes that the event manager is committed to sustainable business practices and environmental responsibility and will use the best efforts available to protect and preserve this reputation from harm.

■ Consulting Agreement

Start with the consulting agreement, the contract in which a meeting or event manager agrees to provide services for a client. This agreement will include many standard legal terms, including definition of parties, consideration clauses, the offer, force majeure, insurance, and indemnification. The *reputation term*, in which both parties agree to preserve and protect each other's reputation, is a perfect place to assert your commitment to sustainability. Consider this example of a reputation section of a greener consulting agreement.

This term tells the client that their event manager is committed to producing greener events, and that they need the support of the client to do so. To get the client to agree to a more detailed set of sustainable policies, the event manager will most likely need to create a *sustainability rider*, or contractual attachment regarding sustainability. Be sure to note in the original contract that this agreement is subject to the terms of all attached riders.

All clients are different, and may require different sustainability riders. While some clients might want you to ban water bottles and plastic bags from the event site, others may not be ready to take this leap. Make clear your basic moral stance to the client, and outline any specific polluting or unethical practices that you refuse to support. Increasingly, event managers are banning polystyrene cups and trays. Perhaps you will not serve fish harvested from unsustainable sources, such as Chilean sea bass, or controversial foods such as foie gras (fattened duck liver). Make sure to also explain your alternatives to these banned practices, which may include biodegradable cups and trays or the serving of sustainable fish such as salmon.

In addition to the unethical practices that your sustainability rider might ban, you may also include several suggested practices, which, although not mandatory, should be given "first priority." These practices may include composting food waste, using energy-saving devices such as LED lights, and facilitating group transportation options. Over time, you might transition these policies from "preferred" to "mandatory" with trusted clients. A detailed sustainability rider, as well as many other greener contracts, can be found in the appendices of this book.

■ Other Agreements

Other agreements that may require sustainability riders are *exhibitor contracts*, in which exhibitors lease space for a booth at a tradeshow or exhibition, *hotel contracts*, where hotels provide rooms, space and services for events, and *vendor contracts*, in which vendors provide services or products.

Exhibitors want to make the most of their time at a tradeshow or exhibition, and to attract the most people to their booths. Unfortunately, this often results in purchasing far too many fliers and disposable giveaways, which are either thrown out by attendees or left in the convention center after the event. The exhibitor contract is your chance to welcome exhibitors to the green agenda and teach them how to be a responsible exhibitor. Give them attendance figures, which might help them produce a responsible number of fliers. Encourage them to use double-sided printing, and on recycled paper. Suggest recycled or organic giveaways that have an actual purpose (bottle openers are useful—plastic toys are not).

Similar to the exhibitor contract, the vendor contract is your chance to get vendors on board with your strategic green plan. Make sure that they recognize the importance of environmentally friendly practices to your organization, and that they will be expected to follow such practices. You might even set a regulatory framework, so that any instances of pollution or litter are policed.

Hotels are typically one of the largest businesses that meeting and event planners deal with. If you can't find a greener hotel, as described in Chapter 9, you can negotiate with your hotel to consider environmental practices through a greener hotel contract. You may request that the hotel offer guests the choice of not having their towels washed every day (to save water). Ideally, the hotel would use organic cleaning supplies, energy-saving lightbulbs, and bulk toiletries (instead of small, wasteful plastic bottles of shampoo and conditioner). You might not convince your hotel to go completely green at first, but you can ask them to take the first step.

Aside from these contracts, there are other legal documents that can have sustainable language inserted without requiring an entire sustainability rider. Employment agreements should make the sustainable ethos of your company clear to any prospective employees, and should ask them to support your green mission statement. Similarly, employee handbooks should outline green office policies such as avoiding disposables, conserving electricity, using double-sided printing, recycling, and even promoting public transportation.

Be very detailed in your *purchase orders*, or requests for vendors to provide services or products, to specify the sustainable credentials required. You may wish to specify which types of organic cleaning products that you require from your general services contractor. Organic or local flowers may be requested from the florist. Lighting designers might be required to deliver a certain percentage of LED lighting instruments. Be as specific as possible, and when you receive a vendor invoice for services or products rendered, make sure that it matches the original remit of the purchase order. Aside from improving the event, you are teaching vendors how to green their business, and also supporting the green economy.

Risk Management

Possibly the most important part of the entire event management process, *risk management* can be defined as the process of carefully planning to avoid any dangerous or harmful incidents during the meeting or event. Common event risks include people tripping on wires, carpeting, or stairs, people becoming overly inebriated, or evacuation in the case

Rating	Impact	Probability
1: Low	Low impact: no physical injury, but event enjoyment disrupted	Unlikely to occur, save for exceptional circumstances
2: Medium	Medium impact: potential for low to medium physical injury	Could possibly occur under normal circumstances
3: High	High impact: very dangerous or lethal activity	Likely to occur

Figure 3.6   Risk Assessment Rating

of a fire. Greener meetings and events have their own inherent risks. For instance, event pollution discussed in Chapter 2, such as turf destruction and deforestation, pose a threat to outdoor meetings and events.

The key to risk management is to think of every possible situation that could go wrong, and take precautions to eliminate these potential risks, well ahead of the event. Gather the green team and engage them in blue sky thinking about any potential risks. It may help to divide risks by potential environmental impacts to earth, water, air, and animal life, or to simply divide risks by area, such as stage, backstage, audience, meeting rooms, bar, and entrance. Visit the event site and investigate all areas that might be affected by the event. Once you have a long list, at least two pages, of risks, rate the potential impact of each one and the probability that it might occur, on a scale of 1 to 3, as explained in Figure 3.6.

Use decimal points when necessary—for instance, to give a risk rating of 2.5 for impact or 1.2 for probability. Discuss these ratings with the group to ensure that they are accurate, and then multiply the impact by the probability to derive the priority of the risk. For instance, a risk with an impact of 2 and a probability of 3 should have a priority of 6, meaning it is a dangerous risk and precautions should be taken.

Events carry hundreds of potential risks, but Figure 3.7 reveals common risks that are specific to greener meetings or events. These are risks to the environment or the sustainability of an event, or risks that environmental initiatives may carry. Hypothetical impacts and probabilities have been assigned to these greener risks, and they have been accordingly prioritized.

Looking at this prioritized risk assessment, ask your green team to brainstorm several different ways in which to mitigate each of these risks. For the biggest risk, turf destruction, you can seed the grass far in advance, create temporary walkways in high-risk areas and encourage all staff and attendees to wear sturdy boots. To avoid bicycle accidents, provide bicycle safety instructions for attendees through the Web site, and provide signage and a bicycle steward on location. Attendees can be warned about chicken bones, but ultimately you will need first-aid-trained staff on hand in case of any medical emergency. Your green team should develop multiple solutions for each of these risks through research and investigation.

Risk	Impact	Probability	Priority
Turf destruction creates slippery mud	2	3	**6**
Bicycle accident	2.5	2	**5**
Attendee chokes on organic chicken bone	3	1.5	**4.5**
Noise pollution	1.5	3	**4.5**
Lack of wind/sun negates wind/sun energy	1.5	3	**4.5**
Organic produce rots	2	2	**4**
Organic cleaning product creates slippery floors	2	2	**4**
Weakened by excess climbing, tree branches fall	2	2	**4**
Attendees or staff demand water bottles at a water-bottle-free event	1.3	3	**3.9**
Staff injured while sorting waste in dumpster	2.5	1.5	**3.75**
Compost produces unpleasant odors	1.2	3	**3.6**
Litter	1.2	3	**3.6**
Air pollution from outdoor barbecues or grills	1	3	**3**
Waste streams contaminated	1	3	**3**
Overflowing waste receptacles	1	3	**3**
Compost uncollected in time	1	2.5	**2.5**
Endangered animals found on menu	2	1	**2**
Bicycle theft	1	2	**2**
Local youth volunteers misbehave	1.7	1	**1.7**
Garbage workers strike	1.2	1	**1.2**
Protest by special-interest group	1	1	**1**

Figure 3.7   Risk Assessment for Greener Meetings and Events

In *Event Risk Management and Safety*, Dr. Peter Tarlow says, "All events carry two risks, (1) the risk of a negative occurrence both on site and off site, and (2) the negative publicity that comes from this negative occurrence" (Tarlow, 2002). This negative publicity is even more dangerous for greener meetings and events, where attendees may blame accidents on environmental initiatives. Ensure that your environmental initiatives are completely safe and free from danger. Always put safety before other considerations.

Coordination

The coordination stage is your chance to execute your environmental initiatives and sustainable planning in the actual event environment. Don't set yourself up for any surprises: In addition to being ambitious and innovative, your environmental initiatives should be eminently *practical*, so that various levels of staff can understand and implement them in the event environment. Underpromise and overdeliver.

The Armory, home to Oregon's Portland Center Stage, is a spectacular venue for Greener Events. *Courtesy of Portland Center Stage.*

The American Society of Association Executives (ASAE) (www.asaecenter.org) has more than 22,000 members who represent trade and professional associations, and many of these members are responsible for organizing meetings and events for their associations. John Graham, president and CEO of ASAE, understands the importance of being realistic with environmental practices. When we spoke in May 2010, Graham explained that water bottles cannot be banned completely from all ASAE events, saying, "It's just impossible from the logistical and operational point of view. The truth is we do need some water bottles; we also need some paper. So it's important to evaluate what can and cannot be done and avoid making promises we can't keep."

Engagement

Get your attendees involved in the greening. One of the greatest possible outcomes for any greener meeting or event is the changed perceptions of attendees. The potential for education begins when your attendee opens his or her e-vite and reads that invitations have been sent via e-mail to reduce paper waste, and continues throughout the entire event as the attendee uses recycling bins and enjoys local, organic foods.

When we spoke in May 2010, Nancy (Wilson) Zavada, CMP, principal at MeetGreen, recalled an outstanding instance of customer engagement at the Doubletree Portland hotel: "A woman served me a beverage with a straw, and she said, 'This is a cornstarch straw, and it will be composted after it is used.' When the bar staff can tell you the hotel's sustainability policy, that's progress. During this economic downturn, they are doing very well."

Use signage to explain all environmental initiatives. For instance, in the restrooms of San Francisco's Moscone Center (www.moscone.com), signs above trash cans say, "Paper Towels Only: We are composting to reduce waste." Attendees need to be told exactly what to do when it comes to trash and recycling receptacles. You might even use clear receptacles and clear trash bags, so that attendees may see exactly what types of trash go in which bin.

Ethical Problem Solving

Even after the most thorough of risk assessments, problems will inevitably arise at any greener meeting or event. A subway strike might interfere with plans to use public transportation. A change in the weather might adversely affect local produce due to be served. Perhaps the garbage is not collected on time. Greener meeting and event pioneers deal with these problems swiftly, effectively, and ethically.

Ethical problem solving requires taking the time to consider various courses of action. In the event of a subway strike, can you encourage attendees to take a bus, or to carpool? If a certain food is unavailable, can you replace it with another local food? If garbage is uncollected, can you hire a separate contractor? Choose the solution that best supports your green mission statement and has the least negative environmental impact.

John Graham knows the importance of having clearly defined environmental ethos and sticking by them in difficult circumstances. "Actions speak louder than words," says Graham, "and one of the biggest challenges regarding the environment and social responsibility is for organizations to act as they preach. With so many ways to understand terms like social responsibility and greener events, organizations need to be careful to remain committed to what they proclaim."

> It's easy to proclaim one's commitment to a cause. It's not as easy to revamp an entire strategy to actually act and operate on new guidelines.
> —*John Graham, ASAE and The Center, interview, May 2010*

The ethical way in which you solve problems during your meeting or event will show your clients and attendees that you operate with diligence and integrity.

Evaluation

Greener meeting and event pioneers know that once an event is over, it isn't over. There remains the task of evaluating any success and examining areas for improvement. Valuable lessons can be gleaned from the event experience that can be used to feed forward into future events. To put it simply: How did it go? This is the question that the evaluation stage seeks to answer.

Survey the Scene

The evaluation process should actually begin during the meeting or event, not after. Data gathered during the event experience will prove critical when analyzing success postevent. Greener pioneers may use participant observation research or survey methods to gather data during the event.

Participant observation describes research conducted by someone while actively participating in the meeting or event. A meeting planner who takes notes on staff service or attendee behavior during the meeting is engaging in participant observation. Bring a notepad to your next meeting or event, and, when there is a free moment, take notes of things you observe that might be of use in later evaluations.

Participant observation is an easy way to gather data, but not the most accurate. In order to get a broader perspective, consider administering either written or verbal *surveys*, strategically conceived questionnaires, to event attendees. Surveys require more preparation and coordination than participant observation but provide more reliable data.

Surveys generally rely on two types of questioning. *Closed-ended questions* allow for quick but limited responses, such as yes/no questions or multiple-choice questions. *Open-ended questions* allow the respondent to answer freely however he or she chooses, such as, "Why did you choose to attend this greener meeting or event?" Closed-ended questions may also use rating systems, such as a *Likert scale*, that charts the level of agreement or disagreement with a statement, or a *semantic differential scale*, which asks the respondent to choose between two opposing qualities.

Question Type	Bad Example	Good Example
Leading questions: Do not attempt to persuade the respondent to agree with you, or to lead them to answering in a desirable way.	"Would you say our recycling policy is incredibly effective?"	"How would you rate our recycling services?"
Difficult questions: Quick and easy questions will get more responses than long or difficult questions that require too much contemplation, memory, or mathematics from the respondent. Keep it simple.	"How many miles did you travel to and from the event today?"	"Where did you travel from today?"
Long questions: Do not tax the patience of your respondents with overly long questions.	"What were your top ten favorite things about this conference, and why?"	"What was your favorite part of this conference, and why?"
Vague questions: Overly general, unclear questions will not draw out useful answers.	"Are you green?"	"Do you recycle at home?"
Sensitive questions: Do not invade the privacy of survey respondents, at risk of offending them or driving them away.	"What race are you?" or "What is your annual income?"	"What is your chosen profession?"

Figure 3.8 Five Question Types to Avoid in Greener Meeting and Event Surveys

Because there are so many different ways to create a survey, there is no one right way. There are, however, a few wrong ways, and Figure 3.8 points out a few types of questions to avoid.

Effective surveys are brief, clear, and to the point. Quick and easy surveys will get many more responses than long and difficult surveys. Figure 3.9 provides an example of a written survey with these qualities that uses a variety of question types.

The survey in Figure 3.9 collects a wide variety of data with just five easy questions. It begins with a clear title and explanation, and thanks the respondent at the beginning and end. Each of the five questions is phrased clearly and simply, without using any complex vocabulary, and each question leads into the next one. At the end, the respondent is given an incentive to submit the survey with his or her name and contact information. This survey could be easily completed in about two minutes, while an attendee is entering or exiting the event.

Thank you for attending EcoEvent. Please take a moment to answer this survey, which will help us to better serve you.

1. [Multiple Choice] How did you travel to EcoEvent?

☐ Walk   ☐ Bike   ☐ Car   ☐ Bus   ☐ Train   ☐ Plane

☐ Other: _____

2. [Yes/No] Would you be more inclined to use the subway if the event was located closer to a subway stop?   ☐ Yes ☐ No

3. [Semantic Differential] Please indicate your awareness or unawareness of the following greener initiatives at EcoEvent:

Recycling

Unaware   1   2   3   4   5   Aware

Local Foods

Unaware   1   2   3   4   5   Aware

Ban on Water Bottles

Unaware   1   2   3   4   5   Aware

4. [Open-Ended] How could we make EcoEvent greener in the future?

5. [Likert Scale] Will you attend future EcoEvents?

No   Unlikely   Not sure   Most likely   Yes

Thank You! For a chance to win two free tickets to the next EcoEvent, and to join our mailing list, write your name and email address below.

Name: _____

Email: _____

Figure 3.9   Greener EcoEvent Survey

As executive director of the International Centre for the Study of Planned Events (www .qmu.ac.uk/be/research/ICSPE), Professor Joe Goldblatt has conducted research on several major UK events, including The Gathering, a celebration of Scottish culture and heritage held in Edinburgh's Holyrood Park in 2009. At The Gathering, Goldblatt led a team of researchers who canvassed the event grounds, engaging attendees in verbal surveys. The researchers would politely approach attendees, engage them in a few brief, clearly enunciated questions, and write the respondents' answers as clearly and accurately as possible. Verbal surveys such as these are perfect for the many respondents who are more comfortable talking face to face with someone, or who would just rather not write. Surveys can also be conducted via phone or e-mail, but these tend to have a much lower response rate.

In 2010, Dr. Goldblatt conducted similar research at The Big Tent (www.bigtent festival.co.uk), an environmental music festival in Fife, Scotland. Fife Council commissioned Dr. Goldblatt before the event to design and implement a research strategy so that

Model Greener Event: MeetGreen

Nancy (Wilson) Zavada, founded Meeting Strategies Worldwide in 1994 with the simple objective of providing expert meeting management with sustainable ethics. Little did she know that 16 years later, the company would become MeetGreen, a major sustainable meeting consultancy, with mega-event clients like Live Earth and Oracle OpenWorld, or that she would play a critical role in founding the Green Meetings Industry Council (GMIC) and creating America's first national standards for sustainable meetings, the APEX standards.

"We're from Portland, Oregon, and we do things sustainably," says Zavada, "but when I was traveling around the country in the Midwest, I found out that it's not always the norm. It's very difficult to do a meeting in a responsible way in a lot of places. We thought that there was a huge impact that meeting planners could have by the different choices they made, and we wanted to go out and train people how to do that."

Zavada's tipping point was when a client requested Styrofoam cups instead of china service. "Our company rule has always been 'absolutely no Styrofoam, under any circumstances,' so I had to bring in my own cups," she says. "That group, in one week, would have used 75,000 Styrofoam cups, so imagine the number of cups used by all the other meeting planners in all of the other cities at that very same time. For me, that was a huge awakening of the impact of my choices."

Zavada notes that although the 2009 economic recession caused meetings to come under attack, as some viewed them as expensive boondoggles, green meetings have endured. "I thought that green meetings would certainly take a hit," she says, "but interestingly, they've become more mainstream, because they save money. People are looking at green for cost-cutting strategies, and to save their corporate image, because if they are still holding meetings in a recession, they need to be good stewards of the planet, to be sustainable, and to look at social issues." Zavada says that, while the early adopters were associations, green meetings have now moved on to corporations, who seek an enhanced image.

this outstanding festival could be properly evaluated in the future. It is never too early to plan how you will evaluate a future event.

Measuring Up

In addition to the ethnographic research that may be gathered from surveys, *quantitative data*, or data expressed in numbers, can be gathered to measure the success of certain strategies. Gas, electricity, and water bills can be mined for signs of reduction from attempts to conserve resources. Complex equations can calculate the total carbon emissions from car travel to and from the event. Chapter 4 will give you the mathematical tools needed to calculate your carbon footprint and to measure the success of your event.

The evaluation of this quantitative data should feed forward into the research phase of the next event. Ask your green team questions like, "Why did we use this much electricity

"For the most part, green meetings are either cost-neutral or cost-savings," says Zavada, who explains that any extra costs can be balanced by the savings. "Large shows may incur a cost for hauling to recycling, in case the center doesn't have a recycler. But look at the other ways that green practices can save money: by not producing a program, by not producing handouts, by doing without a shuttle system. There are many ways to make up for any costs."

MeetGreen Project Manager Shawna McKinley spends many hours training meeting planners on sustainability. She told me, "It's great when you hear a comment from your client or their vendors that tells you that now they're completely owning this themselves. The biggest challenge is to make it cultural, so that there's a permanent shift in the organization." McKinley recalls a member of the janitorial staff who saw her leaning over a dumpster to remove a plastic bottle which was contaminating a compost stream, and who then actually got into the dumpster himself to assist.

Selecting a destination is one of the most important decisions a meeting planner will make, and that is why McKinley developed a guide to the Best Places to MeetGreen (www.bestplacestomeetgreen.com), which helps clients to understand the carbon footprint and the local infrastructure issues in a destination. McKinley says that this guide was created based on demand by clients. "Our clients have done so many events in so many different cities, we know that when we're going to a city that has green infrastructure, our life will be so much easier than if we go to a city that doesn't have recycling or composting."

Zavada advises meeting planners considering sustainability to take the first step, even if it's a small one, and not to get overwhelmed. "Maybe choose to recycle, and ask for that at all future events. Get that down, and build on it," she says.

McKinley and Zavada's dedication to advancing the green meetings industry and their strong work ethic might come down to the fact that they love their job. As Zavada says, "It's really my personal passion, and when I can combine that with my work, it's a fabulous place to be." Thanks to the passion of Zavada and her team, MeetGreen is making big waves in the green meetings industry.

on this day?" and "How can we reduce electricity use at the next event?" In this way, greener meetings and events are cycles, with each event helping to make the next one greener.

Quantitative data are also great for impressing clients. When we spoke in May 2010, Nancy (Wilson) Zavada shared that translating your meeting statistics into something more consumer-friendly can help to get the point across. "Frame it as something helpful or visual, such as the number of trees saved, or the weight in elephants recycled, or the water in swimming pools saved."

Zavada advises greener meeting and event pioneers to "talk about your story and share your successes." The stages of management in this chapter should assist you to produce a successful sustainable meeting or event, and to tell your story, one of continual improvement in event sustainability.

Summary

Greener meetings and events follow the same basic management stages as every meeting or event: research, design, planning, coordination, and evaluation. In the research stage, assemble a diverse green team and engage them in blue sky thinking, assessing the strengths, weaknesses, opportunities, and threats to sustainability for the future meeting or event. Use this research to define your triple bottom line commitment to people, planet, and profit, and to create a strategic green plan consisting of prioritized tasks and a green mission statement. This strategic green plan should be put into action through greener contracts and risk assessment. During the meeting or event, engage staff, stakeholders, clients, and attendees with a common purpose. Sustainability and event success can be evaluated through participant observation, survey research, or quantitative measurement.

Key Terms and Definitions

- **Blue sky thinking**: open-minded and imaginative discussion, unhampered by realistic constraints.
- **SWOT analysis**: a list of strengths, weaknesses, opportunities, and threats for your meeting or event.
- **Triple bottom line (TBL)**: your commitment to people, planet, and profit to ensure event success.
- **Green mission statement**: a prose summary of your commitment to the values of sustainability.
- **Strategic green plan**: a green mission statement and list of prioritized strategic goals. It is supported by planning documents, including SWOT analysis and triple bottom line commitment.
- **Risk management**: the process of carefully planning to avoid any dangerous or harmful incidents during the meeting or event.
- **Reputation term**: section of a contract in which both parties agree to preserve and protect each other's reputation.

- **Sustainability rider**: contractual attachment regarding sustainability.
- **Exhibitor contracts**: agreements in which exhibitors lease space for a booth at an exposition.
- **Hotel contracts**: agreements where hotels provide rooms, space, and services for events.
- **Vendor contracts**: agreements in which vendors provide services or products.
- **Purchase orders**: requests for vendors to provide services or products.
- **Participant observation**: research conducted by someone while actively participating in a meeting or event.
- **Survey**: strategic questionnaire.
- **Closed-ended questions**: allowing quick but limited responses, such as yes/no questions or multiple choice questions
- **Open-ended questions**: allowing the respondent to answer freely however he or she chooses, such as, "Why . . .?" questions
- **Likert scale**: rating scale, usually showing amount of disagreement or agreement
- **Semantic differential**: a scale where the respondent chooses between two opposite qualities
- **Quantitative data**: information expressed in numbers

Blue Sky Thinking

An association of Colorado brewers is organizing a sustainable beer festival in Denver, and it has hired you as its risk management consultant. Some of the electricity will be powered by giant solar panels that patrons can touch. Other electricity will be powered by an array of stationary bikes that patrons can ride. Beer from over 20 breweries will be served from 12 P.M. to 8 P.M., and jazz band Kermit Ruffins and the Barbecue Swingers is scheduled to perform at 6 P.M. Bison burgers will be served all day, grilled on outdoor barbecues. Create a risk assessment for this beer festival with at least 20 risks, then rate the impact and probability of each risk. Which risks have the highest priority, and what precautions will you take to mitigate these risks?

Renewable Resources

Best Places to Meet Green: www.bestplacestomeetgreen.com.

Elkington, John (1998). *Cannibals with Forks: The Triple Bottom Line of the 21st Century Business.* Stony Creek, CT: New Society Publishers.

Hoyle, Leonard H (2002). *Event Marketing: How to Successfully Promote Events, Festivals, Conventions and Expositions.* Hoboken: John Wiley & Sons.

Jones, Meegan (2010). *Sustainable Event Management.* London: Earthscan.

Mazur, Laura, and Louella Miles (2009). *Conversations with Green Gurus: The Collective Wisdom of Environmental Movers and Shakers.* Chichester: John Wiley & Sons.

Sustainability Law Blog: www.sustainabilitylawblog.com.

The Big Tent not only reduces the festival footprint, it helps attendees to reduce their own carbon emissions as well.

CHAPTER 4

Measuring "Green"

"We could have saved the Earth but we were too damned cheap."

—*Kurt Vonnegut, Jr, Novelist (1922–2007)*

In this chapter you will learn:

1. How to create and use key performance indicators (KPIs) for your event

2. How to find and use benchmarks with which to compare your greener event progress

3. How to gather data that can help tell the story of your environmental initiatives

4. How to measure your event's carbon footprint

5. How to calculate the carbon emissions of transportation to and from your event

6. How to write and manage an eco-budget for your event

As always in business, measurements reveal values. A corporate event that includes only financial data in its annual report shows different values than an educational conference that measures the number of students from disadvantaged neighborhoods who attended. No matter how many environmental initiatives you have at your meeting or event, only those initiatives that have been planned, measured, and recorded will have lasting future impact.

Gene Columbus, producer of many high-profile events at Walt Disney World, believes that measurement and budgeting are foundational aspects of event planning. "You can only manage what you can measure" (Columbus 2010).

Greener meeting and event pioneers are increasingly using innovative strategies and comprehensive measurement tools to plan environmental initiatives and to chart their progress along these plans. This chapter will demystify these financial and organizational measurement tools and explain concepts such as key performance indicators (KPIs), carbon footprint, and eco-budget.

Key Performance Indicators (KPIs)

The best way to set and track strategic environmental goals is by creating *key performance indicators (KPIs)*, or specific, measurable outcomes that your strategies will affect. For example, two common KPIs used by greener events pioneers are "volume of trash send to landfill" and "volume of trash sent to recycling." Remember to make your KPIs *SMART*—specific, measurable, achievable, realistic, and timely. Figure 4.1 shows some good and bad examples of SMART KPIs for greener meetings and events.

KPIs may be organized by department or other categories brainstormed, or according to the three tiers of the triple bottom line (see Chapter 3): social KPIs, environmental KPIs, and financial KPIs. Social KPIs might describe guest experience or employee

	Good	Bad
Specific	Pounds of waste sent to landfill per conference attendee	Bags of trash removed
Measurable	Number of green projects managed by nonsenior staff within previous 12 months	Employee enthusiasm
Achievable	Reducing landfill deposit to 50% within 12 months	Zero landfill deposit
Realistic	Purchasing renewable energy from a provider as part of a larger energy plan	Switching to 100% self-generated solar power
Timely	Kilowatts used per hour of event	Total electricity used last year

Figure 4.1   SMART KPIs for Greener Meetings and Events

satisfaction, and may use qualitative research such as interviews. Environmental KPIs mostly use quantitative data to track environmental impact, which could include carbon emissions, electricity and water usage, miles traveled by gas power, and square footage of soil erosion. Financial KPIs rely on quantitative data and show all the standard accounting figures as well as greener numbers—for instance, "percentage of income donated to charity" and "total amount spent on reforestation."

When dealing with environmental data, you may have to learn new measurements. For instance, it is important to know that *kilowatt hours*, abbreviated as kWh, is a standard measurement of electricity use.

Figure 4.2 shows some classic categories, strategic goals, and KPIs that could be used to measure these goals for greener meetings and events.

Environmental Audits

Most businesses undergo an annual *financial audit,* which is a review of all financial data that results in an evaluation of the company's current financial position. Increasingly, businesses are now undertaking *environmental audits*, or audits that analyze not just profit but also a commitment to people and the planet, resulting in a portrait of the company's current environmental and social impact. If you have created KPIs that are truly specific, measurable, achievable, realistic, and timely (SMART), then you should be able to begin collecting data immediately, in order to achieve *baseline indications,* which show the current position of your KPIs.

Unlike financial data, environmental or social data may not be available to review, other than perhaps last month's electricity bill. It may take several months to collect enough data to gauge an accurate baseline indicator of your current status. Do not be daunted by the unfamiliarity of this environmental research, and remember that it is a learning process. Use your mistakes as opportunities to better understand the techniques for collecting this data in the future. Figure 4.3 shows some innovative ways to collect data to chart KPIs for greener meetings and events.

Measuring sustainability is a journey, not a destination. Data collection for an environmental audit is not a one-off activity, but a year-round strategy that should be built into standard operating procedures. Continue to evolve your data collection techniques as you find out what works for you.

Benchmarks for Success

Once you have enough data to provide an accurate and reliable portrait of your current position, you will need some points of comparison, or *benchmarks*, in order to assess your proximity or distance from your strategic goals. Benchmarks provide validity for your internal data collection and help you to set appropriate strategic goals.

Finding specific benchmark statistics in a field as new as greener meetings and events will be understandably difficult, but not impossible. You should be able to glean some

Category	Strategic Goal	KPI
Social	Delegate green responsibility among staff.	Number of green projects managed by nonsenior staff within previous 12 months
	Contribute to local youth groups.	Number of local youths involved at event per attendee
	Educate public on greener events.	Number of different types of media featuring educational information provided for public at event
		Percentage of attendees exposed to educational media
Environmental	Convert to renewable energy.	Percentage of total energy from renewable providers
	Maximize public transport use.	Percentage of attendees traveling by car or taxi to event
		Percentage of attendees traveling by public transportation to event
	Develop water filtration system.	Number of bottled waters consumed at event per attendee
		Number of sources of purified drinking water on event site per attendee
Financial	Cut costs through energy efficiency.	Kilowatt hours used over previous month Amount paid for electricity over previous month
	Attract environmental sponsors.	Number of environmental sponsors over past 12 months
		Number of nonenvironmental sponsors over past 12 months
	Attract new clients with sustainability plan.	Number of new clients engaged with new sustainability plan over last 12 months
		Number of new clients engaged without sustainability plan over last 12 months

Figure 4.2 Categorized Goals and KPIs of Greener Meetings and Events

KPI	Data Collection Methodology
Number of green projects managed by nonsenior staff within previous 12 months	Survey all staff.
Number of local youths involved at event per attendee	Appoint a person-counter at event.
Number of different types of media featuring educational information provided for public at event Percentage of attendees exposed to educational media	Observe media distribution at event or conduct postevent survey.
Percentage of total energy from renewable providers	Measure kilowatts per hour from renewable and nonrenewable sources (different venues may use different providers).
Percentage of attendees traveling by car or taxi to event Percentage of attendees traveling by public transportation to event	Survey attendees.
Number of bottled waters consumed at event per attendee	Count bottles of water before, then after the event, to find the number used.
Number of sources of purified drinking water on event site per attendee	Consult a water quality expert to gauge purity of water sources.
Kilowatt hours used over previous month Amount paid for electricity over previous month	Check electricity bills.
Number of environmental sponsors over past 12 months Number of nonenvironmental sponsors over past 12 months	Survey sponsors to gauge their environmental policies.
Number of new clients engaged with new sustainability plan over last 12 months Number of new clients engaged without sustainability plan over last 12 months	Survey clients to find if sustainability played a role in their decision to hire you.

Figure 4.3 Data Collection Techniques for Greener Meeting and Event Audits

Measuring Success at the Edinburgh International Conference Centre

Over the past several years, the Edinburgh International Conference Centre (www.eicc.co.uk) has earned a reputation for sustainable conference management. On a cold December day in 2010, I decided to check out the EICC for myself, and braved the snow to meet with Reynaldo Guino-o, human resources and total quality management, who has measured and improved sustainable practices over the years. Guino-o believes that sustainability is a key to EICC's success, saying, "With repeat business, there is great opportunity to chart progress in sustainable event management."

Using simple but accurate calculations, EICC found that, at a major four-day event held annually, energy usage per-delegate was reduced by more than 75 percent from 2007 to 2010, from 1.42 kWh in 2007 to 0.34 kWh in 2010. Guino-o is also happy to report, "Despite more than doubling the number of covers from 1,100 in 2007 to 2,500 in 2010, total solid waste from the kitchens was down over 12% in this period, from 1,666 kg to 1,463 kg."

Recently, a prestigious Food and Drink Industry Conference, with a Scottish produce theme, wanted to know the sustainable performance associated with its 275-cover fine-dining event. The conference sponsors were impressed by EICC's detailed report, which revealed:

- 220 kilograms (kg) of food came into the kitchen, excluding packaging.
- Food waste in preparation was kept to 20 kg.
- 200 kg of actual food was sent out.
- Catering packaging waste in kilograms was kept to 8 kg.
- 2 kg packaging waste was returned to suppliers for reuse.
- 6 kg of catering packaging waste went to recycling.
- 22 grams of waste per delegate was recycled.
- 18 grams of food waste per delegate went to compost.

Additionally, the EICC also reported that energy usage per delegate was just 0.90 kilowatt hours, and water usage was 0.006 cubic meters per delegate. "EICC can monitor sustainable events down to the most minute detail," says Guino-o. By using SMART KPIs to monitor and measure sustainability, you too can impress clients and encourage them to come back next year to see how the numbers can be improved.

useful comparative data from the featured greener events that appear at the end of every chapter in this book. Web sites and contact information for greener event organizations are provided throughout this book to encourage you to contact the real people making greener meetings and events happen and to gather more specific data from them. Following are some useful places to find benchmarks for greener meetings and events, and you can find more contact information in the appendices of this book.

The central foyer of Gerding Theatre at The Armory.
Courtesy of Portland Center Stage.

Charles Henderson, managing director of the consultancy Climate Futures (www
.climatefutures.co.uk), provides benchmark data analysis for environmental meetings
and events in the United Kingdom. Speaking at a seminar on Greener Events hosted by
EventScotland (www.eventscotland.org) in April 2009, he said, "It can be useful to say
that we are greener than 80 percent of our competitors. The ultimate goal is zero carbon
and zero waste throughout the entire life-cycle of your event."

Sources for Greener Meetings and Events Benchmarks

- *Similar meetings or events:* Contact one of the many greener events featured in this book, most of which collect extensive data on their sustainability plans. MeetGreen (www.meetgreen.com) publishes a superb annual report.
- *Meeting and event industry reports:* Meeting Professionals International (MPI) (www.mpiweb.org) publishes several different annual reports, which include useful statistics. Also try International Conference and Convention Association (ICCA) (www.iccaworld.com), Convention Industry Council (CIC) (www.conventionindustry.org), International Festivals and Events Association (IFEA) (www.ifea.com), American Society of Association Executives (ASAE) (www.asaecenter.org), and International Special Events Society (ISES) (www.ises.com) for useful industry reports.
- *Industry news: Events Solutions* (www.event-solutions.com) and *Special Events* (www.specialevents.com) are two major magazines in the events industry that regularly feature information on greener events.
- *Government reports:* See what the U.S. Environmental Protection Agency (EPA) has to say (www.epa.gov/opptintr/green-meetings/), or try local government initiatives such as Broadway Green Alliance (www.broadwaygreen.com) or the Mayor of London's reports on greening the arts, titled *Green Theatre*, *Green Music* and *Green Screen* (http://www.london.gov.uk/who-runs-london/mayor/publications/culture).
- *Standards:* BS 8901 (www.bsigroup.com) or the APEX/ASTM Green Meetings Standard (http://www.conventionindustry.org/StandardsPractices/GreenMeetings.aspx).

You may not be able to find benchmark statistics that exactly mirror each of your KPIs. In these situations, try to adapt a related benchmark, and use your own baseline KPI measurement as your point of reference. For instance, on January 29, 2010, President Obama announced that the U.S. federal government would reduce its greenhouse gas pollution by 28 percent by 2020 (White House Office of the Press Secretary 2010). Taking into consideration your current total gas transportation and coal energy usage, could you similarly reduce your greenhouse gas pollution within the next ten years?

Once you have numbers for your own baseline indicators and corresponding numbers as benchmark indicators, compare the two numbers and give yourself a rating as to your progress toward your strategic goals. An easy way to do this is to use a simple rating system with five options:

Figure 4.4 compares a few sample KPIs with hypothetical benchmarks and provides a rating.

KPI Rating Scale

1. Far-below-average performance. Wasteful event practice with a large and negative environmental impact. Baseline far below benchmark.
2. Below-average performance or standard. If limited data or benchmarks are available, 2 should be a standard KPI rating.
3. Average performance for a greener meeting or event. Baseline meets benchmark.
4. Above-average performance. Baseline above benchmark.
5. Outstanding performance. Industry-leading, model practice of a greener meeting or event. Baseline far above benchmark.

---------1---------2---------3---------4---------5 →

Sample KPI	Benchmark	Rating
5 green projects managed by nonsenior staff within previous 12 months.	Statistic is identical at comparison organization.	3
12 local youths were involved in an event with 330 attendees, meaning 3.6% of attendees were local youths.	Amount of local youth involvement at NFL event.	2.5
34% of attendees reported awareness of educational media.	Live Earth exposed 100% of attendees to educational media.	2
Our office uses a renewable provider, but our event venue does not. Of the total kilowatts used for the event, approximately 28% were from renewable sources.	The 2007 Super Bowl used 100% renewable energy.	2
15% of attendees used public transportation.	70% of attendees used public transportation at comparison event.	1
The average attendee consumed 1.4 bottles of water.	No bottled water was consumed at comparison event.	1
Last month we paid $581 for 2,200 kilowatt hours of electricity.	Goal: reduce electricity use by 5% each month.	1
In the past 12 months, 20% of our sponsors were environmentally motivated.	Comparison organizations claim 50% of sponsors are environmentally motivated.	2
In the past 12 months, 50% of our clients were environmentally motivated.	Comparison organizations claim 40% of sponsors are environmentally motivated.	4

Figure 4.4   Benchmarks for Greener Event Success

Action Planning

With your KPIs rated according to their baseline and benchmark, your position in regard to your triple bottom line should be readily apparent. How many of your KPIs are below average, and how many above? Which KPIs are rated the lowest, and which the highest? These ratings point you toward where there is the most room for improvement.

If the baseline KPI measurements in Figure 4.4 relate to one specific event, that event's environmental credentials have an average rating of 2, or below the average rating of benchmark comparisons. The areas in need of the most improvement are increasing use of public transportation, decreasing bottled water, and conserving more electricity.

Now go back to your original strategic goals and assign tasks, which can be measured according to KPIs, to achieve these goals. This list should be much longer than your original list of goals, as it should now include several different specific options for improving each KPI. Consider the bullet list showing just a few tasks that could be gleaned from the goals and KPIs set out thus far.

Now that you have a full and varied list of potential strategies to improve your KPIs, prioritize these tasks, trying to highlight those that are most needed, most effective, and most achievable. Tasks aimed at KPIs with the lowest ratings should be given the highest priority. Discuss these tasks with your green focus panel and try to create a top ten list, with 1 representing the most critical, most effective, and most achievable task, and 10 representing the least. Make a schedule of when each of these tasks will be designed, implemented and completed, with 1 beginning immediately, and 10 on the back burner until a later date. Figure 4.5 provides an example of how to prioritize your goals.

These prioritized strategic goals, based on KPIs, can be generated during the research and design stages of the event management process, in addition to the processes already discussed in Chapter 3. These SMART goals will help you achieve your ambitious agenda for sustainability.

Dale Hudson, head of project development at IMEX, reminds green event pioneers that this kind of detailed strategic planning, using KPIs to track initiatives, is a long-term project. "We started with a step by step approach," she says. "We did not try and do everything overnight, and what we have now is a nine-year program which incorporates three or four initiatives per year" (Hudson, interview, March 2010).

Strategic Goals Expanded into Specific Tasks

- Increase prominence of educational media, so that 100 percent of attendees are aware.
- Incrementally reduce electricity usage by 25 percent within the next 12 months.
- Increase public transportation at events by 50 percent over next 12 months.
- Increase use of filtered tap water at events by 50 percent over next 12 months.

Priority	Strategic Goal	KPI	Schedule
1	Incrementally reduce electricity usage by 25% within the next 12 months.	Total kilowatt hours, from monthly electric bill	This week: Create prioritized list of energy saving initiatives, from "easy" to "hard." This month: Begin to implement "easy" initiatives. Future: Increase initiatives as needed to meet 25% reduction goal.
2	Increase use of filtered tap water at events by 50% over next 12 months.	Number of bottles of water used per attendee	Two months: Gather infrastructure for safe tap-water drinking service at event venue. Four months: Test and gradually increase tap-water service. Future: Transition towards only serving filtered tap water.
3	Increase public transportation at events by 50% over next 12 months.	Percentage of attendees using public transportation	Two months: Create partnership with local public transportation corporations Four months: Create marketing plan to promote public transportation. Future: Position public transportation as a core element of your event experience.
4	Increase prominence of educational media, so that 100% of attendees are aware within 6 months.	Percentage of attendees aware of educational media	This month: Create marketing plan for increasing educational media at events. Next month: Execute marketing plan. Future: Monitor progress and revise.

Figure 4.5   Prioritized Strategic Goals

Measuring Your Event's Carbon Footprint

The total amount of greenhouse gases emitted, both directly and indirectly, in service to your event, is your *carbon footprint*, so called because carbon dioxide is the major gas emitted. Finding your carbon footprint provides you with an excellent baseline with which to measure your progress in cutting down that footprint. Check out the three *carbon calculators*, or computer programs that take diverse statistics to calculate a total carbon footprint, designed specifically for the meetings and events industry.

Available online, these carbon calculators allow you to input data from your meeting or event in order to ascertain an average carbon footprint for your overall event. Be aware that these carbon calculators are based on average assumptions, and that the most accurate way of calculating your carbon footprint is do the math yourself with the help of a qualified consultant. For instance, some of the calculations in this section are based on the work of Mark Lynas, a researcher at the University of Oxford, and a bestselling author on climate change and carbon calculations. You can measure your meeting or event's carbon footprint on your own by using a little simple arithmetic.

Please note that the following calculations are designed to give you a basic understanding of the carbon footprinting process, and are based on a wide variety of average assumptions.

Gas and Electric

The easiest place to start is the one measurement you most likely already have: your gas utility bill. Request the gas bill of your event venue, meeting hall, or convention center. The gas should be measured in *British thermal units* (BTUs) or *therms* (100,000 BTUs). If your event has already occurred, get the total amount of gas used during the preevent, event, and postevent time period. If you have not used the venue yet, try and find a measurement of gas usage taken at a time when the venue was occupied in a way similar to your event. If you cannot get a daily breakdown of gas usage from your provider, take the weekly or monthly total and create a daily average. For instance, if your venue used

Three Carbon Calculators for the Meetings and Events Industry

1. Australian Centre for Event Management (calculator.noco2.com.au/acem)
2. Doubletree Hotel (www.doubletreegreen .com)
3. MPI Sustainable Event Tool (mpi.sustain-ableeventtool.com)

22,500 therms of gas during August, divide this by the number of days in the month (31) to get a daily average of 726 therms per day.

$$\frac{\text{Monthly utility usage}}{\text{Number of days in the month}} = \text{Daily utility usage}$$

If you only used part of a venue, for instance a conference room, you will have to calculate the size of your area in relation to the entire venue, by dividing the square footage of the area you used by the total square footage of the venue. For example, if you used a 2,000 square foot conference room within a larger 200,000 square foot convention center, divide 2,000 by 200,000 to get .01, or 1 percent. You used 1 percent of the convention center, and thus can estimate that you are responsible for 1 percent of the convention center's total gas usage. This, however, assumes that the rest of the convention center was used at full capacity. If yours was the only event on, then you may well assume responsibility for 100 percent of the gas usage.

$$\frac{\text{Area of event use}}{\text{Total area of venue using utilities}} = \text{Percentage of venue used by event}$$

Once you have calculated your event's total gas usage, in therms, you will need to translate this number into total carbon emissions. Pacific Gas and Electric Company (www.pge.com) provides a simple multiplier to calculate the carbon emissions of gas usage. Multiply total event gas usage, in therms, by 13.4 to find your total event gas carbon footprint, in pounds.

Electricity is measured in *kilowatt hours* (kWh). One kWh is equal to using 1,000 watts of electricity in one hour, so using a 100-watt light bulb for one hour would use 0.1 kWh.

$$1 \text{ kilowatt hour} = \frac{1{,}000 \text{ watts of electricity}}{1 \text{ hour}}$$

Calculating your emissions from electricity follows the same process as for gas. Take the venue's monthly electricity bill and calculate your event's usage in terms of how many days and how much of the venue you used. Once you have calculated your event's total electricity usage, in kWh, multiply it by 1.3 to derive the total event electricity carbon footprint, in pounds. 1.3 is quoted by the carbon calculator and offsetter Carbon Fund (http://www.carbonfund.org) as the average pounds of carbon emissions per kWh. This assumes your electricity comes from coal energy, and not renewable sources such as solar power, which can bring your carbon emissions as low as zero.

Figure 4.6 summarizes the basic formulas for calculating gas and electricity carbon footprints.

Total Usage	Multiply by This Number	Carbon Footprint (pounds)
Gas (therms)	13.4	
Electric (kWh)	1.3	

Figure 4.6 Gas and Electric Carbon Calculations

Carbon Miles

As you may have noticed by now, calculating kilograms of carbon emissions from reliable data is as easy as basic math. It's the actual data collection of gas and electricity usage over a specific time period and within specific areas of venues that poses a greater challenge. This is even more true in calculating *carbon miles*, or the greenhouse gas emitted by transportation.

Calculating your meeting or event's carbon miles poses two basic challenges:

1. Finding out the specific types of, and numbers of, different modes of transportation used
2. Calculating the miles these vehicles traveled for your event

Different types of vehicles, including different makes of cars, can emit vastly different amounts of carbon dioxide. Generally speaking, vehicles with larger engines use more gas and therefore emit more carbon dioxide, but this is not always the case. The good news is that there are several Web sites that can provide rough estimations of carbon emitted by various types of transportation if you input the mileage.

Start with the biggest section of your carbon footprint: air travel. Find out how many people flew on planes for your event, and how far they flew. Input this mileage into one of the online calculators to find the total carbon emissions, in pounds. Planes use excessive gas during takeoff and landing, which these Web sites should take into consideration. As Mark Lynas notes in his book *Carbon Calculator*, because airplanes emit carbon so very high in the atmosphere, the Intergovernmental Panel on Climate Change estimates their

Three Free Online Carbon Mile Calculators

1. Choose Climate (www.chooseclimate.org/flying).
2. Transport Direct (www.transportdirect.info). Click on "Tips and Tools," then "CO2 emissions calculator."
3. The Carbon Neutral Company (tools.carbonneutral.com/cncalculators/flightcalculator.asp).

Distance Traveled (miles)	Multiply by This Number	Carbon Footprint (pounds)
Train	0.287	
Bus	0.198	
Large Car	0.882	
Small Car	0.22	
Urban Rail System	0.154	
Boat	1.04	

These calculations are based on average global assumptions. Contact your local transit authority for more exact estimations.

Figure 4.7 Carbon Mile Calculations

emissions to be at least 2.7 times as harmful as emissions on the ground (Lynas 2007). If your Web site has not already done so, multiply your total by 2.7.

Transport Direct (www.transportdirect.info) provides rough estimates of carbon miles travelled by train, bus, or large or small car. Lynas recommends multiplying mileage on the London Underground, London's electric underground railway also known as The Tube, by 0.07 to find kilograms of carbon emissions. We can convert this number to pounds by multiplying by 2.205 to get 0.154 (Lynas 2007). All urban rail systems vary, but multiplying urban rail mileage by 0.154 can provide an average number of pounds of carbon emitted. Similarly, ferries and cruises come in many different shapes and sizes, and large, luxurious cruise ships generate more carbon than small, efficient ferries. Also, ultrafast boats use more gas as they push against water drag.

To do the math yourself, try the following basic calculations listed in Figure 4.7. Keep in mind that these calculations provide per-person carbon emissions, assuming that the vehicle is largely occupied. In other words, an urban rail system has the lowest carbon emissions per-person when it is completely full during rush hour. Always calculate carbon emissions per-person, rather than per-vehicle. For instance, if 98 people took the train, multiply the distance traveled, in miles, by 0.287, and then by 98, to get the total carbon footprint for that group, in pounds.

The greenhouse gas emissions of all transportation and energy use make up the majority of your meeting or event's carbon footprint. You can also use the same formulas to calculate the year-round emissions of a meetings or events organization by measuring these figures over the course of a year. To calculate a carbon footprint over a year, you may have to make some assumptions, such as estimating your average weekly staff car miles, then multiplying by 50, the average number of U.S. work weeks in a year.

Grand Total

The majority of your event's carbon footprint derives from the energy use and transportation you have just calculated, but there are many smaller, indirect ways that your event causes carbon emissions. Did you serve apples picked from a local orchard, or kiwis flown in from New Zealand? Did you recycle? Instead of calculating the carbon emissions of every piece of trash sent to landfill, or the carbon miles of every kiwi flown in from abroad, you can add a lump sum based on your event's general level of consumption.

Lynas recommends adding 3,000, 2,000, or 600 kilograms to a person's annual carbon footprint, based on levels of consumerism and waste over the course of an entire year (Lynas 2007). Our daily event multipliers of 18.1, 12.1, and 3.62 are derived by converting Lynas's annual figures to pounds and then dividing them by 365, the number of days in the year. Multiply your total event attendance by the number of days of your event, and then multiply by 18.1, 12.1, or 3.62, depending on the level of consumerism and waste. For lack of a better word, Figure 4.8 will affectionately call this final addition an event consumption penance.

If undertaking a comprehensive, professional carbon audit, you generally would not add this final sum because it is an estimation not based on hard data. This final sum can be useful for beginners to understand their footprint, but I do not advise you to include it in a professional audit, which may result in professional or financial action.

Amount of Event Consumerism/Waste	Additional Carbon Footprint Kilograms (multiply by number of attendees and by number of days)
"We bought all rare imported foods, shipped from abroad with excess packaging and served on disposable plates, which were sent to landfill. There was no recycling, and all decorations were thrown out post-event. Litter was a problem."	18.1
"We used biodegradable plates and cutlery and recyclable water bottles. We encouraged recycling. All event decorations, such as linens, were rented from a vendor and reused. Most food was purchased locally, but certain elements, such as bananas and coffee, were shipped from abroad."	12.1
"We used all local, organic food, made from neighboring farms, and served on vintage porcelain plates, with glassware and silverware that was washed and reused. All cleaning supplies were organic. All decorations were made from organic materials, and reused afterward. There was minimal waste, which was composted."	3.62

Figure 4.8 Event Consumption Penance

```
         Gas
   +     Electric
   +     Air travel
   +     All other travel
   +     Event consumption penance
   ─────────────────────────────────
   −     Total event carbon footprint (kilograms)
```

Figure 4.9 Total Event Carbon Footprint Calculator

You are now ready to calculate the grand total of your event's carbon footprint, as shown in Figure 4.9. All amounts should be in pounds.

You now have your total event carbon footprint, in pounds. To convert it to U.S. short tons, multiply by 0.0005. To convert it to kilograms, multiply by 0.454. Remember that this figure should represent the carbon footprint not just for you or your staff, but for the entire event, including every attendee's travel, consumption, and waste.

If appropriate, you may also calculate the total carbon footprint for specific groups, such as staff, exhibitors, or attendees. Divide the total attendee footprint by the number of attendees to deduce the average carbon footprint of each attendee.

Although carbon footprint calculations for meetings and events are still rarely published, you may be able to find appropriate benchmark comparisons by contacting the greener events featured in this book, or through specialized consultants to greener meetings and events. MeetGreen provides one of the few online carbon calculators specifically tailored to meetings and events (calculator.meetgreen.com).

Your Eco-Budget

Just as the first step to a diet is a weigh-in, a measurement of your carbon footprint represents the first step to lowering it. Make a pie chart that breaks down the various categories (gas, electricity, transportation) of your carbon footprint. Which were the largest areas? In which areas could you improve the most? Which areas align best with your strategic green plan? One of the most useful tools for understanding how to lower your carbon footprint is the one you already possess: your budget.

Ian Garrett, executive director of The Center for Sustainable Practice in the Arts (CSPA) (www.sustainablepractice.org), gives professional environmental advice to arts events and festivals. When we met during the Edinburgh Festival in August 2009, he noted that most events calculate cash, but not carbon: "When they do their budget they don't look at resources." He recommends that events document and make transparent their use of energy and resources with a similar level of detail reserved for financial accounts. "The biggest hurdle for greening initiatives is getting people to spend some time to look at what they're actually using, in terms of materials and energy," he says.

In recognition of their triple bottom line, greener meeting and event pioneers measure not just financial cost but also carbon cost. These *eco-budgets* include an additional line

Greener Festival: Manchester International Festival

The Manchester International Festival (MIF, www.mif.co.uk) is a cutting-edge, citywide arts festival held biannually in the UK city of Manchester. Not only does MIF feature a vast array of performances and exhibitions—everything from opera to free public art displays, from world music to international conferences, from classical music to Kanye West—but it is also a pioneering greener event, having helped to develop the British standard for sustainable events (BS 8901) since its inception in 2007, when it served 200,000 attendees on a budget of £10 million.

MIF implements many industry-leading practices, such as diverting food waste away from landfill through composting. Promotional vinyl banners are creatively recycled into designer handbags, which have proven popular. Local, seasonal produce is sourced for catering, and recycled paper from sustainable sources is used for printed materials. Most importantly, MIF hosted The Manchester Report, a creative symposium and conference dedicated to environmental issues.

When I spoke with her in August of 2009, Jennifer Cleary, head of creative learning for MIF, said that environmental strategies become easier over time: "Translating environmental standards to a specific event is challenging if you don't have a background in sustainability, and nobody on our team did. As soon as things are implemented for the first time, it starts to become second nature."

She knows that creating a strategic green plan will surely take some time, and that it helps to delegate responsibility among staff, saying, "It absolutely requires an investment of staff time to critically analyze how the organization is working, and how it might be able to

work differently. It really helps to departmentalize things on a certain level, so everyone can think about how their own team can manage it." She explains that staff motivation is key, saying, "Generally, everyone is really enthusiastic about our environmental initiatives, and are quite proactive toward them."

Cleary advises greener meeting and event pioneers to pursue the low-hanging fruit of simple office efficiencies first. "There absolutely have been cost savings," she says. "We saved around £2,000 just by double-sided printing. The basic organizational stuff, like making sure we're not overprinting brochures, has been pretty good." Another big success was the recycling of promotional banners into designer bags. "We've had lots of positive feedback on the banner bags," she says. Everybody, from artists to staff to audience members, has been loving them."

Not all initiatives were so simple or profit-making, however. "Making the festival site more environmentally friendly has had cost implications," Cleary says. "Small things like installing a bike rack clearly have a cost. It also cost more to compost waste than to send it to landfill, and more to source the compostable tableware than the conventional plastic goods."

Composting is perhaps MIF's most ambitious green initiative and greatest challenge. "There was a real learning curve for us, for the composting company, in terms of a large-scale, city-center event, and for the caterers," says Cleary. She explains the composting process, saying, "We set up a partnership with a local composting company. They allocated a separate composting furnace for us, so that if there were things in our waste stream, like plastic bottles, that shouldn't be in there and would contaminate the whole batch of compost, it would only affect our waste."

Cleary acknowledges some of the challenges, saying, "We were working with a new location, and a new process for separating waste streams. Because of this it was hard to anticipate how much compostable waste would be generated and at one stage some waste that could have been composted had to be cleared off the site because it couldn't be picked up in time."

Having been one of the first major events to use the BS 8901 standard's organizing tools, MIF now has some experience in setting and tracking key performance indicators (KPIs) for environmental sustainability. Cleary recommends that greener meeting and event pioneers find the system that works best for their event, saying, "It's about finding simple systems that make tracking easy, so that it isn't an onerous task at the end of the festival to go back and figure out, for example, that this show used X number of international or UK flights."

Cleary says that finding appropriate benchmarks and using them correctly can prove difficult. "With a festival like ours, which has upwards of 25 different venues and hundreds of partners and suppliers throughout the city, we have to discover the measurements that are meaningful in terms of our environmental sustainability. But just as importantly, we need to discover the new partners and suppliers who want to work with us to find new solutions to minimize the impact of our events on the environment."

Cleary lists travel as one of the largest challenges to MIF's environmental strategy, saying, "As an international festival which attracts artists and visitors from across the UK, Europe, and the rest of the world, we recognize that our event has an environmental footprint, in particular through carbon emissions, resource use, and waste.

"Our aim is to minimize this footprint whilst ensuring that the Festival continues to be a world-class Festival with positive social and economic impacts for the city. Within this, there are lots of challenges around transportation but we try to bring artists and visitors into the city in the most effective way possible, whether that is a direct flight to Manchester, or if they are coming from London, to come by train, and then to use public transport."

Systems of measurement are critical for reducing carbon emissions from travel, says Cleary. "What we're looking at now is whether we can track travel-based carbon emissions more effectively through our financial systems, pinpointing how much transport we use, in terms of staff and artists, and how we can try and reduce it. We're also trying to figure out how to most easily and accurately be able to pull those figures out."

In recognition of the inevitable carbon footprint of international travel, MIF donates a percentage of funds per festival to an environmental nonprofit. Cleary avoids the controversial and disputed term *offset,* and instead refers to *carbon compensation:* "This year, based on figures from the 2007 festival, we made a donation to a local climate fund to compensate for the staff and artist travel. It's not an offsetting fund, so to speak, but a compensation fund called Foundation, which invests the money in local, community-based carbon-reduction projects."

MIF is a great example of a major festival with deeply held environmental values. By organizing environmental initiatives into a strategic green plan, MIF ensures that it will meet its goals and, year by year, move closer to sustainability. It is thanks to the passion and dedication of Jennifer Cleary and the staff of MIF that this festival can achieve such ambitious goals.

Budget Item	2010 Expenditure	2011 Expenditure	2010 Carbon (kilograms)	2011 Carbon (kilograms)
Rental car hire	$950	$300	*352 miles × 0.882 (large car) = 310*	*273 miles × 0.22 (small car) = 60.06*
Gas Utility	$500	$250	1200 therms × 13.4 = 16,080	980 therms × 13.4 = 13,132
Cutlery	$150	$750	1,640	320
TOTAL:	$1,600	$1,300	18,030	13,512

Figure 4.10 Sample Eco-Budget

measuring the carbon cost of each item. Use the equations previously listed to calculate the carbon cost of transportation or gas and electric utilities, or use a reliable online carbon calculator. Figure 4.10 shows how a multiyear eco-budget might help you incrementally lower your carbon footprint.

Looking at the eco-budget in Figure 4.10, what changes did the event planners make from 2010 to 2011? By renting a smaller car and driving it less, they saved cash and carbon. They also turned down their thermostat to save on gas. For cutlery, however, they spent five times as much, while using five times less carbon. Perhaps they purchased silverware, instead of buying cheap disposables, thus diverting large amounts of waste from the landfill. By purchasing their own reusable silverware, these event planners may incur an initial cost, but save money over time. Now that they own their own silverware, the 2012 expenditure on cutlery may be quite small. Not all environmental strategies are immediately cost-saving. Greener meeting and event pioneers should pick and choose those strategies that are most important to their green mission statement and their triple bottom line.

The measurements in this chapter are primarily for internal use, so that you can steadily improve the sustainability of your meetings or events for the betterment of people, planet, and profit. However, these measurements have an extra benefit: they enable you to share your success with others.

When asked for the single most important piece of advice for future green event pioneers, Shawna McKinley, Project Manager at MeetGreen (www.meetgreen.com) said, "Measure each step you take. The only way to get affirmation and buy-in is to ask yourself along the way, 'How am I going to measure this to tell the story?'"

Summary

Measurements are an important way to tell the story of your greener meeting or event. Establish key performance indicators (KPIs), or specific, measurable results that may come from your green initiatives, and track them throughout the life cycle of your meeting or event. Compare your initial baseline measurement of specific KPIs to that of other benchmark organizations, such as comparable events, and create strategic plans for improving the KPIs that need the most attention. To measure your event's carbon footprint, gather as much detailed data as you can regarding gas and electricity usage and transportation type and mileage, and convert these diverse numbers into pounds of carbon dioxide emitted. These conversions can be done using the calculations in this chapter, or through on online carbon calculator. Finally, an eco-budget tracks carbon emissions alongside financial expenditure, helping you to monitor your emissions throughout the event process.

Key Terms and Definitions

- **Key performance indicators (KPI)**: specific, measurable outcomes that your strategies will affect.
- **SMART**: acronym for intelligent goals. These goals are specific, measurable, achievable, realistic, and timely.
- **Kilowatt hours (kWh)**: a standard measurement of electricity. One kWh equals 1,000 watts of electricity used in one hour.
- **Environmental audit**: an analysis of not just profit but also a commitment to people and the planet. It results in a portrait of a company's current environmental and social impact.
- **Carbon footprint**: the total amount of greenhouse gases emitted, both directly and indirectly, in service to your event.
- **Carbon calculator**: a computer program that calculates total carbon footprint based on diverse statistics.
- **British thermal units (BTUs)**: standard unit of measurement for natural gas usage in the United States.
- **Therms**: 100,000 BTUs.
- **Carbon miles**: greenhouse gases emitted by transportation.
- **Eco-budget**: a standard financial budget, but with an additional line measuring the carbon cost of each item.

Blue Sky Thinking

The National Banjo and Accordion Conference and Tradeshow (NBACT) in Atlanta, Georgia, attracted a total of 6,000 visitors, including staff, attendees, and exhibitors. A survey revealed that 3,800 came by car, 500 by airplane, 700 by train, 200 by urban rail system, and 100 walked. 700 were unaccounted for. How would you calculate the total carbon miles of all transportation? How would you complete the carbon footprint study by factoring gas and electricity usage? Create three strategic goals for NBACT, each based on SMART KPIs. How will you measure NBACT's progress on these goals over time?

Renewable Resources

APEX/ASTM Green Meetings Standard (www.apexsolution.org/green.htm).

BS 8901 (www.bsigroup.co.uk).

Climate Futures (www.climatefutures.co.uk).

Lynas, Mark (2007). *Carbon Calculator*. London: Harper Collins.

Manchester International Festival (www.mif.co.uk).

Swallow, Lisa (2007). *Green Business Practices for Dummies*. Hoboken, NJ: Wiley.

White House Office of the Press Secretary (2010). "President Obama Sets Greenhouse Gas Emissions Reduction Target for Federal Operations" (January 29). http://www.whitehouse.gov/the-press-office/president-obama-sets-greenhouse-gas-emissions-reduction-target-federal-operations.

PART TWO

Conservation

METRO light rail in Phoenix, Arizona helps meeting attendees to reduce their carbon footprint when attending conferences.
Courtesy of METRO Light Rail.

CHAPTER 5

Green Light: Sustainable Transportation

"Everywhere is within walking distance if you have the time."

—*Steven Wright, Comedian* (1955–)

In this chapter, you will learn:

1. How transportation helps to define the event experience
2. How meeting and event locations shapes transportation needs
3. How to partner with existing public transport infrastructure for event success
4. Why it's better to travel together
5. How biofuels work to promote environmental sustainability for your meeting or event
6. How to ride a bike (to your next meeting or event)
7. When to travel by airplane, and when not to
8. How telecommuting and web-conferencing are changing the way we conduct and attend meetings and events

Greener Wheels

After calculating your event's carbon footprint in Chapter 4, you might notice that transportation can easily make up half or more of a meeting or event's carbon emissions, meaning that most of the damage is done before the attendees even arrive. Excessive traffic not only pollutes the air with carbon emissions, it also disrupts natural terrain, clogs streets and denigrates the event experience. A Greener Festival (www.agreenerfestival .com), a UK organization advocating for environmentalism at festivals, surveyed attendees of music festivals and found that 70 percent of them considered traffic to be a negative event outcome.

Ian Garrett is the executive director of the Center for Sustainable Practice in the Arts (CSPA) (www.sustainablepractice.org). When I met him at an Edinburgh Festival Fringe venue on Edinburgh's Royal Mile in August 2009, he said, "The biggest challenge for an event is still getting people to a place where they can congregate."

For many meetings and events, attendees actually spend more time traveling to and from the site than they spend once they are there. The journey to and from the meeting or event bookends the attendee experience. How many times have you driven to a major concert or sporting event, only to find yourself stuck in bumper-to-bumper traffic in the parking lot afterward? Figure 5.1 shows that greener meeting and event pioneers work to move away from inefficient, individual gas transport and toward efficient group transport powered by renewable energy.

With efficient group transport powered by renewable energy, greener meeting and event pioneers seek out new and exciting ways of getting people from Point A to Point B

High-Impact Travel		Low-Impact Travel
Inefficient	→	Efficient
Unnecessarily large engines, airplanes, and idling vehicles all waste fuel.		Appropriately sized engines, used only when necessary
Individual	→	Group
Empty seats are wasted opportunities. All multiple-occupancy vehicles are most efficient when fully occupied.		Full trains and busses are among the most efficient vehicles, while empty trains and busses are among the least.
Gas-powered	→	Renewable Energy
Most traditional transportation relies on fuels that produce carbon emissions, including electric trains powered by coal-burning plants.		Innovative technology, such as electric cars, as well as the more old-fashioned bicycle

Figure 5.1   Greener Pioneers Move Toward Low-Impact Travel

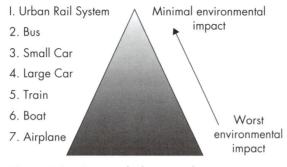

1. Urban Rail System

2. Bus

3. Small Car

4. Large Car

5. Train

6. Boat

7. Airplane

Minimal environmental impact

Worst environmental impact

Figure 5.2   Green Vehicle Hierarchy

without costing the earth. The simplest way is to favor transportation choices that emit the least amounts of carbon. Figure 5.2 provides a hierarchy of green vehicles, starting with the most favorable and ending with the least. This hierarchy assumes that vehicles are operating at maximum capacity, with no empty seats. A bus is only greener than a car if it is full of people.

Whenever possible, use urban rail systems before driving a car. Take a train instead of a plane: When you factor in the ride to the airport and airport security, a plane ride may be longer, and more stressful. When driving a car, carpool. Empty seats are the enemy.

The increasingly prohibitive financial and environmental costs of air travel are changing the way we look at traveling to and from events. The 2008 recession popularized the *staycation,* where one stays home for vacation. Event attendees may wish to minimize travel in order to save funds and minimize their carbon footprint. Does the Kansas City Rotary Club really need to hold its annual meeting in Chicago, or can it be held right there in Kansas City, putting the cost savings from travel toward other local event amenities?

Research where your clients are located and search for venues convenient to them. Don't make attendees drive an hour both ways to attend an event at an arbitrary location. Events that require multiple venues, like hotels and a conference center, can use venues within walking distance of each other. For destination events and conferences, discourage your visiting attendees from renting private cars by providing a shuttle service. When factoring transportation into the event experience, location becomes even more important. For example, urban and rural meetings and events have very different transportation needs.

Urban Infrastructure

Because they are more accessible, urban meetings and events often carry less of a negative environmental impact from transportation. Paul Tollett founded Coachella Music Festival (www.coachella.com) in a remote area of Southern California, which, although beautiful, is more than two hours driving distance from Los Angeles. When producing an East Coast version of the event, All Points West (www.apwfestival.com), he made the critical decision to set it in the urban landscape of Liberty State Park, New Jersey, just across the Hudson River from Lower Manhattan and easily accessible by ferry, light rail, or train. Battery Park Ferry tickets could be purchased online alongside concert tickets, making it easier than ever for thousands of local residents to enjoy a major pop music festival after just a short ride on public transportation.

Urban meetings and events should harness every bit of public transit infrastructure that their city provides. At the least, you should notify your local public transit officials of your event in case it affects their services. Go a step farther and partner with these public transit corporations, positioning public transit as the preferred mode of travel to your meeting or event. Arrange specialized public transit services at discounted rates for your attendees. The Washington, DC, Metro Rail partners with most local cultural events, offering shared advertising that promotes Metro as the preferred way to travel to the meeting or event. For the Olympic Games in Atlanta, Sydney, and Athens, the local authorities actually created additional public transit infrastructure to support these mega-events.

Ian Garrett laments the number of events in urban areas that fail to provide patrons with public transportation directions. "When you try to get somewhere via bus, especially in a city that doesn't have transparent public transit, there's no information there. No one's taken the time to look at which buses stop nearby." Using Los Angeles as an example, Garrett notes that driving directions are far more prevalent than bus directions. He sees major growth opportunities for events that reach out to public transit users:

> Events using public transportation would engage a whole other group of people, because it's accommodating to the choices people make. People are trying to make that choice: between traffic, the cost of everything and environmental sensibilities, people want to turn to public transit when they can. It's all about making it easy for your patrons to do better.
> —Ian Garrett, Center for Sustainable Practice in the Arts, interview, August 2009

Capitalize on the public transit amenities offered in your local city. More and more cities are providing innovative public transit services, such as hybrid and biofuel airport shuttles. Remember that every empty seat on a public bus or a train is a wasted opportunity, and work to fill these seats with the attendees of your meetings and events.

Rural Roadtrips

In 1978, actor Robert Redford organized the Sundance Film Festival (festival.sundance.org) in Park City, Utah, a town that offers attendees inspirational mountain views. Although Sundance has implemented an extensive environmental policy that includes recycling and renewable energy, one thing it cannot do is build a train line to Park City, and so attendees will be flying into Salt Lake International Airport, then making the

45-minute drive to Park City for the near future. No one would dare suggest that Sundance leave its picturesque location for a more accessible major city, but transportation will remain an issue for its environmental team.

Similarly, Garrett recently computed the carbon footprint of all patron transportation to and from the Oregon Shakespeare Festival, finding that, of 400,000 patrons, around 40 percent come from the San Francisco Bay Area, which is close enough that most of them drive. Based on the average car's energy use and the average household size, billions of watts and millions of pounds of carbon dioxide are expended in travel to the Ashland, Oregon, festival. "There's no way, without a massive change in how to get to Ashland, in having the festival offset any of that," says Garrett. Until they build a solar-powered railroad, the Oregon Shakespeare Festival, like Sundance, has to accept a negative environmental impact from car travel.

Although not the greenest vehicle, a car filled with passengers is much more efficient than one with only one or two persons, and so, by encouraging car-pooling and organizing group transportation, even rural meetings and events can lessen their environmental impact. After all, meetings are essentially opportunities to be together, so why not travel together as well?

Encouraging attendees to carpool is a simple place to start. Many UK music festivals now provide online forums for attendees to advertise rides offered or wanted to the big event. Carpool networks may already exist in your area: search for your event location on the following Web sites and share your findings with staff and attendees.

Carpooling is a great way to instill community within a group, or to break the ice between meeting attendees. If you manage a recurring meeting or event, challenge attendees to find someone with a similar commute, and carpool together next time. When encouraging carpooling, be sure to also provide the following tips for a smooth ride.

Carpooling is a fun, simple way to increase fuel efficiency and lower carbon emissions per person, but remember to be safe and respect people's differences.

Even more efficient than a full car is a full bus, and chartered buses can add a lot to the event experience. When booking tickets for the 2008 Connect Music Festival in rural Argyle, Scotland, attendees were strongly encouraged to also book a ticket on one of 35 buses running from various locations around Scotland directly to the festival site. The benefits of this scheme were huge: attendees could eat, drink, relax and socialize while a driver navigated difficult winding highland roads. Not only was the bus ticket cheaper than the gas required for the car journey, the bus also delivered attendees closer to the

Three Free Online Carpool Directories

1. Carpool World (www.carpoolworld.com)
2. RideshareDirectory(www.rideshare-directory .com)
3. iCarpool (www.icarpool.com)

Smooth Ride Carpool Tips

- Get to know your carpoolers first. Social acquaintances or work colleagues should be given priority over strangers.
- To make sure your drivers are calm, safe, and responsible behind the wheel, ask them how they would react in potentially stressful traffic situations.
- Share the cost of gas and/or tolls.
- Get appropriate contact information for everyone in the group, to avoid delays.
- Set a schedule that works for everyone, and stick to it.
- Set some ground rules as a group regarding smoking, eating or drinking in the car, music, cell phones, and lateness.

For Attendees	For Staff
Chance to socialize with other attendees	Potential to begin meeting or event during journey, using onboard microphone, music, or movies
Freedom to relax, eat, and drink	Less time needed for pre- and post-event traffic direction
No worries about following directions to unfamiliar locations	Less turf destruction from cars
No worries about parking	Less air pollution from cars
Bus drop-off location generally closer to event site than public parking lot	Smaller parking lots needed
Potential onboard amenities, such as toilet or television	Fewer parking attendants needed
Can be cheaper than gas for individual trip	Increased assurance against reckless driving
Increased safety	Increased safety for staff
Fewer carbon emissions	Fewer carbon emissions

Figure 5.3   Group Transportation Benefits

event site. The event organization also benefited, with less disruptive traffic to manage, fewer parking lots to maintain, and increased assurance against car accidents. Figure 5.3 summarizes the benefits of group transportation at meetings and events.

Wolf Trap, America's National Park for the Performing Arts, located just outside Washington, DC, encourages public transit use by providing a shuttle bus system from

Wolf Trap Shuttle Pluses

- Fewer cars to park
- Slightly better air quality
- Goodwill with local government officials
- Avoiding a wait in traffic after the concert, because the shuttle gets priority

- Avoiding a long walk from the parking lot; the shuttle delivers directly to the main entrance
- Camaraderie on the shuttle, which is exclusive to Wolf Trap
- Cost savings for attendees

the nearest Metro Rail station. When I spoke with Wolf Trap CEO Terrence Jones in July 2009, he listed the following benefits of this shuttle, including the obvious one of increased access:

The success of Wolf Trap's shuttle shows that it really is more fun to travel together—the party begins early! Although urban events generally have much more efficient transportation options, rural events are uniquely positioned to offer attendees a unique group travel experience, loaded with benefits for staff and attendees.

Biofuels

Biofuels are farm-grown fuels made out of agricultural products such as corn or vegetable oil, which can be used to power engines. Like coal and oil, biofuels emit carbon. Unlike coal and oil, biofuels come from renewable agricultural sources, which, in their raw form (e.g., wheat or corn), also absorb carbon. However, because very few automobiles can run on *pure biomass* (pure organic matter), most biofuels are *biodiesel*: a combination of regular diesel and biomass. All diesel engines can run on a biodiesel mix that uses at least 10 percent biomass, and many can run on much more. Biodiesel is labeled according to its percentage of biomass, so B20 biodiesel contains 20 percent biomass and 80 percent diesel.

With most diesel engines, you can actually take the *waste vegetable oil* (WVO), or used cooking oil, straight out of your local fast-food joint's deep fryer, filter it through a sifter, and put it straight into your gas tank. This is especially green when you consider the vast amount of WVO thrown away by restaurants and food manufacturers every day. How's that for free gas? Companies like Grease Car (www.greasecar.com) can help you convert your car to WVO, and there are several online networks dedicated to the growing WVO market. Smarter Fuels (www.smarterfuel.com) will save you the work of finding WVO, and deliver it straight to your door.

A *firm note of caution*: Consult your car manufacturer, and biofuel experts, before converting your existing car to biofuels. Although many biofuels are certified by the U.S.

Three Free Online Biofuel Directories

1. Oliomap (www.oliomap.com)
2. Fill up 4 Free (www.fillup4free.com)
3. Good Grease (www.goodgrease.com)

EPA as having passed emissions standards for the Clean Air Act, most WVO is uncertified. Check out the EPA's guide to biofuels at www.epa.gov/otaq/fuels.htm.

The eccentric and eco-centric music legend Willie Nelson started his own biodiesel business in 2005, selling his own branded BioWillie fuel from a truckstop in Texas called Willie's Place. Sadly, BioWillie fuel is no longer sold, which may reflect changing public opinion on biofuels: Although WVO is free, harvested biofuels can deplete corn and grain crops. I visited Willie's Place in 2009 and was impressed at the display of rare country music memorabilia, the classic southern food restaurant, and the professional theatre and bar venue for touring country western bands.

Although America is still a car-country, heavily dependent on gas-powered vehicles, and biofuel may not greatly improve this situation in the near future, Willie's Place stands to show how creative entrepreneurs can confront environmental issues. An iconic crossroads where entertainment meets the environment, this little truck stop delivers hope for the future.

Hybrid Highway

Because both regular gas and industry-certified biofuels have become expensive in recent years, there is increasing consumer demand for a car powered not by gas, but by electricity. Recently, both the Nissan Leaf and the Chevrolet Volt have emerged as successful electric cars. *Hybrid cars*, those powered by a combination of electricity and fuel, have achieved great popularity, most notably the Toyota Prius, driven by Al Gore. Hybrid cars generally use power from an electric battery for low speeds, switch to fuel power at medium speeds, and use both electricity and fuel at high speeds. The year 2010 saw the debut of the Nissan Leaf, a car powered by 100 percent electricity.

Following are the top five energy-efficient cars on the U.S. market today, as ranked by the American Council for an Energy-Efficient Economy (ACEEE). The U.S. Environmental Protection Agency also provides a handy Green Vehicle Guide on its Web site at www.epa.gov/greenvehicles.

Among the 2010 market trends for greener cars, ACEEE listed greater fuel efficiency, decreased size, more electric power, clean diesel engines, and, you will be particularly pleased to learn, lower prices, as green cars become increasingly affordable.

Five Lean Green Eco-Machines

1. Honda Civic GX Natural Gas Vehicle
2. Nissan Leaf
3. Smart for Two Convertible

4. Toyota Prius
5. Honda Civic Hybrid

Source: www.greenercars.org/highlights_greenest.htm

Pedal Power

Every summer, Barbara Neff produces Sailfest (sailfest.org), a fantastic outdoor event that brings live music, food, and family fun to the city of New London, Connecticut. Despite its large urban population, New London has insufficient commuter rail transport, resulting in congested traffic and car exhaust air pollution. When Neff visited the Edinburgh Festival in August 2009, she told me, "We have so much traffic at the end of our fireworks display that it clogs the streets for about an hour." She cites local government inaction as one obstacle for increased commuter rail service.

Taking traffic reduction into her own hands, Neff decided to promote bicycling to and from Sailfest. On the Sailfest Web site and in the program, she provided information for attendees on how to bike to and from the event, and advertised a bike valet service for $1. Showing the true spirit of environmentalism, Neff donated all money from the bike valet toward buying much-needed bike racks for the city. Not only did she cut down on traffic, she impressed attendees. Neff recalls, "People were very surprised we did it and they wanted it to be done at more festivals."

Increasingly, greener meetings and events pioneers such as Barbara Neff are harnessing *human energy*, the most sustainable power source of all, to transform their event transportation plans.

Encouraging Exercise

Neff's bike valet at Sailfest achieved two positive civic goals for New London: reducing traffic and encouraging exercise. Show your attendees the fun, active side of environmentalism by incorporating bicycling into your next meeting or event. Following are just a few examples of ways in which you can engage meeting or event attendees with cycling.

As with any exercise activity, bicycles should be tested, riders instructed and supervised, and helmets worn at all times. Bike rides are a great opportunity to hand out reusable branded clothing or water bottles. Finding safe, well-managed ways to incorporate cycling into your next meeting or event can provide attendees with that most basic of human pleasures, and a powerful motivational tool, exercise.

Fresh Ideas for Cycling at Meetings and Events

- Walt Disney World provides bicycle rentals for patrons to travel around the various locations on its sprawling Florida resort (disneyworld.disney.go.com/recreation/bike-rentals/).
- Bicycle Sport Shop of Austin, Texas (bicyclesportshop.com), provides a free bike valet for attendees of the South by Southwest music conference.
- In addition to standard bicycle rentals, Pedal Bike Tours of Portland, Oregon (www.pedalbiketours.com), organizes corporate bicycle outings that can vary from a team-building ride around public parks to an educational tour of Portland's outstanding environmental infrastructure, including their array of sustainable buildings. Portland is the home of MeetGreen and is consistently ranked as one of America's top cities for cycling.
- The 2007 Outsider Festival combined music and comedy performances with bicycle racing activities amid the stunning scenery of Cairngorms in Scotland.

Pedicabs

Many events employ expensive transportation devices such as Segways (personal motorized scooters) or golf carts when a simple bicycle will do. *Pedicabs* are just simple rickshaws pulled by bicycles, but they offer passengers an exciting, novel, and eco-friendly travel experience. Pedicabs can be used to take attendees between meeting or event venues, or even around a convention or exhibition center. When liquor conglomerate Diageo threw the 200th birthday party for Johnnie Walker Scotch Whisky in New York City, it hired pedicabs from Manhattan Rickshaw Company (www.manhattanrickshaw.com) to elegantly take tipsy patrons home. New York's Revolution Rickshaws even offers cargo pedicabs that can transport 500 pounds of materials through Manhattan streets faster than a taxicab (www.revolutionrickshaws.com). In our zest for innovation, humankind has forgotten that the complex automobile is often less convenient and useful than our most ancient of inventions, the wheel. As with all new transportation methods, a comprehensive risk assessment must be undertaken when using bicycles and pedicabs at your meeting or event.

Air Travel

At the bottom end of the green vehicle hierarchy flies the airplane, which uses more resources and emits more hazardous pollution than any other commercial vehicle. Still, budget airlines have made short-distance flights increasingly affordable, and airlines such as RyanAir and EasyJet occasionally offer promotional fares as low as £1, or a couple of dollars. Although low prices can be tempting, traveling by plane can easily double your carbon footprint. Short-distance flights are the most wasteful because of the excess fuel used in takeoff and landing, so trains, buses, or cars should always be favored before planes in these cases. Not only do trains, buses, and cars deliver you closer to your destination (unless your destination is an airport), they also save you from the stress of airport security and airplane food!

There are, of course, many situations where air travel is the only option—namely, long-distance or overseas journeys. International arts festivals, like the Manchester International Festival (MIF) (www.mif.co.uk), have a remit to present international artists, most of whom come from overseas. Now chief executive of the Edinburgh Festival Fringe (www.edfringe.com), the world's largest performing arts festival, Kath Mainland first began implementing environmental policies at the Edinburgh International Book Festival (EIBF) (www.edbookfest.org.uk). One of the highlights of her time at EIBF was a lecture on climate change by Al Gore. "Al Gore on a private jet from America is okay," Mainland said at a 2009 seminar, recognizing that such a cultural and educational opportunity could not logistically happen any other way. Although this is changing, some celebrities require a private plane for security reasons.

Carina Bauer, CEO of IMEX (www.imex-frankfurt.com), also acknowledges that an international exhibition such as IMEX requires international travel, but she is not resigned to the fate of mass air travel. On the contrary, IMEX's Frankfurt location allows exhibitors and visitors to arrive by train, bus, or car from many different locations across Europe—like its sausages, Frankfurt is well linked.

Offsetting Air Travel

Carbon offsetting refers to making a charitable donation to an environmental project in order to balance negative greenhouse gas emissions. Various commercial activities with negative environmental impacts can warrant carbon offsetting, but air travel is by far the most common. Greener meetings and events offset air travel in a variety of ways. Based on their calculations of air travel emissions, MIF donates a *carbon compensation* to an environmental charity. IMEX provides a facility for exhibitors and visitors to offset their travel.

Matt Grant, festival director of Peats Ridge Sustainable Arts and Music Festival in Australia (www.peatsridgefestival.com.au), supports IMEX's strategy of encouraging attendees to offset their own carbon emissions. When I spoke with him in December of 2008, Grant said, "People should buy their own carbon. If you offset your patrons' carbon then you are saying it's okay to not take responsibility for your actions." Grant's rule of thumb is to reduce first, offset second.

Along with environmental strategies, carbon offsetting plays a critical role in a meeting or event's commitment to corporate social responsibility (CSR), as Chapter 10 will discuss.

Telecommuting

The best way to cut down on transportation is to cut it out completely. *Telecommuting*, or working from a remote location, connected by phone or Internet technology, continues to evolve as the technology does. Video conferencing has never been easier and can save event professionals an expensive drive or flight for business meetings. Products such as Skype, GoTo Meeting, and Cisco Telepresence are rapidly changing the way that people

Three Video Conference Technology Systems

1. Skype: (www.skype.com)
2. GoTo Meeting (www.gotomeeting.com)

3. Telepresence by Cisco (www.cisco.com; type "telepresence" in search window)

meet. *Webinars*, or seminars delivered and experienced on the Internet, continue to evolve as competition to live lectures.

This increased access to online communication tools means that international meetings and events can be held online, which forces meeting and event planners to redefine the value of face-to-face interaction. After all, there is nothing like the human touch. Ian Garrett has held a number of video conferences wherein he experienced a time-delay. He told me, "You can't really see what's going on. It's hard to have a really effective immediate conversation." Garrett concludes, "Being there in person is still important."

Greener meeting and event pioneers will need to assess the value of webinars and online meeting technology in order to restate the value of face-to-face conferences. As technology continues to deliver more isolated communication options, the demand for real-life human interaction increases.

To Meet or Not to Meet?

Some meeting planners have already embraced new online meeting technology, while others are fearful that this poses a threat to the live meetings industry. To test out this new technology, I interviewed Shawna McKinley, project manager, and Nancy (Wilson) Zavada CMP, principal, of MeetGreen (www.meetgreen.com), via a Skype online conference call in May 2010. I was in Edinburgh, Scotland, McKinley in Canada, and Zavada in Portland, Oregon. The conversation was fraught with interruptions and disconnections, which encouraged our conversation on the enduring value of face-to-face meetings.

McKinley begins by saying, "I think we have a choice right now. Technology's not going away. Virtual means of connecting are not going away, especially for the generation that

now has more relationships that are virtual than in-person. We, as meeting professionals, have a choice to figure out how it's going to work for us, and how it can be harnessed to change our profession in a fundamental way, but still allow us to do what we do, which is to build relationships and connections with people and to give them the forums to do that."

She continues, "It may be that we have to change our thinking a little bit to realize and accept that the model for meetings is changing. It is less about booking properties and the various commission and budget structures associated with that, and changing our thinking to what the new virtual business model is."

Zavada agrees, saying, "Travel's going to change, and people aren't going to be traveling

Make It Worth the Trip

Transportation remains a central challenge for greener meetings and events. It can be distressing to recognize that the mere arrival of the attendees is one of the most negative environmental impacts of any meeting or event. Bear in mind, then, that, once arrived, attendees might actually use fewer resources and carbon than if they had stayed at home. Ben Challis, founder of A Greener Festival (www.agreenerfestival.com) and lawyer for UK music festival Glastonbury (www.glastonburyfestivals.co.uk), understands the negative environmental impact of the thousands of attendees driving to the remote festival location of Glastonbury. For Challis, however, the cloud of car exhaust has a silver lining:

> Once people drive in, they park their cars for three or four days, they live in tents, they don't have cookers or radiators and they share catering, which is very efficient. We think that it is possible that we're actually carbon negative. When people are here, they are using less carbon than they would in their normal lives. Perhaps that is a green event.
>
> —Ben Challis, A Greener Festival, interview, April 2009

Although Glastonbury encourages public transit and carpooling, they are willing to accept some negative impact from transportation if it means a more positive impact in

as much in the future. The smart people in this industry are adapting to that, and finding a way to host those meetings, even though they will look a little bit different. The smart ones are also looking into the technology, so that they become the download site."

Zavada sees the next step as hybrid meetings, which she describes as live meetings across several geographic regions that can interact with each other through video conferencing. In this format, groups can communally enjoy a keynote presentation from far away, disconnect for a breakout session, then reconnect for another presentation. "You still have the face-to-face meeting connection," she says, "yet you're able to gather a larger group of people, and the carbon footprint is much, much smaller."

McKinley adds, "What's always key is the intention of the gathering, the connection being formed and the audience's needs. A lot of our clients are getting strategic about who needs to come together and what is the best way, given who they are, how comfortable they are with technology and what the objective is that they want to achieve."

Considering the impact on the meetings industry, McKinley concludes, "There are those people who are fighting it, and there are those people who are saying that we have to make it work in this new environment, and those people will be the ones that create a very new face for the industry."

Video conferencing technology is certainly changing the way in which people meet, but after a crackly conference call with many disconnections, I am inclined to agree with Zavada, who concludes, "The impact of humans connecting face-to-face is never going to change."

Model Greener Event: Capital Fringe Festival

Since 2005, the Capital Fringe Festival has transformed the cultural life of Washington, DC, by presenting an annual summer festival of performance, which anyone can participate in (www.capitalfringe.org). Featuring hundreds of performances and serving more than 20,000 audience members, the festival is managed by just two full-time staff members, Scot McKenzie and Julianne Brienza, who are committed not just to telling DC's stories and supporting local talent, but to protecting the environment as well.

Considerations for transportation figure highly in the Festival's environmental commitment. After three years at separate venues all over DC, in 2009 the Festival centralized all venues into a three-block radius, accessible from two Metro Rail stations, four Metro Rail lines, and several Metrobus stops. When I spoke to her following the July 2009 Festival, Brienza described the way a centralized location vastly improved patron experience, saying, "They loved it. We sold so many more passes this year. People were just jumping around because they could. You could literally end the show at four forty-five and go to a five o'clock show, no problem. And get a drink on the way."

A centralized location also decreased staff travel, cutting costs and the carbon footprint. Whereas in 2008 the Festival spent roughly $2,000 to rent two cargo vans, in 2009 they spent around $1,000 to rent one truck, which was driven about half as much.

Festival Director Scot McKenzie has a firm belief in reusing old materials to create new experiences. He created the sensational Baldacchino Gypsy Tent Bar out of reused domestic doors. Funky vintage furniture was sourced at little cost from reused building materials warehouse Community Forklift (www.communityforklift.com). Church pews, donated freely from a defunct congregation, became the most popular seats in the house. Instead of buying expensive new theatrical sandbags, Production Manager Zoia Wiseman made her own from local Virginia sand and reused bags, at a fraction of the cost.

Brienza knows that going green isn't always a walk in the park, and Brienza recalls the disappointing patron attitudes toward recycling, saying, "One thing I was very surprised at was that recycling was something that needed to be managed at the bar. We had to instruct patrons to recycle. Numerous times, myself and five to six other staff members would go around and take bottles out of the trash, or see someone throwing their bottle in the trash and say, 'No, really, you want to put that in the recycling, right next to it.'"

Brienza discovered that certain environmental policies, like the use of organic cleaning products, were hard for the staff to get used to. She says that, "In using cleaning supplies that are good for the environment or might just be old fashioned, it can require extra arm strength. There were some secret bleach attacks." She turned this staff challenge into an educational opportunity, saying, "I would find out and talk about it with them."

She believes that environmental managers must be firm in order to generate respect and understanding for environmental alternative work methods. Brienza reflects that, "I could have loosened up, but I didn't. In the end it was more meaningful." This firm policy spread throughout the culture of the organization, ensuring staff compliance. Brienza recalls that, "At the bar they used all green cleaning supplies. I didn't even tell them that they had to,

Capital Fringe Festival repurposes neglected buildings in Washington, DC, such as the former A.V. Ristorante Italiano, now Fort Fringe, into vibrant art centers.
Courtesy of Paul Gillis.

they just thought it was the law." She believes that discussing environmental policies is critical to staff acceptance, saying, "The biggest benefit was just making staff aware. We had 40 staff who were exposed to that and what they choose to do with that is up to them. I think five of them will take that into their daily lives, which is pretty good."

In 2009, I served the Capital Fringe Festival as Environmental Officer, and began by creating three documents. The first was our *Strategic Green Plan*, which included a prioritized list of environmental goals. The second was called *How to Be a Green Audience*, and gave patrons advice on everything from where the nearest

bus stop was to how to recycle. Lastly, we sent all participating artists *How to Be a Green Artist*, which included advice on sourcing reused costumes and limiting paper waste.

Brienza and McKenzie remain actively committed to reducing their carbon footprint and to engaging their audiences in discussions about the environment. An upcoming performance, Wattage, will tackle issues of energy, natural resources, and responsibility to the planet. Thanks to their commitment to innovative event experiences and their fierce determination, they are helping to raise the profile of the arts and the environment in Washington, DC.

the long run. Similarly, make sure that your meeting or event offers significantly positive environmental outcomes for all attendees, making it truly worth the gas to get there.

Summary

Transportation is the greatest challenge and often the greatest environmental impact for any greener meeting or event, with vehicle emissions making up the largest percentage of a typical carbon footprint. Greener meeting and event pioneers work to move away from inefficient, individual gas transport, and toward efficient group transport powered by renewable energy. Urban rail systems are the greenest method of transit, with the smallest carbon footprint, followed by buses, cars, trains, and boats, with airplanes ranking as the highest-polluting vehicle. Urban events should partner with local authorities to capitalize on the public transportation infrastructure already in place, while more remote or rural events can organize group transportation to lessen their carbon footprint and provide superior travel experiences for attendees. Car-drivers can consider biofuels, hybrid electric vehicles, or the simple bicycle, which can be used to transport people or objects around event sites while incorporating exercise into the event design. Although air travel should be avoided when possible, it can be offset with charitable contributions. Telecommunication technology is changing the way we meet.

Key Terms and Definitions

- **Staycation**: staying home on vacation.
- **Biofuels**: farm-grown fuels made out of agriculture such as corn or vegetable oil that can be used to power engines.
- **Pure biomass**: pure organic oil used as fuel.
- **Biodiesel**: a combination of pure biomass and diesel fuel.
- **Waste vegetable oil (WVO)**: used cooking oil that can be filtered and used as fuel, if certified.
- **Hybrid car**: a car powered by a combination of both fuel and electricity.
- **Pedicab**: a taxi-cab bicycle that can cart passengers or cargo. It is similar to a rickshaw.
- **Carbon offsetting**: charitable contribution to environmental projects in order to balance negative greenhouse gas emissions.
- **Carbon credits**: financial units in which carbon offsetting is measured.
- **Telecommuting**: working from a remote location, connected by phone and Internet technology.

- **Webinar**: seminars delivered over the Internet. They can be streamed live or downloaded.
- **Hybrid meetings**: live meetings across several geographic regions. Those in the meetings can interact with each other through video conferencing.

Blue Sky Thinking

The United States Conference of Mayors has hired you to organize its 2011 annual meeting. The theme is green cities. How would you plan the meeting in a way that would reduce transportation emissions as much as possible? Write a one-page travel plan that chooses the location of the event, the transportation to and from the event, transportation during the event, and event activities that will produce the least amount of carbon emissions. How will you communicate this plan to the delegates and ensure that it is followed?

Renewable Resources

A Greener Festival (www.agreenerfestival.com).

Main Street Pedicabs (www.pedicab.com).

Skype (www.skype.com).

Starbuck, Jon (2008). *Run Your Diesel Vehicle on Biofuels: A Do-It-Yourself Manual*. New York: McGraw-Hill.

Well-labeled bins and environmental stewards help make sure waste is sustainab
managed at The Big Tent.

CHAPTER 6

Waste Management

"I only feel angry when I see waste. When I see people throwing away things we could use."

—*Mother Teresa, Humanitarian (1910–1997)*

In this chapter you will learn:

1. How event waste can be directed into reuse, recycling, and composting streams

2. How to divert waste away from the landfill

3. How to organize attractive and effective trash receptacles

4. How to minimize event waste through precycling

5. Tips for managing a comprehensive recycling program

6. How composting can add to a greener meeting

7. How meeting planners can use innovative ideas to create a greener event

Greener Events Are Cleaner Events

Susan is hosting a dinner party for her work colleagues. She sources all her own organic vegetables from a garden in her backyard, prepares the food in her kitchen, and serves it on beautiful porcelain plates with stainless steel silverware and cloth napkins. Afterward, she saves the leftovers in the refrigerator, and recycles the empty glass wine bottles. The following week, one of her colleagues hosts a pizza party. Pizza is delivered in cardboard boxes and eaten on Styrofoam plates with paper napkins. Box wine is served in Styrofoam cups. Which event would you rather attend?

After transportation and energy use, waste management is one of the most important issues for any greener meeting or event. Greener meetings and events minimize waste using many of Susan's strategies—avoiding disposables and recycling—as well as a host of other innovative techniques. Reduce the rubbish, and remember that greener events are cleaner events.

Event Waste

Modern events are built around waste. Every Styrofoam plate, plastic spoon, confetti blast, helium balloon, and paper tablecloth that is thrown out after one use is wasted. Not only are high waste levels unsustainable, but they degrade the patrons' experience. Claire O'Neill's study of UK music festivals, "A Greener Festival," available at www.agreenerfestival.com, surveyed 649 festival patrons and found that 71 percent agreed that waste was a negative environmental impact of festivals.

Disposable items make for disposable events; don't let your event's greatest outcome be an overflowing dumpster. Make *waste minimization*, the process of reducing waste, a priority for your event. Figure 6.1 shows a hierarchy of waste management strategies, with prevention, minimization, and reuse being the most preferred methods of dealing with waste. For event waste that cannot be reused, composting or recycling (both discussed later in this chapter), should be considered before sending waste to landfill.

Figure 6.1 Event Waste Hierarchy

Although waste prevention should be your goal, very few meetings or events can avoid waste completely. It is how these greener meetings and events manage their event waste that matters. The various ways to deal with waste, such as reuse, recycling, composting, or landfill deposit, are called *waste streams*. *Waste diversion* is the environmentally friendly practice of keeping as much waste out of the landfill stream as possible. Glass can be recycled, food composted, and signage reused.

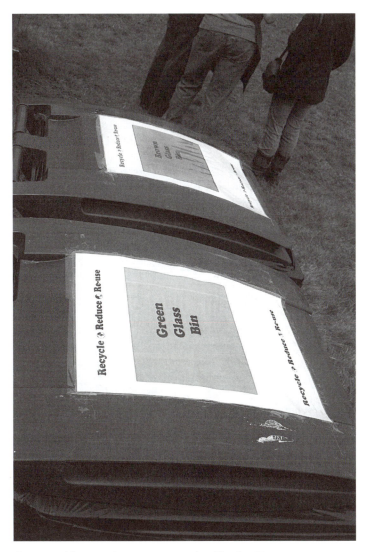

Green and brown glass is separated at The Big Tent.

Paul Salinger, vice president of events for Oracle, has helped Oracle OpenWorld divert 67 tons from the waste stream in 2008, 140 tons in 2009, and is looking to increase this diversion in 2010. "We aggressively work with the venue, hotels, and the city to make sure that we are really thinking about our overall waste stream and how we can reduce what goes into landfill," says Salinger. "We are fortunate to be in San Francisco, a city that has very forward-looking plans on reducing waste, as well as a waste hauler, Recology (www.recology.com), that is also focused on working with the city and with our venues to move toward a 'zero waste' state in the future."

Although *zero waste*, or a 100 percent rate of diversion from landfill, provides a great target for green meeting pioneers to reach for, Salinger urges caution when using this language:

> We are not big fans of promoting terms like zero waste and carbon neutral, as they can easily be claimed without the right set of data and right understanding of the complexity of our systems to back them up. We prefer the term responsible meeting management.
> —*Paul Salinger, Oracle, interview, May 2010*

Waste management means taking responsibility for all the items we might normally disregard. Event waste comes in four categories, each of which can be closely managed for cleaner, greener meetings and events: litter, standard, recyclable, and biodegradable.

Litter

According to the anti-litter organization Keep America Beautiful (www.kab.org), U.S. roadways receive over 51 billion pieces of litter per year, or over 6,000 pieces of litter per mile of road, which costs the United States $11.5 billion each year (Keep America Beautiful 2010). With the modern widespread availability of garbage disposal options, why is *litter*, or unlawful disposal of garbage, still such a problem?

One reason is that our consumer culture produces so many disposable materials, such as plastic wrappers, that we are accustomed to immediate disposal. Also, modern garbage services remove personal responsibility: Throw away as much as you like, and once the garbage man arrives, it's out of sight and out of mind.

Ben Challis, lawyer for the UK music festival Glastonbury (www.glastonburyfestivals.co.uk), described this mindset in those attendees who litter not just food wrappers but larger objects as well. At an April 2009 seminar, Challis said, "We end up with thousands of tents left on site, which aren't recyclable." He believes part of the problem is the availability of cheap, disposable goods such as tents, saying, "People get them for £10 and leave them behind. We have huge amounts of poles and tents, which go straight to landfill." Challis is often surprised by the things festival attendees litter, saying, "People bring sofas to festivals and leave them behind. It is quite extraordinary." Glastonbury is working to educate patrons on reducing their waste. "We try to stop people bringing stuff they don't need," Challis says.

Staff at the Edinburgh International Conference Centre clean up their urban environment.
Courtesy of the Edinburgh International Conference Centre.

Although abandoned tents and furniture pose a problem for large outdoor festivals, the majority of greener meetings and events are more likely to experience litter in the form of discarded paper, food packaging and drink containers, and the number one weapon against this type of standard litter is the humble trash receptacle. Figure 6.2 shows how greener meeting and event pioneers cut down on litter by positioning plenty of waste receptacles, which are exceptionally well labeled, well positioned, and well maintained.

San Francisco has a mandatory recycling program that requires a three-bin trash receptacle system (Wollan 2009). Naina Ayya, communications manager at Moscone Center, created Figure 6.3, first published in Moscone Center newsletter *Changing Conventions*, to demonstrate the bins to stakeholders. At the recent convention at Moscone, Oracle OpenWorld hired Green Angels to help attendees figure out which bin to use (Ayya 2010).

Well Labeled	Well Positioned	Well Maintained
Divided by waste category (recycling, trash, etc.)	At all entrances and exits	Supervised by environmental stewards
Using simple words ("glass," "aluminum cans," "paper," "trash")	At *transition points*, or points where attendees move from one activity to another	Emptied regularly
Using pictures	At all food and drink service locations	Clean
Shaping entry slat to fit waste type (rectangular slat for paper, circular slat for aluminum cans)	At all restrooms	Attractive and aesthetically pleasing

Figure 6.2   Exceptional Waste Receptacles

What trash goes into which bin?

Trash

Very few items actually belong in the trash. These include: Styrofoam, plastic coffee cup lids, candy wrappers, condiment packets, potato chip bags, plastic bags, and "aseptic packaging" such as juice boxes, also called Tetrapaks.

Recycling

Recycling includes all clean office paper, glass bottles and jars, aluminum foil and cans, steel/tin cans, and plastic jugs and containers. Blue recycling bins have a slot at top for paper and round openings on the sides for cans and bottles. No *soft* plastics like bags and wrappers belong in the blue containers.

Compost

Most of the material that used to go in the trash can now be composted including paper take-out containers, paper coffee cups, used napkins and towels, milk cartons, leftover food, and compostable plastics. All of the serveware provided by SAVOR such as boxed lunches and cutlery is made from certified compostable PLA or vegetable resins.

Figure 6.3   Moscone Center Three-Bin Program
Graphic by Naina Ayya, communications manager, Moscone Center (www.moscone.com)

When I spoke with Kathleen Hennesey, recycling manager at Moscone Center, in July 2010, she explained:

> During this green meeting three-bin pilot, the bins are outside restrooms, and elevators and in the lobbies on each of the three floors for attendees. An objective of the pilot is to determine the best placement and also the appropriate number needed on each floor. For instance, outside rest rooms allows a permanent location and provides a place for attendees to drop beverage containers before going into the rest room, where we collect paper towels for composting. Hopefully, the three-bin set-up will prevent beverage containers going into the paper towel bin inside the restroom. (Hennesey, interview, July 2010)

Receptacles need to fit in with the atmosphere and decor as much as possible so as not to denigrate the event. At the same time, they must be widely available and clearly labeled. Obviously, high-traffic areas necessitate receptacles, but try to predict the more unusual areas that patrons may require receptacles. Monitor all receptacles during the event, making adjustments or additions as needed in a manner unobtrusive to the event

The Edinburgh International Conference Centre (EICC) uses colorful waste receptacles that are easy to identify. *Courtesy of the Edinburgh International Conference Centre.*

experience. After the event, record the locations that collect litter so that you can add receptacles to these locations in future events.

Events like Glastonbury, where attendees consume alcohol, which clouds their judgment, tend to have increased litter. Greener meetings and events serving alcohol, thus, need to make their trash receptacles extra obvious, so as to be spotted even by an inebriated attendee in the dark. Be creative with your waste receptacles and make the process fun for your attendees. Paint your receptacles bright colors, or make them look like monsters or animals that are swallowing the trash or recycling. This is a perfect opportunity to make your attendees feel good about managing their waste responsibly.

Another way to increase awareness of litter is to have environmental stewards roaming the meeting or event site and supervising event activity. At Sailfest (sailfest.org), members of the Green Team wear green shirts with the recycling symbol on them. The UK charity Oxfam (www.oxfam.org.uk) organizes volunteers to act as environmental stewards at music festivals. These volunteers dress up like green fairies, superheroes, or green police officers and interact with attendees. These stewards might confront litterers in a playful discussion about the environment, but sometimes just the sight of staff picking up litter is enough to discourage attendees from littering.

Although cities are increasingly moving to ban indoor smoking, cigarettes are still the most-littered item in America, according to Keep America Beautiful (www.kab.org), and cigarette butts, which are generally not biodegradable, are extremely damaging to the environment. Greener meeting and event pioneers offer smokers numerous ways to bin their butt, rather than litter it.

Running, biking, and other athletic events seem to become more popular and more accessible every year, and they have a difficult relationship with littering. For health reasons, runners may need to consume water or protein from disposable packages while running through remote areas without access to trash receptacles. Well-organized races have volunteers collect litter post-event, but rarely, if ever, will every piece of litter be found.

The Austin Marathon (www.youraustinmarathon.com), named America's greenest race in 2008 by *Runner's World* magazine, discourages littering, but realizes that some litter is inevitable during a major public race. To this end, organizers install "Gutter Buddies," blockades that keep litter out of street gutters. They also take the innovative approach

Help Smokers Bin Their Butts

- Provide ample ashtray receptacles in likely smoking areas at the meeting or event site.
- Hand out pocket ashtrays, or small containers that can hold used cigarettes, with your brand or promotional message printed on them, from a company like Boodi (www.boodi.co.uk).

- Have environmental stewards assist smokers with finding ashtrays.
- Display signage with friendly reminders to "Bin Your Butt."

San Francisco's Moscone Center features a large array of solar panels on the roof.

Courtesy of the Moscone Center.

Solar panels on the roof of San Francisco's Moscone Center provide energy to the convention center.

Courtesy of the Moscone Center.

Because of its central location, it is easier for many attendees to walk than drive to San Francisco's Moscone Center.

Courtesy of the Moscone Center.

Low-energy lighting creates an intimate atmosphere for the Capital Fringe Festival.

Courtesy of Paul Gillis.

The Armory, a certified LEED Platinum building, home to Portland Center Stage.

Courtesy of Uwe Schneider.

Reynaldo Guino-o and staff of the EICC plant trees in the Scottish Borders as part of their environmental charity efforts.

Courtesy of the Edinburgh International Conference Center.

Attendees of The Big Tent were greeted by hostesses who provided fresh organic strawberries for those who traveled by bicycle or public transportation.

At the Capital Fringe Festival, I created The Free Store, a free swap shop for used music, books, and clothing.

Friends of The Earth Scotland brought environmental awareness to attendees at The Big Tent.

Guerilla Cinema provides pedal power for a movie screening at the Take One Action film festival.

Beesy's Beeswax Candles
were sold at The Big Tent.

Fayre Earth Gift Shop
presents colorful picture
frames and accessories
made from recycled paper.

At The Scottish Seabird Centre, visitors can observe wildlife through remote cameras powered by solar power.

Courtesy of Hans Bouwmeester.

The Scottish Seabird Centre, a wildlife observation center and venue for greener meetings and events.

Courtesy of Simon Heath.

An enormous origami crane sculpture, titled Ascension, was powered by solar energy at Coachella festival.

Courtesy of Coachella.

Solar panels powered Ascension at Coachella.

Courtesy of Coachella.

Top Tips for Litter Prevention

- Provide well-labeled, well-positioned, and well-maintained waste receptacles.
- Minimize the amount of disposable materials distributed to attendees.
- Advise attendees on what disposable items *not* to bring to the meeting or event.
- Have environmental stewards roam the meeting or event site and interact with attendees.
- Provide appropriate receptacles for smokers.

of having a team of kayakers laying in wait under a bridge, to quickly remove anything thrown in the water. Greener racing events can encourage participants to avoid littering while racing, while also taking precautions to minimize the damage of any litter.

Standard Waste

The most common waste receptacle is for *standard waste*, or garbage sent to landfill, also known as municipal solid waste (MSW). Although programs such as the United States Environmental Protection Agency's (EPA) Landfill Methane Outreach Program (LMOP) (www.epa.gov/lmop) help to convert landfill waste into energy, landfills remain a major blight on the earth's environment. Put simply, materials such as glass and plastic are not meant to be buried in the earth.

The best way to reduce standard waste is to reduce disposable items. Plastic wrap, cigarette butts, plastic cutlery, Styrofoam, aerosol cans, and plastic bags are all nonrecyclable, nonbiodegradable, and, at least in the case of cigarette butts, nonreusable. These items are used once, and then spend many years decomposing in landfill.

Your garbage man is also an important stakeholder in your meeting or event. Contact your local waste collection service to discuss the most environmental way to dispose of your standard waste. Here are some top tips on how to arrange the best standard waste collection.

Standard Waste Collection Tips

- Give preference to any members of LMOP who can convert your standard waste into energy.
- You may find private companies that can provide you with better waste services for a small fee.
- Confirm the exact date, time, location, and manner in which trash will be collected.
- Ensure that you have more than enough dumpsters to store all standard event waste before it is collected.
- Keep standard waste sealed in dumpsters, stored in remote locations, so as to not disturb the event's atmosphere.

Recyclable Waste

Many waste items, such as glass bottles and aluminum cans, can be separated from standard waste and *recycled*, or sent to a factory and turned into something new. Unfortunately, many meetings and events provide attendees with *only* standard waste containers, meaning that all recyclable waste is sent to landfill unnecessarily. Greener meeting and event pioneers provide attendees with a kaleidoscope of waste disposal options, and encourage them to consider recycling before standard waste disposal, aiming for recycling containers that are more full than those for standard waste.

Biodegradable Waste

Biodegradable waste describes organic matter that naturally decomposes, and includes most food and drink waste, as well as products made from organic materials such as cornstarch or soybeans. If it cannot be composted, biodegradable waste can be included in standard waste, having less of a negative landfill impact than that of nonbiodegradable waste such as plastic.

Patrons could use this receptacle to compost their biodegradable cups, food packaging, and food waste at The Big Tent.

Avoid: Nonbiodegradable and Nonrecyclable	Compost: Biodegradable	Recycle: Recyclable
Plastic bags	Food waste	Glass bottles
Cigarette butts	Biodegradable containers	Aluminum cans
Aerosol cans	Soy-based paper	Nonglossy paper
Plastic silverware	Biodegradable cutlery and plateware	Cardboard
Styrofoam	Cornstarch bags	Plastic bottles

Figure 6.4 Common Biodegradable/Recyclable Waste Items at Meetings and Events

For meetings or events requiring disposable items, biodegradable products are an increasingly accessible alternative to plastic. The company Vegware (www.vegware.us) provides meetings and events with biodegradable and compostable products that include cutlery, bags, napkins, straws, both hot and cold cups, and food containers. Figure 6.4 shows some of the most common items of waste at meetings and events that are biodegradable or recyclable, as well as those that are neither and should, thus, be avoided.

Precycling

In recognition of the amount of energy that recycling requires, a new word has recently emerged to describe a strategy to minimize all waste, whether biodegradable, recyclable, or disposable. *Precycling* means sourcing reused or recycled materials, and greener meeting and event pioneers precycle before they recycle. Salinger explains how Oracle OpenWorld is moving from recycling into precycling:

> When we started this process, our goal was to recycle as much as we could. Over the last three years, we have begun to expand this thinking to try to better understand how much waste is being created, and then looking at how much could actually be diverted from landfill by reducing what is produced.
>
> —*Paul Salinger, Oracle, interview, May 2010*

In addition to this reduction, Salinger also sources materials that are reusable, recyclable, or compostable ahead of time.

Figure 6.5 describes five ways in which greener meeting and event pioneers can minimize waste through precycling. The central goal is to minimize disposables. Buying in bulk, for instance, can minimize extraneous disposable packaging.

Buy Retro	Buy Real	Buy Recycled	Buy Bulk	Biodegradable
• Antique furniture gives an elegant touch. • Vintage arcade games provide retro fun. • Dated decor can take your attendees back in time.	• Disposable items make for disposable events. Avoid one-use-only products. • Invest in reusable products such as silverware for long-term cost savings. • Hand out reusable thermoses with your company logo on them.	• Recycled paper now comes in every color of the rainbow. Use it not just for invitations but also for streamers, banners, signage, tablecloths, napkins, and confetti. • Tradeshow exhibitors should be encouraged to print their handouts on recycled paper.	• Ask suppliers to minimize packaging. • Bulk buys are often cheaper. • Bulk foods can be arranged in real dishes for an elegant look. Nothing is tackier than a pile of individual packets of ketchup.	• Containers for food and drink, cutlery, dishes, and other food accessories are all now available in biodegradable form. • Buy organic cleaning products instead of chemicals.

Figure 6.5 Five Precycled Buys

Recycling

Greener meetings and events place recycling bins next to every trash can. Glass and plastic bottles, aluminum cans, and paper are just some of the many materials that can be recycled for later use. The key to effective recycling management is communication with your collection agency. Contact your local authority's waste management office and find out the exact date, time, location, and manner in which your event's waste and recyclables will be collected and processed. The two key issues for collection are what to contain recyclables in (government-issued bins? paper sacks?) and how to separate recyclables.

The Washington, DC, Department of Public Works (dpw.dc.gov) offers single-stream recycling, in which residents combine all recyclable materials in government-issued blue bins, for the recycling plant to separate the various materials into plastic, glass, and so on. The City of Edinburgh Council (www.edinburgh.gov.uk) requires residents to separate their own recycling. Get to know your local waste officers to ensure that your recyclables are processed correctly. Recycling stations are one of the most visible ways to market your event's environmental ethics, so make them look good!

Composting

Much of your standard waste, such as solid and liquid food waste, need not ever see the plastic lining of a garbage bag. Composting, the process by which biodegradable organic matter is decomposed into fertilizer, is becoming increasingly accessible to greener meetings and events. Composting has never been easier since the advent of indoor composting tools like Nature Mill, available at www.naturemill.com, an easy-to-use electric composter that fits under your kitchen sink. Simply scrape your dishes into the Nature Mill and let it decompose the food matter into plant soil, which you can remove and use in your garden.

Outdoor composting sites need to be created in coordination with local government and event site managers, and generally require more cost and effort than standard waste collection. Still, they are an impressive addition to any greener meeting or event, and more sustainable than standard landfill systems. If creating a compost heap is out of your reach, consider collecting your biodegradable waste and donating it to a local farm for its composting.

Waste Innovations

Waste management is a key area for greener meeting and event pioneers to use their imagination and create innovative strategies. Here are just a few of the many opportunities to surprise attendees with unique ways to cut down on waste.

Cup Deposit Schemes

Many UK music festivals now have a cup deposit scheme. For every purchase of a pint of beer in a plastic cup, patrons pay an extra £2, which is refunded upon the return of the plastic cup. Nearly all patrons will return the cup for their refund, a second sales interaction that often results in another pint purchased. There are no littered plastic cups to be seen anywhere on the event grounds, as savvy patrons are happy to recycle them for £2. In the German Market at Edinburgh's Winter Festival grounds, patrons pay an extra £2 for every mug of mulled wine, money that is refunded upon return of the mug. Many patrons choose to keep the souvenir mugs, thus effectively making a second purchase. Cup deposit schemes are good for the environment and good for business. Matt Grant, director of Peats Ridge Sustainable Arts and Music Festival, described to me in December 2008 the vastly enhanced atmosphere instilled by a cup deposit scheme:

> The psychology of putting a value on a piece of waste can change behavior. If a can is worth one dollar, then someone will pick it up. There are no cans on the floor, and so that creates a psychology as well: there are no cigarette butts on the floor and people generally litter less. If anyone doesn't care, then they pay a dollar for not caring.
>
> —*Matt Grant, Peats Ridge Sustainable Arts and Music Festival, interview, December 2008*

Bring Your Thermos to Work

Buy a reusable thermos: It sounds like such a simple idea, but yet millions of disposable cups get sent to landfill every day. While some coffee cups are now made from recycled or biodegradable material, the energy spent on creating and then disposing of these products far outweighs their brief, fleeting use. Imagine how much time and energy it takes to create a disposable cup, then to decompose or recycle it, compared to the half hour of usage that you actually get from the cup.

Encourage mass participation in a Bring Your Thermos to Work (or Bring Your Thermos to the Meeting or Event) campaign by providing free coffee for anyone who has brought a

Waste stewards were on hand at The Big Tent to teach attendees about reducing their landfill stream.

thermos. Companies like Biobadge (www.biobadge.com) can even make reusable coffee cups from organic sources, with a company logo on them.

E-Cycling

Electronic goods, which contain precious metals and nonbiodegradable plastics, are one of the worst things to end up in landfill. E-cycling is the recycling of these electronic goods, so that their valuable materials and machinery do not go to waste. E-cycling can prove to be an intriguing and exciting addition to any greener meeting or event: Green Festival (www.greenfestivals.com), a green economy conference, has impressed both attendees and the media by providing e-cycling receptacles at its events.

Cell phones have become a very popular item to e-cycle, and the EPA even hosts a National Cell Phone Recycling Week. Check out the EPA's guide to e-cycling at www.epa .gov/osw/conserve/materials/ecycling. Cell Phones For Soldiers is a nonprofit that collects used cell phones and sells them to an e-cycling company. All profits are used to buy pre-paid phone cards for soldiers to call home (http://cellphonesforsoldiers.com).

Terre Jones, CEO of Wolf Trap (www.wolftrap.org), America's National Park for the Arts, has made a number of environmental innovations during his tenure, one of which was an e-cycling swap that allowed patrons to bring used electronics to Wolf Trap to be recycled. In return for very little work, Jones lists the following positive outcomes: "3.5 tonnes of electronic equipment was safely and responsibly recycled, new audiences made their way to our space and were directed to the box office, and ultimately our education department will receive a portion of the fee from each recycled item." When I spoke with him in July 2009, Jones said that through strategic planning, not only does Wolf Trap gain new audiences and new income, it cleverly draws parallels between its typical arts events and an e-cycling electronics swap; Wolf Trap aligns its brand with the positive ethos of recycling.

Greener Toilets

Waste management means human waste as well, and several pioneering vendors are making great headway in the field of green toilets, or portable toilets that conserve water and do not pollute the event site. Australian vendor Natural Event (www.naturalevent.com .au) provides outdoor festivals with portable toilets that meet the twin goals of increasing sustainability while also improving the attendee experience. These toilets are completely

Three Ways to E-cycle

1. Give used but working electronic goods to a friend, to a charitable thrift store, or post them on a free online swap shop such as Freecycle (www.freecycle.org) or Craigslist (www.craigslist.org).
2. Send used electronic goods back to the manufacturer. Increasingly, electronics companies are implementing recycling programs and accepting used goods.
3. Contract a third party such as Eclycing.com (www.ecycling.com) to recycling electronics on your behalf.

waterless, as all waste is composted into soil, which can be planted. They are also odorless, providing a clean, green experience.

Australia's Peats Ridge Sustainable Arts and Music Festival (www.peatsridgefestival .com.au) proved the feasibility of composting at large, outdoor festivals when it initiated composting toilets. These were initially waterless toilets from Natural Event, but in 2010, Peats worked with Splashdown and SITA Environmental Services to develop a low-flush toilet:

> Composting toilets, when well managed, are odor free and need no water for flushing, making them ideal for festival environments. That said, 10 000 people make quite a lot of business over the course of our event so in 2010 we are very pleased to have developed a new composting toilet system for the event industry system. . . . Due to the low water to solid matter ratio this material can then be dewatered and composted in-vessel to generate the same high quality compost.
> *www.peatsridgefestival.com.au/sustainability/toilet-technology*

Share Your Surplus

Many meeting and event caterers operate on the principle of always making more than enough food, rather than running out. This only makes sense so long as the extra food is made use of, and not simply thrown out at the end of the day. Donating unserved food to local charities is complicated, but can be arranged with a little preparation. Other materials, such as signage, office supplies, decorations, and tradeshow handouts, are easier to donate.

Shawna McKinley, project manager at MeetGreen (www.meetgreen.com), describes the process of creating a donation program:

> All of our clients have a vendor, often the general services contractor, who are required as part of the terms of their agreement to facilitate a donation program. There are several general services contractors in the US who now are creating standard donor relationships with organizations that they can tap into in different cities. Very often, we will use these contractors to donate exhibit materials or decorator materials that are left in the host community.
> —*Shawna McKinley, MeetGreen, interview, May 2010*

In finding recipients for redistributed goods, McKinley recommends nationally based organizations, such as Habitat for Humanity or Boys and Girls Clubs of America, as well as local groups such as local schools, arts programs, and drama groups. "Theater folks take a lot of signage and counter tops, framing, and fabrics," she advises.

Finding an appropriate recipient for used goods can be challenging, but don't give up. Nancy (Wilson) Zavada, principal at MeetGreen, recalls a particular hotel chain that was trying to get rid of thousands of large hotel bed cushions. After much trial and error, it was finally put in touch with the Burning Man Festival (www.burningman.com) a free-spirited arts festival in the Black Rock Desert, which used the cushions for attendees to sleep on.

Exhibitions may donate unused pencils, pens, notepads, and other supplies to local schools. Untouched box lunches can be sent to local homeless shelters. Even plastic fencing

Eleven Places to Donate Goods

1. After-school programs (www.afterschool
   .gov)
2. American Veterans National Service Foundation(AMVETS)(www.amvetsnsf.org/
   stores.html)
3. Art schools (www.artschools.com)
4. Boys and Girls Clubs of America (www
   .bgca.org)
5. Habitat for Humanity (www.habitat.org)

6. Kiwanis Clubs (www.kiwanis.org)
7. League of Resident Theatres (www.lort
   .org)
8. Little League Baseball and Softball Clubs
   (www.littleleague.org)
9. Rotary Clubs (www.rotary.org)
10. Salvation Army (www.salvationarmyusa
    .org)
11. Thrift stores (www.thethriftshopper.com)

and temporary staging can be contributed as raw materials to a local festival or theatre company. Contact charities in your area and create meaningful partnerships with them to ensure that your event does not gratuitously waste useful items. By creating strategic partnerships with charities, you will enhance your public image and impress your attendees.

Donation plays a major role in the ambitious recycling program of San Francisco's Moscone Center. Of the nearly 2 million pounds of materials that Moscone Center annually donates from the city's landfill, around 20 percent is donated to local nonprofit organizations. Figure 6.6, created by Moscone Center Recycling Manager Kathleen Hennesey,

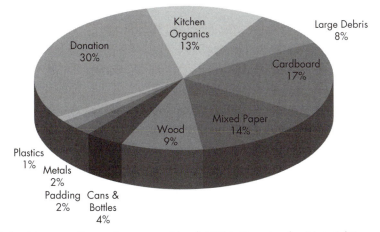

Figure 6.6   Moscone Center January to March 2010 Diversion by Material Type
Graphic by Kathleen Hennesey, recycling manager, Moscone Center (www.moscone.com)

Greener Convention: Greenbuild

Greenbuild (www.greenbuildexpo.org) is the annual conference and tradeshow of the United States Green Building Council (USGBC) (www.usgbc.org), or as Kimberley Lewis, vice president for conferences and events, likes to call it, the green building industry's tent revival. I spoke to her in May of 2010 to talk about Greenbuild.

Lewis, the daughter of a preacher, is passionate about her work. "Greenbuild is USGBCs largest vehicle to educate the building industry on sustainability," she says. "Our mission is to transform the built environment, and it is our job to inspire people to move to action. We use this event as a way to get the message out far and wide. We need to get people to realize that the time is now and that every person has a hand in making a difference."

Lewis recalls that when the show launched in 2002, the USGBC was so focused on education and content that it didn't realize the opportunities for sustainable event management. MeetGreen (www.meetgreen.com) approached the USGBC with a proposal to transform Greenbuild into one of the world's greenest conferences, and the rest is history. "In the early days, people looked at me like I was crazy," recalls Lewis. "In the hospitality sector, there were very few cities that understood sustainability."

Greenbuild has come a long way, and continues to raise the bar for green conventions every year. The year 2009 saw an estimated 70 tons of material donated or recycled, a 27.5 percent increase in recycling from the previous year. 79 percent of waste from the opening party was diverted away from landfill. There was a 50 percent reduction in energy consumption from the previous year, and 459 free light rail passes were distributed to attendees.

With the support of MeetGreen, Lewis carefully tracks Greenbuild's progress each year, including any setbacks. "You have to share the good and the bad," she says. "Our founding governance is on transparency. If you cannot be open and honest on the good and the bad, then you cannot move forward, because you learn from the bad. That is the powerful story behind Greenbuild. We're honest about our learning curve and we've been able to grow forward."

Lewis knows that MeetGreen shares this commitment to transparency. "Most consultants will tell the best story possible to keep the contract," she says. "We don't want the story where everything was great but nothing changes. From the very first year, MeetGreen has helped us to go beyond the minimum requirement. Each year we tell them that we know we can take the lessons learned to a new region and push the envelope."

USGBC is perhaps most famous for its LEED green building certification system, and convention centers that have been LEED-certified by USGBC hold an obvious appeal for Greenbuild. "That is definitely something we consider when choosing a destination," Lewis says. "In the early days, there weren't that many LEED convention centers. We had a wonderful show in 2003 at the Pittsburgh Convention Center, the first LEED Gold-certified convention center, and we won the IMEX award that year."

Transportation infrastructure is another major consideration in choosing a destination for Greenbuild. "Walkable cities are the best possible places to have a show," says Lewis. Proximity to the airport is also important, and Lewis recalls, "When Phoenix, Arizona, started courting us, we were unsure how attendees could get from the airport to the site. They planned to have a new light rail system in place, and said it would be there in time for Greenbuild. I said, If you can commit to that in writing, along with getting your convention center LEED-certified, I will push for this."

In Phoenix, Boston, and Chicago, guests could take the light rail straight from the airport to the convention center doors. Lewis says, "I always tell folks, anyone who wants to get on that freeway to the airport in rush hour traffic is crazy, when there's public transportation right here."

Local agriculture and composting facilities are another big consideration. "In Chicago, composting was easy because there's a lot of farms surrounding the city, and our facilities could create relationships with the farmers," Lewis says. She describes the way in which these local farms sourced food for Greenbuild, and how Greenbuild then delivered the compost for the farms to use as fertilizer. "All meat and produce for our evening events were sourced from a local farm, and all of the compost was given right back to them. It was a circle," she says.

Although it was easy to make that happen in Chicago, it was less so in the Arizona desert. "We had 27,000 people in Phoenix, and finding someone to take that amount of compost was a challenge," she says. Lewis is grateful that her organization supports practices such as composting, despite these challenges. "I have the leeway to say, this is an expense that we need to take, so that in the Arizona desert, they can learn how to compost, where they haven't before," she reflects.

Lewis sets aside a contingency fund in her Greenbuild budget to make sure that any challenges to sustainability are met head on. "It isn't just about me, it's about how can I help this facility, this hotel or convention center, or supplier to improve performance, so that they can support the next event planner that comes along wanting the same thing," Lewis says.

"Our board wants Greenbuild to be an educational tool, not just for the attendees, but for the staff of the hotels and convention centers we visit," Lewis says, "so that they can learn how to support a show of this size. We see our team as moving the industry forward."

Lewis does not want Greenbuild to become just another tradeshow. "It isn't just about the numbers," she says. "We want Greenbuild to help transform the building industry, to empower people, to change behaviors, and to make things better for the next generation." When she considers this grand agenda, Lewis smiles and says, "Who would have thought that an event planner could be part of that?"

Lewis came to the USGBC when it had just 15 staff members, and it now has over 250, with 80 chapters and over 100 green building councils across the world. "When I came here, I knew I had found my life's mission, and it has changed my life," she says. "Being an African American woman, I understand that environmental disasters often debilitate low-income neighborhoods where resources can be scarce. I am proud to play a role in educating people on how to improve their worlds. When you ask me, how did I get here, I think it was my purpose."

shows the vast array of materials diverted from landfill deposit in early 2010, 30 percent of which was donated to local groups for reuse.

Moscone Center's secret to diverting so much waste material is to get the stakeholders involved. Exhibitors are given stickers with which to mark all leftover materials. Green stickers mark materials to be recycled, such as unused print materials, and blue stickers mark materials to be donated, such as pencils and pens. Hennesey believes in getting clients and exhibitors involved in the waste diversion process from the start. "Green meetings begin with them!" she says. "The choices they make and materials they select actually determine what enters our doors. By the time materials and products come into our facility, it is too late."

Hennesey recommends that exhibitors establish goals and measurable objectives at the outset with input from key players. "Make these goals an integral part of the design, manufacture, transport, installation, and service of displays and exhibits," she says. "Choices made during the initial planning and design stages can minimize environmental impact. It takes partnership and communication to produce success."

Summary

Greener events strive to be cleaner events by minimizing event waste, which comes in the form of litter, standard landfill waste, recyclable waste, and biodegradable waste. Avoid disposable materials through precycling, or sourcing reused materials such as vintage or recycled goods. Provide plenty of different waste receptacles for standard, recyclable, and compostable waste that are well labeled, well positioned, and well maintained. Greener pioneers make waste management fun and easy for attendees with innovations such as cup deposit schemes and the promotion of reuse.

Key Terms and Definitions

- **Waste minimization**: the process of reducing waste.
- **Waste streams**: the various ways of dealing with waste, such as recycling or composting.
- **Waste diversion**: the act of keeping waste out of the landfill stream.
- **Zero waste**: 100 percent landfill diversion rate.
- **Litter**: unlawful disposal of garbage.
- **Transition points**: locations where attendees move from one activity to another. These are generally areas of high waste generation.
- **Standard waste**: garbage sent to landfill, also known as municipal solid waste (MSW).

- **Recycling**: sending waste items, such as glass bottles, to a factory to be turned into something new.
- **Biodegradable waste**: organic items that naturally decompose.
- **Precycling**: sourcing reused or recycled materials.
- **Composting**: decomposing biodegradable organic matter into fertilizer.
- **E-cycling**: recycling electronic goods.

Blue Sky Thinking

An exercise club in Miami wants to produce the city's first Green Triathlon. The race will challenge hundreds of participants to swim in the ocean, bicycle along the boardwalk, and then run to the finish line in downtown South Beach, Miami. The main event areas include the starting point on the beach, the entire race course, where participants will be provided with water and spectators will line up to cheer, and the finish line, where participants will be given medals, food, and prizes. Write a proposal for a waste management plan for the Green Triathlon that will keep litter and landfill waste to a minimum, while ensuring a safe and practical event. Include precycling, recycling, composting, and your own innovative waste solutions to make this successful event clean and green.

Renewable Resources

America Beautiful, Inc. (January). Accessible at kab.org/research09.

Ayya, Naina (2010). "WMWorld and Oracle Step Up Recycling Stations with Green Angels." *Changing Conventions* 8 (3) (August–November).

Freecycle Network, The (www.freecycle.org).

Keep America Beautiful (2010). "Litter in America: Results from the Nation's Largest Litter Study." Prepared by the MidAtlantic Solid Waste Consultants for Keep

Mobiles 2 Recycle (www.mobiles2recycle.com).

National Recycling Coalition (www.nrc-recycle.org).

Royte, Elizabeth (2005). *Garbage Land: On the Secret Trail of Trash.* New York: Black Bay Books.

TerraCycle (http://www.terracycle.net).

Wollan, Malia (2009). "San Francisco to Toughen a Strict Recycling Law." *New York Times* (June 10).

Participants pedal stationary bicycles to power a movie at Guerilla Cinema in Edinburgh.

CHAPTER 7

Energy and Water

"I'd put my money on the sun and solar energy. What a source of power! I hope we don't have to wait until oil and coal run out before we tackle that."

—Thomas Edison, Inventor (1847–1931)

In this chapter, you will learn:

1. How to save electricity in the office and at events by focusing on energy efficiency

2. How direct sunlight (passive solar power) can enhance the event environment while providing light and heat

3. How renewable energies such as solar, wind, water, and biofuel can provide energy while adding to the event atmosphere

4. How human energy can power devices that traditionally run on electric or battery power

5. How government grants can support renewable energy

6. How to support renewable energy initiatives with renewable energy certificates (RECs)

7. How to conserve water in the office and at events

8. How to harvest rainwater using landscaping techniques

Can you imagine a major heavy metal concert powered by sunlight? How about an outdoor cinema where the audience pedals bicycles that power the screen? Can you picture a dance floor that uses the kinetic impact of the dancing feet to power the lights?

These are not visions of the future; they are real attractions, brought to meetings and events today by companies such as Firefly Solar (www.fireflysolar.co.uk), Magnificent Revolution (www.magnificentrevolution.org), and Sustainable Dance Club (www.sustainabledanceclub.com). Renewable energies such as solar, wind, hydro, and even human power are becoming increasingly accessible, and the meetings and events industry is looking at the use of and support for these energies as a major trend.

Arlene Campbell is general manager, sales and events, for the Direct Energy Centre in Toronto, as well as former chair of the Environmentally Responsible Exhibitions and Events Committee of the International Association of Exhibitions and Events (IAEE) (www.iaee.com). When I spoke to her in August 2010, she said that she saw renewable energy gaining in popularity for the exhibitions industry: "I think greening your energy consumption either by purchasing green power or instituting energy conservation measures in consultation with your facility is a key initiative."

This chapter will explore the many ways in which you may conserve existing energy, purchase renewable energy, or even create your own energy from solar panels or pedal power.

Energy Efficiency

On Saturday, March 27, 2010, at 8:30 P.M., over 128 nations turned off the lights of some of the world's largest and most iconic buildings, including the Eiffel Tower, Buckingham Palace, the Las Vegas Strip, the Empire State Building and the city of Rio de Janeiro. They were participating in Earth Hour (www.earthhour.org), an initiative of the World Wildlife Fund (www.wwf.org) that asks people across the world to turn off their lights for one hour every year. Hundreds of millions of people and businesses annually take part, drastically altering the world's visual landscape, saving vast amounts of electricity, and making Earth Hour the world's largest global climate change initiative.

All this, just for turning out the lights. One of the most important things that greener meeting and event pioneers can do is to do less. Small things like using less electricity, turning off appliances, and reusing water can have big results, in the office and on site at meetings and events.

Office and Venue Controls

Start with your own meeting or event organization office, venue, or other areas that you control or occupy. A quick examination will reveal some initial low-hanging fruit, simple efficiencies that can save energy and money. For useful tips, check out Energy Savers (www.energysavers.gov), the U.S. Department of Energy's (DOE) guide to energy efficiency. Making small changes to the way you use lighting, heating and air conditioning,

Area	Action
Electronics	Turn off computers and monitors when not in use. Plug all electronic devices into power strips, and turn strips off when devices are not in use. Screen savers do not save energy. Instead, switch computers to sleep mode or turn off monitors.
Temperature	Lower your hot water heater thermostat to 120 degrees Fahrenheit. Set your thermostat as low in winter and as high in summer as is comfortable. Clean or replace filters on furnaces once a month or as needed. During winter, keep south-facing windows unshaded during the day and shaded at night to maximize heat gained from sunlight. Avoid placing lighting fixtures or large electronic devices near an air-conditioning thermostat, as the heat from these devices may interfere with the thermostat temperature.
Lighting	Install *compact fluorescent light bulbs* (CFLs). Open blinds to use direct sunlight instead of indoor lights when possible. Install occupancy sensors, dimmers, or timers to lighting fixtures.

Figure 7.1 Simple Energy Savings in Buildings

Check out Energy Savers (www.energysavers.gov)

appliances, and electronics can reduce your energy use considerably. Figure 7.1 provides some simple ways to find savings in basic office or venue maintenance.

You can make some of these changes yourself, immediately, such as replacing all light bulbs with *compact fluorescent light bulbs* (CFLs). These energy efficient devices use about 75 percent less energy than standard light bulbs, and last up to ten times longer. Other changes will require buy-in from all occupants of the building. Consider creating a new policy whereby all computers are to be powered off by the user if he or she will be away for more than a half hour (e.g., in a meeting). New policies such as these will require enforcing at first, but over time they may become second nature.

■ Insulation

Insulation, material that prevents heat loss, is one of the best investments that owners of older buildings can make. According to Energy Savers, only 20 percent of homes built before 1980 are well insulated. By investing in cavity insulation or insulative sheathing with various *R-values* (a rating system for insulation), which may include rolls and batts, loose-fill insulation, rigid foam insulation, and foam-in-place insulation, building owners can conserve significant energy.

Area	Action
Walls	Investigate cavity insulation or insulative sheathing. Consider the options of rolls and batts, loose-fill insulation, rigid foam insulation, and foam-in-place insulation of various R-values.
Air ducts	Seal leaks with heat-approved tapes such as foil or butyl tape. Consider heat-resistant insulation. Add vapor barriers to retain moisture.
Radiators and hot water heaters	Place heat-resistant radiator reflectors between exterior walls and radiators.
Water pipes	Consider heat-resistant insulation to retain heat in hot water pipes.
Leaks	Look for air leaks in dropped ceilings, recessed lights, water and furnace flues, ducts, doorframes, sill plates, or electrical outlets and switches. Seal with caulk, foam, and sealant.

Figure 7.2 Top Insulation Tips

Installing cavity insulation in your walls is a big, long-term project, but you can also carry out smaller installation projects, as shown in Figure 7.2. Radiators, hot water heaters, hot water pipes and air ducts can all be insulated to ensure that they are performing at maximum efficiency. Leaks on air ducts can be sealed with heat-approved tapes such as foil or butyl tape. Install well-sealed vapor barriers outside duct insulation to prevent excess moisture. Buildings may be leaking air from dropped ceilings, recessed lights, water and furnace flues, ducts, doorframes, sill plates, or electrical outlets and switches. You can seal these leaks inexpensively with caulk, foam, and sealant.

Building maintenance crews may be able to handle small projects such as insulating water pipes or sealing air leaks, but you will need a professional insulation specialist to provide large-scale insulation solutions.

■ Windows

Windows are highly desirable features in offices and venues, as everyone wants an office with a window, or a room with a view. However, windows can also allow heat to escape, wasting a lot of energy and money in the winter months. Building owners can consider upgrading single-glazed windows to double- or even triple-glazed glass with *low-emissivity coating (low-e)*, a treatment that reduces heat loss. Window replacements can be expensive, but can save money on heating equipment purchasing and use in the long run.

There are also a number of ways to maximize the energy efficiency of your windows without replacing them outright. To start, make sure that all window frames and sills are

Cold-Weather Windows	Warm-Weather Windows
Install strong storm windows with weatherstripping.	Install awnings on south- and west-facing windows.
Install thick, insulative window shades.	Install white window shades to reflect heat away.
Close at night and open at day window curtains.	Close at day south- and west-facing windows.
Clean south-facing windows to maximize solar gain.	Add sun-control or reflective film on south-facing windows to minimize solar gain.

Figure 7.3 Energy-Saving Windows in Cold and Warm Weather

tightly sealed to retain heat. Strategies differ in cold and warm-climates, and Figure 7.3 outlines these differences.

As with insulation, all major window refurbishment should be carried out by a professional.

Production Efficiencies

With sound, lights, and special effects, the technical production of the show, concert, keynote speech, panel discussion, or awards presentation is typically one of the biggest energy users of any meeting or event. There are a number of ways in which you can reduce this energy use and still produce a high-impact, spectacular show. White Light (www.whitelight.ltd.uk), a major theatrical lighting distributor in the United Kingdom, goes the extra mile to help major West End musicals as well as corporate clients and event planners to work more efficiently. White Light distributes a Green Guide, available on its Web site, to all clients, helping them to save energy while producing spectacular shows.

Most strategies for energy efficiency should have no noticeable effect on the audience experience. Instead, they are merely smarter, more efficient ways of technical stage production. Figure 7.4 summarizes efficiencies to be found in sound, lights, and special effects.

These energy efficient practices should not have any discernible impact on the quality of the show (unless you want them to, to show your audience your energy efficiency). Instead, they should allow you to produce the same show, but with less energy. Arts and entertainment organizations that work heavily with stage production can save considerable sums of money through these practices. According to White Light's Green Guide, London's National Theatre (www.nationaltheatre.org.uk) calculated that it could save around £1200 (about US$1,900) annually just by leaving its moving lights switched off until 35 minutes before the show.

High-Impact, Low-Energy Productions
After testing, leave all equipment switched off until 35 minutes before use. Handle electronic equipment and cords with care to preserve long-term use. Do not use unnecessarily large speakers or lights when smaller ones will do. Use the fewest number of microphones, speakers, and lights required to achieve the desired effects. Position speakers, lights, and special effects strategically to maximize their effects. Reuse lights and microphones during a show when possible. Turn equipment off when it is used last, even if show is not over yet.

Figure 7.4   Event Production Efficiencies

Catering Efficiencies

Catering managers know that the kitchen is a high-activity, high-energy location. As with the technical production, there are several ways to use energy strategically in the catering production for any meeting or event. Caterers, chefs, and kitchen staff may consider the advice in Figure 7.5 to work efficiently in the production, service, and cleaning of any catering operation.

Energy-saving strategies such as air drying dishes may not always be possible in the high-pressure kitchen environment, because they could potentially slow down the

Area	Action
Cooking	Keep your refrigerator at 37 to 40 degrees Fahrenheit and your freezer at 0 to 5 degrees Fahrenheit. Regularly defrost manual-defrost freezers. Make sure refrigerator doors are tightly sealed. Keep items in refrigerator wrapped and contained. Keep a lid on cooking pans to conserve heat. Do not put small cooking pans over large burners. Keep range-top burners clean.
Service	Buffet, French, or family-style service allows diners to choose their own portions, creating less food waste. Keep lids on buffet chafing dishes to conserve heat.
Cleaning	Air dry dishes when possible. Only use the dishwasher when full. Do not wash silverware, dishes, or napkins that you are sure are untouched.

Figure 7.5   Event Catering Efficiencies

operation. Greener caterers will use these efficiencies when possible, and find creative ways to work smarter, not harder, in the kitchen.

Energy-Efficient Products

Increasingly, engineers are designing more energy-efficient appliances and devices, as new energy-saving devices become available every day. Energy Star (www.energystar .gov) is a joint program of the U.S. DOE and the Environmental Protection Agency (EPA), designed to help Americans save energy. One of its most visible campaigns is the certification of energy-efficient products, including vending machines, water coolers, deep fryers, refrigerators, air conditioning units, televisions, and lighting fixtures, among others. In choosing which products to certify, Energy Star uses a set of key guiding principles.

Greener meeting and event pioneers look for energy efficiency when purchasing appliances and electronic devices. Look for the Energy Star logo when purchasing appliances or electronics for your next meeting or event. Not only can these purchases help you to save money and energy, but they are promoting a greener manufacturing industry. Figure 7.6 provides the criteria for a truly energy-efficient shopping list.

Energy Star provides a list of all accredited manufacturers of efficient devices on their website. For instance, Access Lighting (www.accesslighting.com) carries a wide variety of Energy Star–certified lighting fixtures. If you decide to upgrade your existing stock to energy-efficient products, do not throw out your old goods. Donate or e-cycle them to ensure that they receive future use.

Energy Star Certification Guidelines

- Product categories must contribute significant energy savings nationwide.
- Qualified products must deliver the features and performance demanded by consumers, in addition to increased energy efficiency.
- If the qualified product costs more than a conventional, less-efficient counterpart, purchasers will recover their investment in increased energy efficiency through utility bill savings, within a reasonable period of time.
- Energy efficiency can be achieved through broadly available, nonproprietary technologies offered by more than one manufacturer.
- Product energy consumption and performance can be measured and verified with testing.
- Labeling would effectively differentiate products and be visible for purchasers.

Source: Energy Star (www.energystar.gov)

Product	Criteria
Air conditioning unit	High energy efficiency ratio (EER) Correct BTU/hour for size of area to cool (check www.energystar.gov)
Window	Low U-values on National Fenestration Rating Council (NFRC) label
Refrigerators and freezers	Low kilowatt of electricity per year, listed on EnergyGuide label Refrigerators with freezers on top, which are more efficient than those with freezers on side Heavy door hinges create a tight seal
Dishwasher	Low kWh of electricity per year, listed on EnergyGuide label Low amount of water use Booster heaters Smart controls
Clothes washer	Low kWh of electricity per year, listed on EnergyGuide label Water level controls Suds-Saver features Spin Cycle adjustments Large capacity
Lighting	Compact fluorescent light bulbs (CFLs) Decorative light strings use under 0.2W per bulb
Televisions, computers, telephones, CD, and DVD players	Energy Star approved

Figure 7.6 Energy-Efficient Shopping List

Look for the Energy Star logo on each of these products (www.energystar.gov)

Emerging Energies

Since the Industrial Revolution, humans have depended on coal and oil for energy, but these sources are limited because they do not reproduce at the rate at which we use them. These dwindling resources are leading humans to pursue renewable energy, or energy using Earth's natural resources such as sun, wind, and water. In *Hot, Flat and Crowded,* Thomas L. Friedman differentiates between coal and oil, which comes from underground, and sun, water, and wind, which come from above. He calls coal and oil *Fuels From Hell*. By comparison, sun, wind, and water are termed *Fuels From Heaven* (Friedman 2009).

Sun, wind, and water can be turned into solar, wind, or hydropower to provide energy and electricity for greener meetings and events. Although such endeavors can make a spectacular impact, they need to be carefully coordinated with event suppliers, independent experts, and local authorities. Much of the technology discussed here is available for purchase from Green Energy Products at www.green-energy-products.com or ABS Alaskan at www.absak.com, and the appendices of this book have a complete list of renewable energy suppliers. The U.S. DOE provides a guide to renewable energy at www .eere.energy.gov.

Renewable Energy Providers

Switching to renewable energy may be as simple as calling the electric company; the U.S. DOE lists more than 750 U.S. electricity suppliers that already offer alternative energy plans that you can switch to, available online at: apps3.eere.energy.gov/greenpower. There is a broad range of availability between U.S. states; Oregon lists 18 green power options, while Louisiana only one.

Even if renewable energy is not locally available, you may support local or national renewable energy by purchasing *renewable energy certificates (REC)*, or investments in renewable energy. Earth Era (www.earthera.com) is one of several companies with a proven track record in supplying certified offsetting credits to major events.

Events without access to an alternative energy supplier may consider designing their own alternative energy solutions. Renewable energy is still an emerging science, so undertake a thorough investigation into multiple solutions before making any purchasing decisions. Choose Renewables (www.chooserenewables.com), a provider of solar and wind power, provides a free assessment on its Web site, called the MyWatts Renewables Estimator. Simply enter an address, and MyWatts will tell you the potential cost of wind and solar power installation, as well as the potential energy generated in that location. More importantly, Choose Renewables emphasizes conservation first, and sells several low-usage electronic devices.

Solar

At the 2010 Coachella Music Festival (www.coachella.com) in California, attendees partied beneath the wings of a gigantic origami swan that extended over the festival grounds. This was no ordinary swan—it was a solar-powered swan. During the day, festivalgoers relaxed in the shade beneath solar PV panels, which absorbed and stored solar power. As the sun set, generators released this stored energy to power an array of colorful lights that turned the swan into a huge, luminescent attraction that provided light to the festival.

Icon Energy displays solar thermal heating technology at the Edinburgh Jazz and Blues Festival.

Solar power is an increasingly feasible energy source for events. *Solar PV systems* use panels that hold photovoltaic cells (PVs) and transmit sunlight into electricity. *Solar thermal systems*, by contrast, convert sunlight into a fluid that provides heat for water systems. Solar PV uses flat panels, while solar thermal uses panels of tubes containing fluid. As solar PV rapidly develops, it is becoming increasingly accessible to consumers. You can now purchase a handheld solar power generator for as low as $49.95, thanks to companies such as Solio (www.solio.com), which make small, portable generators with solar PV panels that can store electricity and power electronic devices such as portable music devices or mobile phones.

Partner with your local renewable energy company. Icon Energy (www.iconenergy. co.uk) provides solar PV, solar thermal, and wind energy solutions for domestic and business interests, and one of their best marketing tools is live appearances at outdoor festivals. In 2010, it gained visibility by showcasing products at festivals such as The Big Tent (www.bigtentfestival.co.uk) and the Edinburgh Jazz and Blues Festival (www.edinburghjazz-festival.com). Displays of solar PV and solar thermal panels earned the interest of the crowd, and a large wind turbine created a unique addition to the atmosphere. By sponsoring meetings and events, renewable energy companies can greatly increase their visibility.

Firefly Solar

Firefly Solar (www.fireflysolar.co.uk) is the United Kingdom's largest event supplier of portable solar power generators. Housed in a 6 × 6 foot trailer, its Orion generators not only supply up to 5 KVA of solar power each, but also are 100 percent mobile. Firefly's Pictor generators are more compact and easier to handle, better suited for exhibition stands and trade shows. In addition to these generators, Firefly provides audiovisual equipment hire and technical production services to ensure the seamless operation of your solar powered venue.

When I spoke with him in August 2010, Richard Randall, project coordinator, told me, "The benefits of solar are that the generators don't produce emissions, reducing an events carbon footprint, they are completely silent running, and produce a cleaner 100% sine wave current. Solar power removes the need to handle volatile fuels and helps to reduce an event's fuel bill."

At the July 2010 Lovebox festival (www.lovebox.net) in London's Victoria Park, Firefly provided solar power to make sure that artists such as Grace Jones gave a truly electrifying performance. In producing the world premiere of the environmental film *The Age of Stupid* (www.spannerfilms.net), Firefly created a solar-powered cinema in Leicester Square that used just 1 percent of the carbon emissions typically associated with a Hollywood film premiere.

"Events choose solar power as it is a truly viable power source and a very visible indicator of an events effort to go green," Randall said. "In today's climate, event managers are very aware of the need to be sustainable, and there has been a switch to a greener way of thinking." Randall cites a UK festival survey that showed that, for some attendees, environmental policies were an even bigger concern than the price of alcohol.

Randall said that Firefly's biggest challenge was the lack of market confidence and people's perceptions of the reliability of renewable power sources within the events industry. "We have now overcome this particular challenge by proving that renewable power sources are a viable alternative to diesel," he said. "Designing and developing innovative products itself also presents hurdles, as every new project presents a different set of challenges, and, as pioneers of off-grid generator design we have to resolve these issues in house."

"We have also faced the challenge of changing people's behavioral patterns and getting them to think about their attitude towards energy usage." Randall has seen Firefly generators become a huge point of interest at events, engaging the audience in a dialogue about sustainability. "Audience reaction is very positive and people are surprised and interested by the fact that we can run so much equipment from solar power. People are always genuinely intrigued, and we get asked a lot of questions."

Solar Power International (SPI) (www.solarpowerinternational.com), North America's largest business-to-business solar event, showcases solar technology that is available for residential, commercial, and utility-scale applications. I spoke with Director of Communications and Spokesperson Monique Hanis in August 2010. Hanis said, "SPI presents a window on a thriving industry that is creating a domestic manufacturing base, jobs and producing clean, safe energy." While SPI features expert sessions on policy, markets, finance, technology and jobs in the solar industry, the organizers also strive to make

SolarPump

The unofficial motto of Austin, Texas, a unique little city in a big southern state, is "Keep Austin Weird," and perhaps that's why South by Southwest (SXSW) (www.sxsw.com) Music, Film, and Interactive Conferences and Festivals continues to push the envelope each year. In 2010, it commissioned artist Beth Ferguson to reinvent the iconic American gas pump into a renewable energy provider. The result was the hugely successful SolarPump, which enabled festivalgoers to recharge their electronic devices (www.soldesignlab.com).

I phoned Eve McArthur, director of operations, in May 2010, and she explained that materials were sourced locally to build three SolarPumps. "This is completely an Austin prod-

The SolarPump, a solar-powered charging station, in use at South By Southwest 2010.
Beth Ferguson, 2010, SolDesignLab.com.

the show accessible to the general public in order to promote education. She explained, "The show is about advancing the U.S. solar energy market, and so our extensive Expo Hall is open to the public, with free access on the Wednesday evening."

In addition to this commitment to accessibility, SPI has several environmental conferencing policies. Hanis said, "Most of our marketing is electronic; onsite paper distribution is limited; we provide recycling bins onsite; we provide water bottles to refill at water uct," she said. "They have solid welded bodies. We have incorporated safety mechanisms such as cut-offs, in case somebody plugs in something too strong. If the battery gets too low, it turns off." McArthur said, "We have an LED display that tells you how many volts are coming in from the solar arrays, and that tells the user how many volts their item is using while it charges."

Made from actual used gas pumps that have been gutted, refinished, and repurposed, the SolarPumps were designed with reuse in mind. Furniture made from used street signs gives users space to relax and congregate while powering up. McArthur says that these street sign chairs are always full, as the SolarPumps are a hugely popular attraction. "People charge everything. Laptops, phones, Mp3 players, anything that you can plug into a 120-volt socket." The pumps can now charge up to 75 cell phones at a time.

The SolarPumps were so popular that Ferguson has taken them to three other music festivals: Roskilde (www.roskilde-festival .dk) in Denmark, Lollapalooza in Chicago (www.lollapalooza.com), and Coachella (www .coachella.com) in California. At Coachella, a pump installed at the campsite was incredibly well used, and seemed to require no supervision, so Ferguson left it unattended overnight. As McArthur recalls, "One morning, coming down to the campsite, Beth began to smell hamburgers. She walked up and saw that someone had plugged in a portable grill, and was cooking hot dogs and hamburgers. The guy didn't know who she was, and said, 'Want a hamburger?'

"She panicked, because she knew that those things drew a lot of energy, but she didn't know how much," McArthur said. "What if the control mechanisms didn't work? A cell phone pulls 3 volts, a laptop maybe 5 or 7. This thing was pulling 500 volts. Well, our inverters can take that much. It was working fine, although draining the battery. It did not shut down, and that was gratifying." Ferguson later heard that people had been plugging in their electric guitar amplifiers over night, to play music powered by the SolarPump.

McArthur has been delighted by the high energy potential of the SolarPumps. "Our new panels from Sanyo were pulling about 40 volts in full sunlight," she said. "When the sun went back past the buildings, they were pulling 20 to 30 volts, just from indirect light. The most amazing thing was that, at night, with just the ambient light of downtown, they were still pulling 5 to 7 volts. That was really exciting news for us, and I think for Sanyo as well. We're hoping to expand and continue our relationship with them."

Part of the SolarPump's success lies in its design, which reimagines a classic 1950s gas pump with solar panels. McArthur recalls taking it to an energy fair, saying, "People would see it and take dozens of pictures, then come over and say, 'That's cool. What does it do?' It definitely gets people's attention and sparks a dialogue."

"We have huge interest from around the country," says McArthur, citing several festivals and universities that want their own SolarPump. "It's been a very gratifying project to be involved with."

dispensers; and many of our venues are solar powered, as we are this year at the Los Angeles Convention Center." With its commitment to education and sustainability, SPI has seen great growth over the last six years.

Larger events may consider renting or purchasing solar generators from companies such as Wholesale Solar (www.wholesalesolar.com) or Mobile Solar Power (www.mobile-solarpower.net). Solar power providers can be found throughout Europe, and Focus Solar (www.focussolar.de) provides solar power in Germany. If large-scale solar PV rentals are unavailable in your area, try smaller options, such as purchasing handheld generators from Solio (www.solio.com). Solar Home (www.solarhome.com) provides an extensive array of solar-powered lighting fixtures, including garden path lights, glass LED string lights and security spotlights. These individual solar-powered lights make a charming addition to any outdoor meeting or event.

■ Passive Solar Power

Passive solar power is much simpler than solar PV or solar thermal technology; it means using direct sunlight for light and/or heat. The design of an event's architecture can easily be altered to maximize passive sunlight and minimize electric light: using a tent with

The Colorado Convention Center features solar arrays on its roof.
Courtesy of the Colorado Convention Center.

transparent walls can give patrons natural light and a beautiful vista. Similarly, at a recent Green Events Summit at EventScotland (www.eventscotland.org), organizers opened the blinds of the seventh floor conference room to reveal a sparkling view of Edinburgh, Scotland, allowing the sunlight to light the room. South-facing windows are generally best positioned to harness direct sunlight.

Certain floor materials can also absorb heat from the sun better than others. Some of the most innovative new green buildings employ passive solar power with window shades that allow warming sunlight in the winter and keep it out in the summer. Some green buildings even have window shades made from solar PV panels, which collect sunlight for electricity while keeping the building cool. Direct sunlight can also be used to cook things like sun tea: Just put a jar of water outside in hot weather with a few teabags inside.

Wind

In the past few years, the United States has skyrocketed to become the world's leading generator of wind power, thanks to initiatives in California and Texas. Wind power is generated from *turbines*, or windmills placed either on land or offshore that convert kinetic wind movement into electricity. Small-scale wind power can be not only feasible but profitable; citizens of the Danish island of Samso have generated enough wind power from both large municipal turbines and small personal turbines to both power the entire island and sell the remaining energy at a profit (Kolbert 2008).

Icon Energy displays a wind turbine at the Edinburgh Jazz and Blues Festival.

You can also investigate small-scale wind power for events. Try Bergey Windpower (www.bergey.com) or Aerostar Wind Turbines (www.aerostarwind.com) for wind power solutions. Consider partnering with your local wind power provider to either power your event or promote their business. Either way, their wind turbines will make a great addition to the event environment, and leave a stunning impression on attendees.

Some wind energy devices may emit mechanical sounds that could interfere with your event, although probably less so than a typical portable gas energy generator. Always ask about potential noise pollution before you buy or rent new technology, and test it before the event. If necessary, position these devices away from a public area to minimize noise pollution.

Hydro

Hydropower is the harnessing of naturally flowing water to generate hydroelectricity, and it is already a critical part of the Earth's energy supply. As of 2005, hydroelectricity accounted for 19 percent of the Earth's electricity. The nation of Norway runs on 98 percent hydroelectricity, and has the sixth greatest capacity of all nations for generating hydroelectricity. The United States has the fourth greatest capacity, with immense untapped potential hydropower ("Binge and Purge," *The Economist* 2009).

Many hydroplants offer scenic locations with breathtaking views, making them ideal event venues. Smaller refurbished mills offer cozy meeting rooms, while larger civic dams can support major outdoor events. Events held at or near hydroplants may save energy costs by using hydroelectricity. Other events may investigate designing their own microhydropower, simple technology, which can harness local water sources for specific event use. Try Canyon Hydro (www.canyonhydro.com) or Utility Free (www.utilityfree.com) for microhydropower solutions.

Biofuel

Biofuel is fuel made from organic ingredients such as corn oil, and Chapter 5 showed how this resource can power automobiles. Energy specialists are now developing portable biofuel generators that can power meetings and events. Peats Ridge Sustainable Arts and Music Festival (www.peatsridgefestival.com.au) in Australia, was one of the first major events to rely on biodiesel generators. Executive Director Matt Grant told me in December 2008 that, "There was no one in Australia that would do biodiesel. We were talking to generator companies and trying to convince them to do biodiesel, but they couldn't warrant biodiesel. It was an uphill battle, talking to companies that didn't want to void their warrantees."

Grant turned the challenge of persuading suppliers to incorporate risk into their product development into an opportunity for these suppliers to innovate their product and increase sales. The company that voided its warranty in order to supply biodiesel generators to Peats Ridge tripled in size that year, and have now opened another two stores in Australia, selling only biodiesel generators.

Demand for biodiesel generators is now growing rapidly. UK demand was so strong in 2009 that the Manchester International Festival (MIF) (www.mif.co.uk) could not contract any environmentally friendly generators, as all suppliers were fully booked. MIF Head of Creative Learning Jennifer Cleary told me, "There is an issue with suppliers being able to cope with increased demand. You have to have increased demand to make it economical for those suppliers to make the switch."

Biogas is energy created by breaking down organic matter, typically waste, without oxygen, and is one way to generate energy from landfills. Biogaz Europe (www.biogaz-europe .com) is one of the world's largest biogas conferences, and is organized by sustainable events company Bees (www.bees.biz).

Chapter 5 discussed the use of waste vegetable oil (WVO) to power vehicles, but this same substance can power stationary generators at permanent or temporary venues. Vegawatt (www.vegawatt.com) provides a system that allows restaurants to power themselves with their own french fry oil, by refining WVO and turning it into electrical power. The Fairmont St Andrews (www.fairmont.com/standrews), host to such important international conferences as the G20 Summit (www.g20.org), powers its shuttle buses on WVO recovered from the kitchen.

HyLight150

In June 2010, White Light Ltd (www.white-light.ltd.uk) brought a mysterious blue, wheeled flight-case to the Association of British Theatre Technicians (ABTT) (www.abtt.org. uk) annual tradeshow. Operating silently and with no emissions other than a small amount of water, the portable box stunned the crowd by powering high-tech lighting instruments.

This portable energy generator is called the HyLight150, and it uses a hydrogen fuel cell. A tiny amount of the resulting H2O (water) is the only emission from this silent-running, clean energy provider. A joint project between White Light (www.whitelight.ltd.uk), Arcola Energy (www.arcolaenergy.com), and BOC (www. boconline.co.uk), HyLight150 can power low-energy lights such as Pulsar ChromaFlood fixtures or single color worklight floods to create stunning outdoor displays.

Because HyLight currently only provides 150 watts of power, its use is limited, but White Light

Managing Director Bryan Raven sees HyLight as a big step towards energy independence. When I met him at the Edinburgh Festival Fringe in August 2010, he said, "It is showing the way with fuel cell technology. As this technology improves, and efficient lighting uses less power, we may see hydrogen powered performance stages within a couple of years time."

Raven says that he doesn't expect clients to necessarily care about the history or technology of the hydrogen fuel cell. "What we do expect is that they will care greatly that they can have a lighting system that is clean, silent, and portable, perfect for lighting events in gardens and parks," he says. "HyLight perfectly complements the range of low-energy LED lighting equipment that we have introduced over the last few years, and the work we have been doing to encourage sustainability in lighting and event production. We think and hope that those who create lighting outdoors are going to be as excited about it as we are."

Human Energy

Not only do bicycles conserve resources and promote exercise, but they can also be used to generate energy. The 2008 Super Bowl, which was 100 percent powered by renewable energy, hosted a four-day stationary-bike ride event that powered 30 minutes of the pregame show solely by pedal power. You can bike power generators from Windstream Power (www.windstreampower.com) to power your event while giving attendees an exciting, competitive activity. In the United Kingdom, Firefly Solar provides Kinetic Pedal Powered Generators that allow attendees to supplement solar power by pedaling stationary bikes.

Magnificent Revolution is a group of London artists, ecologists, and electricians who have created a series of pedal-powered performances. Its Magnificent Cycling Cinema uses ten bikes to provide 600W of audiovisual equipment for screening films. It also hosts DJ dance nights and live band performances where the sound system is powered by audience members pedaling stationary bicycles. In 2009, Stan's Cafe (www.stanscafe.co.uk), brought *Home of the Wriggler*, a play in which the cast power the lights onstage by cycling, to the Edinburgh Festival Fringe (www.edfringe.com).

Some tasks can be completed by downgrading from electronic devices to human-powered simple machines. People Powered Machines (www.peoplepoweredmachines. com) sells a wide range of hand-powered lawnmowers and other devices. In addition to supplying these simple machines that require no electricity, People Powered Machines also provides renewable energy devices.

Engineers have powered long-lasting electric lighters from the mere click of a finger for years, using the *piezolectric effect*, or the ability for certain materials to generate energy from simple friction. Pioneering engineers are looking to apply this technique to cell phones, using the motor energy generated from fingers when sending text messages to charge the phone battery. It is now possible to buy portable clocks, radios, flashlights, and electrical generators that are powered solely by winding a crank. People Powered Machines sells wind-up radios and other self-powered devices.

The Sustainable Dance Floor

At a nightclub in Rotterdam, Holland, dancers enter a darkened dance floor and begin to boogie. As they dance, the lights grow brighter, and every extra step or move brings new lights on, until the dancers tire out, and the lights dim. These dancers are at Club Watt, home of the Sustainable Dance Floor (www.sustainable-danceclub.com), which powers a full nightclub LED lighting system from the kinetic energy of feet dancing on an energy-sensor dance floor.

Sustainable Dance Club, the makers of this amazing technology, are working to bring low-energy dancing to the masses. It is seeking to feature its dance floor at a major international event in order to power the world's largest LED screen.

Energy	Opportunities
Human	Bicycle pedal power can generate electricity. Simple machines such as push mowers operate without electricity. Wind-up radios and other devices require only a little elbow grease. Bicycles and pedicabs are eco-friendly alternatives to cars and cabs.
Solar	Solar PV power generates electricity with solar panels. Solar thermal power generates water heat. Solar panels create an impressive display. Let the sunshine in! Create skylights and windows to use passive solar power to light and heat a room or tent.
Wind	Wind turbines can provide site-specific wind energy. Turbines make a striking, powerful look on an outdoor event site. Many local energy companies offer wind power already.
Hydro	Hydroplants make scenic and unique venues for events run on renewable energy. Look into microhydropower solutions from either running water or rainwater.
Biofuel	Filtered waste vegetable oil (WVO) from deep fryers can provide fuel. Work with your local generator rental company to find generators that can run on biodiesel.

Figure 7.7 Renewable Energy Opportunities

Renewable energies are rapidly developing as a sustainable way to power greener meetings and events. You can seek out solar, wind, hydro, biofuel, and human power solutions to create new energy sources to dazzle your attendees, lower your carbon footprint, and make a stunning addition to the event environment. Figure 7.7 summarizes the renewable energy opportunities now on offer for greener meetings and events.

Government Grants

The U.S. government, and other governments, are actively supporting renewable energy and energy efficiency at the moment, and there are many government grants and tax incentives available for the installation of renewable or energy efficiency technology. The U.S. DOE operates a Database of State Initiatives for Renewables and Efficiency (DSIRE) (www.dsireusa.org), a complete catalog of government initiatives in this area. Check DSIRE, and contact your local city and state government to find out more about tax incentives and government grants for renewable energy and energy efficiency.

Renewable Energy Certificate (REC) Providers

- Earth Era (www.earthera.com)
- ChooseRenewable(www.chooserenewables. com)

- The Carbon Neutral Company (www.car bonneutral.com)

The DOE also operates a Building Technologies Program (www1.eere.energy.gov/buildings), which funds research and technology that reduces energy use in buildings.

Renewable Energy Certificates

Similar to carbon offsets, renewable energy certificates (RECs) may be purchased by organizations that wish to support renewable energy. Meetings and events without access to renewable energy may purchase RECs in order to drive the green economy and support this burgeoning market, in the hopes that renewable energy will one day be accessible to them.

As with carbon offsets, RECs should be considered after doing everything possible to reduce energy consumption and to source renewable energy. Events without access to renewable energy should seek out professional, accredited REC providers.

Water Conservation

As with energy, scientists are warning that current levels of water consumption are unsustainable. Arlene Campbell believes that meeting and event professionals will have to watch this trend. When I spoke with her in August 2010, she said, "Water conservation is going to become a critical issue for the future, so I see this as an area where the industry has to focus their attention, whether it be in the water used to produce goods at the event, or water conservation practices at the hotels and venues."

Water Efficiency

The U.S. EPA has created a water conservation program called WaterSense (www.epa. gov/owm/water-efficiency), which provides advice on how to save water. The first step to water efficiency should be detecting and repairing any leaks in the plumbing system.

Check toilets for leaks by putting a little food coloring in the tank; if food coloring appears in the bowl within 15 minutes, there is a leak.

Once a certified plumber has repaired all leaks, there are many ways to use water more efficiently. In the kitchen, avoid running the sink constantly for melting or cleaning purposes, and only wash full loads of dishes. Reuse cleaning water when possible, and sweep outdoors instead of hosing. Use sprinklers efficiently, and allow grass to grow to 3 inches for maximum water retention. Figure 7.8 provides a plethora of savings to be found in ordinary water activities.

Area	Action
Catering	Turn off dishwashers when not in use. Only use dishwasher when full. Scrape, don't rinse food off dishes. Melt ice or frozen foods in a still basin, not with running water. Use steam table water to wash down cooking areas. Use water-efficient ice makers.
Cleaning	Only use washing machine when full. Use a rinse water recycle system. Clean pavement by sweeping or blowing, rather than hosing. Reuse indoor cleaning water to clean outdoors.
Outdoors	Use treated wastewater for irrigation when possible. Water trees and shrubs longer than smaller plants. Position sprinklers strategically, so that they do not hit the street or pavement. Install moisture sensors on sprinkler systems. Water the grounds during the early morning to avoid heat evaporation. Add organic matter to soil if needed, to increase water retention. Native plants require less water than ornamental varieties. Only install or use fountains that recycle water, and never operate during a drought. Do not cut grass shorter than 3 inches, as taller grass retains water better. Use sprinklers that produce droplets, not mist.
Plumbing	Detect and repair all leaks. Adjust flush valves on install dams on toilets. Install WaterSense certified ultra-low flow toilets, faucet aerators and high-efficiency showerheads. Minimize water used in cooling equipment in accordance with manufacturer regulations. Shut off cooling units when not needed.

Figure 7.8   Water-Saving Tips

Check out WaterSense (www.epa.gov/owm/water-efficiency)

WaterSense Products

- Perform as well or better than their less efficient counterparts
- Are 20 percent more water efficient than average products in that category
- Realize water savings on a national level
- Provide measurable water savings results

- Achieve water efficiency through several technology options
- Are effectively differentiated by the WaterSense label
- Obtain independent, third-party certification

Source: WaterSense (www.epa.gov/owm/water-efficiency)

Water-Efficient Products

In addition to providing advice, WaterSense also certifies efficient water products. As with Energy Star, for a product to be certified with the WaterSense logo, it must meet strict criteria.

Gerding Theatre features a 10,000-gallon underground cistern that harvests rainwater and redirects it for use in the toilets. Portland Center Stage's performance season occurs during Portland's peak rainy season, to make this rainwater available when it is in highest demand. *Courtesy of the Portland Center Stage.*

WaterSense Product	Comparison	Potential Savings (gallons of water per year)
Urinal	Saves between 1 and 4.5 gallons per flush	4600
Toilet	Uses up to 20 percent less water than standard versions	4000
Showerhead	Uses no more than 2 gallons per minute	2300
Faucet	Reduces sink water flow by 30 percent or more	500

Figure 7.9 WaterSense Shopping List

Look for the WaterSense logo when purchasing these items.

By upgrading your existing plumbing infrastructure to WaterSense products, you may realize great savings over time. Check out the savings from the shopping list in Figure 7.9.

Rainwater Harvesting

Greener meeting and event pioneers can conserve water through landscaping techniques that utilize rainwater, called *rainwater harvesting*. A key benefit of rainwater harvesting is that it reduces *urban runoff*, or excess water that increases flooding and carries pollutants from streets, parking lots, and lawns into streams and lakes. Urban planners, architects, and landscapers are creating a handful of innovative ways to utilize rainwater or stormwater from wet weather, including rain gardens, porous pavements, green roofs, infiltration planters, and rain barrels. Figure 7.10 describes the ways in which these rainwater-harvesting techniques conserve water and improve event venues and sites.

Urban gardens that harvest rainwater may show many more benefits than listed above. The San Francisco Bay Area, in its 2007 report on the State of the Urban Forest, lists the following positive outcomes from its urban forestry program:

You may be surprised at the multitude of benefits that plants and gardens bring to meetings and events. In addition to complex benefits such as harvesting rainwater and helping buildings to conserve energy, plants also improve the event atmosphere in a simple, comforting way. In many ways, live plants are the original and the ultimate event decoration.

Technique	Description	Benefits
Rain gardens	Landscaped areas that absorb rainwater runoff from nearby buildings	Absorbs about 30 percent more water than a plain grass lawn. Reduces stormwater runoff.
Porous pavements	Permeable surfaces such as asphalt or concrete that treat water and allow it to drain into the soil below	Filter oils and heavy metals out of stormwater. Reduce stormwater runoff. Increase groundwater recharge.
Green roofs	Rooftop gardens	Reduce runoff. Increase access to plants and wildlife for urban dwellers and office workers. Keeps buildings cooler, reducing air conditioning costs.
Stormwater planters	Small, contained vegetated areas that collect and treat stormwater using *bioretention*, or mulch and soil systems that filter pollutants	Filter pollutants such as bacteria, nitrogen, phosphorus, heavy metals, and oil and grease out of stormwater. Provide plants and wildlife in urban areas with limited space. Reduce runoff water in streets and sidewalks. Increase groundwater recharge.
Rain barrels	Containers that collect and store rainwater for later use	Can be used for commercial or municipal irrigation. Reduce runoff.

Figure 7.10   Rainwater-Harvesting Techniques

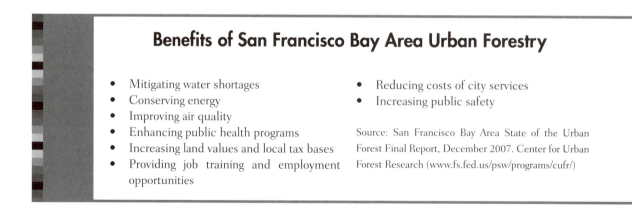

Benefits of San Francisco Bay Area Urban Forestry

- Mitigating water shortages
- Conserving energy
- Improving air quality
- Enhancing public health programs
- Increasing land values and local tax bases
- Providing job training and employment opportunities

- Reducing costs of city services
- Increasing public safety

Source: San Francisco Bay Area State of the Urban Forest Final Report, December 2007. Center for Urban Forest Research (www.fs.fed.us/psw/programs/cufr/)

Consider holding your next meeting or event at a venue with water conservation features such as a green roof or rain barrels. You also might be able to incorporate some of these features in an existing venue or event site with the consultation of a professional landscaper. The U.S. EPA provides a thorough guide to managing wet weather using green infrastructure at www.epa.gov (Search: "Managing Wet Weather with Green Infrastructure").

As president and CEO of the American Society of Association Executives (ASAE, www.asaecenter.org), John Graham manages an institution that advises thousands of association leaders in planning their annual conferences. He believes that energy and water efficiency, and renewable energy, offer events many intangible benefits. When we spoke in May 2010, Graham said, "It's important that our actions have a minimal impact on the environment for numerous reasons, besides the obvious—preserving the limited and often nonrenewable resources. It's really a much bigger picture."

There are many great benefits that are especially useful, like enhancing reputation and visibility of our organizations, attracting and engaging a highly qualified workforce as well as members and customers committed to social responsibility, and the possibility of significant cost savings through increased operational efficiencies and innovations.

—*John Graham, ASAE, interview, May 2010*

Graham believes that water conservation and energy efficiency are key assets for a modern business. "With these benefits, organizations are more likely to become a part of the 'greening' movement," he says, "and although saving the environment should be a priority for everyone, outlining the benefits and having a conversation about them is very helpful in attracting more organizations to join the movement." In many ways, working efficiently with water and energy can help your organization to work smarter in all areas.

Greener Conference and Festival: South by Southwest (SXSW)

South by Southwest (SXSW, www.sxsw.com) started as a small music industry conference and festival in Austin, Texas, attracting 700 attendees in 1987. Having built its reputation as a unique and exciting event, SXSW has become the preeminent showcase for new musical talent, as well as one of the world's most important conferences for the music, film, and interactive

(continued)

(continued)

industries. In 2010, SXSW hosted 27,551 badged registrants from 73 different countries, contracted 56 properties, sold 39,738 hotel room nights, and featured 1,978 musical groups.

A grassroots organization that has always used local suppliers and secondhand goods, SXSW was green before green was trendy. Reusable canvas tote bags are popular now, but SXSW has provided these for registrants for the past 20 years. Eve McArthur, longtime director of operations at SXSW, has managed reuse and recycling programs, transitioned to a paperless office, and implemented high-efficiency heating and cooling systems throughout her tenure. She explains, "Our environmental initiatives are long-standing."

SXSW continues to expand their environmental initiatives each year. When we first met in September 2009, McArthur said, "Last year, we added a solar array to our roof to supplement our electrical usage with clean energy, and in 2005 we put rain collection barrels in place for water control and landscape use." The solar panels have generated 18 percent energy savings, and the rain barrels continue to conserve water resources. A comprehensive energy audit resulted in solar screens, roof insulation, and upgraded air conditioning and light fixtures. By switching to online applications and electronic press kits, paper waste was cut by 70 percent. When it comes down to protecting the planet, McArthur isn't afraid to make tough decisions. "Bottled water has been banned for staff use at the offices and during

the event, with alternatives provided that use city water," she said.

These initiatives are the result of detailed planning. McArthur said, "We initiated a carbon study to measure and try to reduce the major administrative carbon emitters we identified, which included the heating, cooling, and lighting of all of our spaces, including those used during the event, and staff travel. This has been a major tool to keep staff awareness high and to measure our progress."

McArthur reminds event planners to thoroughly investigate all sustainable initiatives: "It is not enough to just have your recycling picked up—you need to know where it goes, or you may be just greenwashing. At SXSW, we visit the dump and our other waste management facilities to see if we are getting the services we are paying to get."

I spoke with Executive Director Mike Shea in May 2010, and he said that a popular new policy this year was a serious restriction on paper flyers. "We tried to cut down on leaflets that people don't really value, and encourage people to put in reusable things that have a value, whether it's a CD or a DVD or a water bottle, a cigarette lighter, or a bottle opener."

Because SXSW has grown into a sprawling, citywide event, with thousands of artists traveling into Austin from around the world and occupying hundreds of different hotels, conference centers, and indoor and outdoor venues, their greatest challenge is stakeholder buy-in. McArthur said, "SXSW's major focus is on our administrative, year-round operations, since that is the place we have the most control. We have made changes where feasible during our event, but where we have less control over space or practices."

McArthur thinks that one of the keys to stakeholder buy-in is to create a public dialogue. "Just by having this discussion about sustainability, making these efforts and publicly reporting the results, we have seen our stakeholders make their own efforts toward improvement," she says. "Notable examples are the Convention Center, where much of SXSWeek takes place, which has become LEED certified in the last two years and which is striving to achieve Gold LEED status." The Austin Convention Center has operationalized its recycling and waste management practices, and McArthur said its back-of-house personnel are trained and knowledgeable. The Convention Center has gone completely to biodegradable serviceware and has added composting.

For the past four years, SXSW has held meetings of the over 50 hotels involved in the event, for them to share information on how their hotels can become greener. Shea said, "What we found was that every hotel, without exception, found something that not only contributed to sustainability, but also that saved money. Every single thing they did turned out to be money saving, whether it was switching to more efficient light bulbs or switching to a recycling system." McArthur noted, "We have seen wider and deeper initiatives in place

each year with this group." One outcome has been a listing of all hotels on the SXSW website, along with a little green leaf that you can click on to see the sustainable initiatives of each hotel.

SXSW reaches out to local companies to help them achieve sustainability. McArthur noted, "We have worked with local providers to improve waste management, and offer alternative transportation options, including an increasing use of biofuel for generators, shuttles, and other transportation for our staff functions and for our attendees."

McArthur makes sustainability a highly visible aspect of SXSW: "Each year we publish an article on our Web site and in our publications that highlights ways to do SXSW greener. Over the past several years, we have added increasing numbers of panels and other programming in the conference end of the event that address sustainability, climate change, and the environmental impact of our choices."

"Sustainability is complicated and ever-changing," says McArthur. "Our challenge is to remain ever mindful of our actions and their consequences, and to recognize that doing something, though small, is better than doing nothing. This is a discussion that is never done, but the actions and decisions we make as a company and as individuals do matter. At all levels of staffing it is important that people be reminded that every job is a green job and that sustainability is never a done deal. We are all in this for the long run."

Summary

You can save energy and money by purchasing energy-efficient products and by making simple changes to the way you use lighting, temperature, electronics, insulation, and windows. Additional efficiencies can be found in catering and stage production. Look for renewable energy providers in your area to provide your meeting, event, office, or venue with clean, green power. On-site solar, wind, or hydropower generators can create startling attractions, and biofuel generators can also lower your carbon footprint. Human energy through bicycle pedal power creates an interactive energy source. By purchasing water-efficient products and making basic changes to your water-handling procedures, you can save significant money and water. Rainwater harvesting techniques such as green roofs and rain barrels can divert urban runoff by reusing stormwater for gardening.

Key Terms

- **Insulation**: material that prevents heat loss.
- **R-Values**: a rating system for insulation.
- **Compact fluorescent light bulbs (CFLs)**: energy-efficient light bulbs.
- **Low-emissivity coating (low-e)**: a window treatment that reduces heat loss.
- **Renewable Energy Certificates (RECs)**: investments in renewable energy.
- **Solar PV**: panels that hold photovoltaic cells (PVs) and transmit sunlight into electricity.
- **Solar thermal**: tubes that convert sunlight into a fluid that provides heat for water systems.
- **Passive solar power**: use of direct sunlight for light or heat.
- **Wind turbine**: windmill that transforms kinetic wind energy into electricity.
- **Hydropower**: energy generated from water.
- **Microhydropower**: simple technology that can harness local water sources for specific event use.
- **Biogas**: energy created by breaking down organic matter without oxygen, usually in landfill.
- **Piezolectric effect**: the ability for certain materials to generate energy from simple friction.
- **Rain harvesting**: landscaping techniques that utilize rainwater to conserve water.
- **Urban runoff**: excess water that increases flooding and carries pollutants from streets, parking lots, and lawns into streams and lakes.
- **Green roofs**: rooftop gardens that absorb stormwater and cool buildings.
- **Stormwater planters**: small, contained vegetated areas that collect and treat stormwater.
- **Bioretention**: mulch and soil systems that filter pollutants.

Blue Sky Thinking

You are organizing a green lifestyle fair in a local park, which will feature local green businesses and artists, and it is important to be as energy and water-efficient as possible. The fair will feature a music stage with theatrical sound and lighting, a public art display, and an interactive event for children. How will you present these attractions while using the least possible amount of energy and water? How will you incorporate solar, wind, hydro, biofuel, or human energy into the fair?

Renewable Resources

People Powered Machines: www.peoplepoweredmachines.com.
Renewable Energy Focus: www.renewableenergyfocus.com.
The Age of Stupid, a film by Franny Armstrong: www.spannerfilms.net.
The Ecologist: www.theecologist.org.
Windstream Power bike power generators: www.windstreampower.com.

Organic food is served on china plateware, with soup served in a bread bowl, at The Big Tent in Fife.

CHAPTER 8

Green Cuisine and Eco-Chic Decor

"Save the Planet—Drink Organic"

—*Tagline for Black Isle Brewery (www.blackislebrewery.com)*

In this chapter, you will learn:

1. How to use sustainable themes such as permaculture, biomimicry, and cradle to cradle in the event design

2. How to source foods that are ethical, local, natural, and seasonal

3. How to work with caterers and chefs to create sustainable menus

4. How to emphasize sustainable food presentation

5. How to minimize food and drink packaging waste

6. How recycled, bioplastic, and biodegradable materials can reduce waste

7. How to source environmentally sensitive giveaways, awards, invitations, and signage

8. How to use sustainable floral arrangements

9. How to engage attendees with sustainability through interactive programs

When attendees arrive at The Big Tent (www.bigtentfestival.co.uk), a sustainable music festival in Fife, Scotland, they are greeted at the gates of the Falkland Estate by friendly volunteers carrying strawberry baskets. "Did you arrive by public transportation?" they ask. If attendees answer in the positive, they are given a cup of organic, locally grown strawberries. This simple practice benefits the event experience in several ways:

- Public transportation use is rewarded.
- Attendees are educated on the benefits of public transportation.
- Organic, local produce is featured.
- Attendees are greeted with a surprise gift.
- The festival is framed from the start as an organic, sustainable experience.

What a great way to start an event! You, too, can frame your event with themes of sustainability by incorporating environmental practices into the catering, décor, and design elements.

Green Themes

When designing a meeting or event, consider incorporating green themes such as sustainability, environmentalism, reuse, or conservation. Make sure that these themes are carried out meaningfully, not superficially. For instance, it is easy to incorporate the color green into the design and decor of an event, but much more difficult to back up this color scheme with serious environmental practices. Painting something green without actually making it environmentally friendly is known as *greenwash*, and can generate negative publicity. Environmentally minded attendees will be more impressed with tablecloths made from organic or recycled materials than they will with standard tablecloths colored green.

One theme to inspire your event designs is *permaculture*, an approach to designing human settlements that mimic the relationships found in natural ecologies. Some organic farms subscribe to the principles of permaculture. For example, by attaching a chicken coop to a garden, the chickens will naturally scratch and peck the ground to clear it of weeds and fertilize the soil with their manure. Permaculture can be applied to outdoor events through organic gardening and natural landscaping, and indoor events can highlight the theme of natural agriculture through composting.

Similar to permaculture, *biomimicry* is the examination of nature to serve human purposes. For instance, Velcro adhesive fabric was invented by examining the tiny hooks that burs use to cling to objects. Greener meeting and event pioneers may examine the complex ecologies around their event site for inspiration. You might engage meeting attendees in a game that mimics local wildlife activity, such as fishing for ideas like a bear fishes trout, or building a strategy out of ideas like a beaver builds a dam.

Another inspirational green theme is *cradle to cradle*, the concept of manufacturing products with a circuitous lifecycle so that their disposal generates future products. This

The Chocolate Tree serves organic delights at The Big Tent.

chapter will show how sourcing recycled, bioplastic, or biodegradable products can support cradle-to-cradle manufacturing. Purchasing live plants that can be replanted after the event also supports cradle-to-cradle systems.

Permaculture, biomimicry, and cradle to cradle are all themes that can meaningfully integrate sustainability into your meeting or event design. Think creatively about the theory of sustainable development and consider unique ways to reflect these values in the event plan. Let's start with everybody's favorite part of the event: food.

Green Cuisine: The Four Ls

Food is not just sustenance. Food is cultural, and, as evidenced by United States First Lady Michelle Obama's campaign for healthy eating, food is political. On February 22, 2009, on the eve of her first State Dinner, Mrs. Obama hosted a discussion in the White House kitchen with White House Executive Chef Chris Comerford, Pastry Chef Bill Yosses, and culinary students from L'Academie De Cuisine. Eventually, the subject of this political debate turned around to a carrot:

When you grow something yourself and it's close and it's local, oftentimes it tastes really good. And when you're dealing with kids, for example, you want to get them to try that carrot. Well, if it tastes like a real carrot and it's really sweet, they're going to think that it's a piece of candy. So my kids are more inclined to try different vegetables if they're fresh and local and delicious."
—*U.S. First Lady Michelle Obama, White House, Office of the First Lady 2009*

As a proponent for healthy eating among children, Mrs. Obama promotes the idea that local and natural produce often tastes better. Similarly, caterers are increasingly sourcing sustainably harvested ingredients to create spectacular menus for meetings and events. Greener caterers source ingredients that are ethical, local, natural, and seasonal, to make outstanding greener menus. Figure 8.1 provides examples of some of these greener ingredients.

Jeff Hall, executive chef at Savor. . . San Francisco (www.cateringbysmg.com), the sustainable catering group serving the Moscone Center, has the following specific criteria for different kinds of sustainable foods:

- Produce: local, organic, seasonal
- Dairy: raised without the use of *recombinant bovine somatotropin (rBST)*, a synthetic growth hormone; local, organic
- Meats: meat and poultry products raised without the use of hormones and/or antibiotics, free grass-fed and/or organic beef, cage-free poultry
- Seafood: select seafood supply in accordance with the Marine Stewardship Council's (MSC) sustainably fished seafood list or lists that are approved by or comparable to the MSC

When we spoke in August 2010, Hall said that, by setting basic criteria for sustainability, caterers can make a huge difference in the environmental impact of any meeting or event: "Because we cater to large groups over multiple days, we can have a noticeably positive impact on our environment."

Ingredients	Yes	No
Ethical	Fair trade coffee Free-range eggs	Products made in sweatshops Third-world labor without human rights Cage-raised poultry
Local	Florida oranges in Orlando Valencia onions in Atlanta	Florida oranges in Toronto Valencia onions in Seattle
Natural	Pesticide-free produce Chemical-free goods	Chemical fertilizers Pesticides Genetically modified foods Chemically enhanced foods
Seasonal	Strawberries in June Apples in January	Strawberries in September Apples in August

Figure 8.1   Greener Ingredients: The Four Ls

Ethical

Above all else, food sourcing should involve the ethical treatment of workers and animals. For workers, this means ensuring that farmers and harvesters have been paid a fair wage for their labor. The Fairtrade Foundation (www.fairtrade.org.uk) certifies goods from the developing world such as coffee, chocolate, and bananas as having been produced under fair working conditions. As discussed in Chapter 1, these conditions include fair pay, investing in projects that enhance workers' quality of life, partnership, mutually beneficial long-term relationships, and social, economic, and environmental responsibility.

The ethical issues concerning animal rights are more complicated. Greener meeting and event pioneers may purchase meat, poultry, and eggs certified as *free range*. For poultry to meet the U.S. Department of Agriculture's (USDA) (www.usda.gov) definition of free range, producers must demonstrate that the poultry has been allowed access to the outside. Meat may also be certified *cage free*, meaning the animals were not kept in cages. Free-range and cage-free meats may cost more than mass-produced or factory-produced meats, but they provide a more ethical dish for attendees concerned with animal rights.

Free-range chicken is an important issue for Andrew Williams, managing director of Seventeen Events (www.seventeenevents.co.uk). When I asked him about the ethics of catering in May 2010, he said, "We do have a red line. We press our clients to only ever serve free range chicken." Williams recalls one event where the budget was such that the only option was to go for non-free-range chicken, saying that Seventeen Events made up the difference themselves in order to afford free-range chicken. "You have to draw a line somewhere," he says.

Sometimes the most expensive foods are the most controversial. Foie gras, or fattened goose liver, is a French delicacy traditionally prepared by force-feeding geese. Although some gourmands crave this dish, many now object to the treatment of the animals. Although eating endangered mammals has always been frowned upon, endangered fish and seafood are now receiving consumer attention. Fish Online (www.fishonline.org) provides a directory of fish to avoid, such as Chilean sea bass, because they are being unsustainably harvested.

Another ethical dilemma for meat eaters is the environmental impact of the U.S. meat industry, as analysts are increasingly warning that current production levels are unsustainable and environmentally damaging. A 2008 *New York Times* article by Mark Bittman called "Rethinking the Meat-Guzzler" compares U.S. meat consumption with that of oil, and calculates that producing a typical beef dish requires 16 times more energy than producing a vegetable dish and generates 24 times more greenhouse gas emissions. Additionally, U.S. livestock annually produce about 900 million tons of waste, or about 3 tons of manure for each American (Iowa hogs annually produce about 16 tons of manure for each Iowan). There is also a vast amount of grain used in feeding livestock (Bittman 2008).

Understanding the complex environmental impact of the meat industry requires research. Paul Salinger, vice president of conferences and events for Oracle (www.oracle. com), describes a multilayered process for considering the ethics of food purchasing: "We are considering moving from beef to lower-impact sources of protein, or at least working with purveyors or farmers to buy only sustainably farmed sources of protein." Salinger recommends thorough research into all possible food sources in order to source the best foods at the best prices.

Understanding the supply chain and the overall food miles gives us the data we need to make trade-offs, when needed, to procure at a price point that is sustainable, while providing and promoting a healthy food lifestyle for our attendees.
—*Paul Salinger, Oracle, interview, May 2010*

Local

Sourcing food locally is one of the most important criteria for greener menus, especially if it comes from small, local farms. More and more, attendees expect to learn the name of the farm, farmer, or region where their food came from. Sourcing food locally not only reduces the carbon footprint of *food miles*, or the distance food travels, it also supports local small businesses and authenticates the ingredients as homegrown.

Salinger has started working with his food and beverage providers to track the total food miles per meal. "We want to understand the whole food chain and how many resources and transport miles it takes to get food to our attendees," he says, "so that we can look at menu planning as another means of reducing the overall impact of our event."

Our ultimate goal is not only to try and get to a high percentage of local and organic food procurement but to work across the supply chain to inform farmers, for example, of our needs well in advance so that we have a ready source of food from local sources at the time we need it.
—*Paul Salinger, Oracle, interview, May 2010*

Williams also sees tremendous value in locally sourced foods, saying, "There are issues around the decreased carbon footprint of local foods; there's a social element, in terms of promoting local businesses, and in terms of delivery, local food is fresher, so that improves what you're serving your guests."

Local sourcing has been a key thing for us, in terms of trying to trace where we're sourcing things from and where it's traveling from. There are issues around the carbon footprint of that, there's a social element, in terms of promoting local businesses, and also, if you're sourcing local food, then it's fresher, so that's better in terms of delivery and what you're serving your guests.
—*Andrew Williams, Seventeen Events, interview, May 2010*

How local is local? In our conversation in May of 2010, Nancy (Wilson) Zavada, principal at MeetGreen (www.meetgreen.com), explained her guidelines on keeping food local: "Try to keep it within a hundred miles, but realize that if it's winter in Minnesota, you're not going to be able to do that. You need to source as locally as you can, but you need to start early." Zavada, cautioned that events should source local crops without monopolizing them, saying, "It's possible for one conference to wipe out a whole spinach crop for a salad."

Work with the local resources available. When accepting requests for proposals (RFPs) from caterers, look for local food providers. Investigate local farms and food manufacturers. You may find that the best local food providers have limited event experience. Look at this as an opportunity to grow the local economy and to provide your attendees with unique foods. Any event can serve a nationally distributed beer, but attendees may be impressed by a limited-edition beer from a small microbrewery that is only available locally.

Natural

At The Big Tent, Black Isle Organic Ale was served in fully compostable Biopac cups made from plant matter.

Organic food has been grown, harvested, and prepared without artificial chemicals. The USDA defines organic production as "a system that is managed in accordance with the Organic Foods Production Act (OFPA) of 1990 (PDF) and regulations in Title 7, Part 205, of the Code of Federal Regulations to respond to site-specific conditions by integrating cultural, biological, and mechanical practices that foster cycling of resources, promote ecological balance, and conserve biodiversity" (USDA 1990).

Some people define organic as food made the old fashioned way: from sun, water, and hands-on farming. You might recognize an organic carrot because it is still a bit dirty, or an organic potato because it is an odd shape, rather than a perfect sphere. Organic meats may lack preservatives, and so expire sooner. It should be noted that while the USDA has tough criteria for certifying *organic* food, the word *natural* can be used without adherence to as many criteria.

Organic foods may cost slightly more to source than nonorganic foods, which can be factory produced by major distributors for low costs. Although gourmet, certified organic delicacies might cost extra, you may find that simple food farmed locally according to organic methods costs the same or even less. Hall says that by serving food that is "in season, in your region," caterers may provide sustainable menus without breaking the budget.

Seasonal

Preservatives and food storage technologies now allow us to eat any food at any time of the year, no matter if it is in season or not. We are increasingly separated from the agricultural processes that produce the food we eat, and one of the results is a decreasing use of seasonal foods. Impress and delight your attendees by serving them foods that are currently in season. Not only does this improve food quality, but it shows a meaningful connection with the agricultural sources of these foods. Try Eat the Seasons (www .eattheseasons.com) for a guide to seasonal produce. Figure 8.2 gives several examples from Eat the Seasons.

The UK Soil Association lists five basic reasons to eat organic foods:

1. *Knowing what's in your food: Hydrogenated fats and controversial additives including aspartame, tartrazine and MSG are banned under organic standards.*
2. *The environment: Organic farming releases less greenhouse gases than non-organic farming—choosing organic, local, and seasonal food can significantly reduce your carbon footprint.*
3. *Animal welfare: Organic standards insist that animals are given plenty of space and fresh air to thrive and grow—guaranteeing a truly free-range life.*
4. *Protecting wildlife: Organic farms are havens for wildlife and provide homes for bees, birds, and butterflies. In fact, the United Kingdom's Government's own advisors found that plant, insect, and bird life is up to 50% greater on organic farms.*
5. *GM-free: Genetically modified crops and ingredients are banned under organic standards. You may be surprised to know that over a million tons of GM crops are imported each year to feed the majority of non-organic livestock, which produce pork, bacon, milk, cheese, and other dairy products.*

Source: www.soilassociation.org (search: Five reasons)

Creating Sustainable Menus

When creating a menu, decide what criteria are most important to your meeting or event. Many caterers would rank the four Ls in this order of importance—ethical, local, natural, and seasonal—but it depends on the details of the ingredients. There are many decisions to make regarding sustainable catering, and Williams concedes that one must set priorities. "Fruits, tea and coffee that are fair trade are much higher up on my agenda than those that are organic," he says, "and that's because of the social issues surrounding fair trade. We look at where the food is coming from and how it's being produced."

Zavada recommends that greener caterers decide what their commitment level is early on. She recommends asking yourself, "How local and sustainable do you want to be? Does it have to be local and organic, or can it just be local?" Looking at potential caterers, Zavada recommends asking, "Do they have sustainable food? What is their service-ware like? What are their sources? How far does the food travel?"

Zavada recommends vegetarian menu options as a way of using local produce, limiting the environmental impact of meat, and saving costs. "One thing we do is have at least one vegetarian meal a day," she says. "But not just some vegetables thrown over a bed of rice. You have to have some protein, and it's got to be a quality meal. It's usually 20 to 30 percent less cost than a meal with meat in it, and the chefs get to design something new."

Food	Season
Zucchini	May to Early September
Blueberries	June, July, August
Tomatoes	Late June to October
Lobster	July to October
Butternut squash	Late September to Early March
Sweet potatoes	Late September to January
Kiwi	November to May

Figure 8.2 Seasonal Foods
Source: www.eattheseasons.com

Vegetarian options must be wholesome, high-quality meals, not afterthoughts. Although caterers may be hesitant to try vegetarian or organic options, Zavada has found that chefs often enjoy this unique challenge:

> Chefs are really excited about this. They're excited not just about sustainability, but about not working off the same banquet menu day after day after day.
> —*Nancy (Wilson) Zavada, MeetGreen, interview, May 2010*

Sustainable menus present a challenge to the catering team at any meeting or event, but creative caterers will turn this challenge into an opportunity. Figure 8.3 presents the unique challenges and opportunities of creating sustainable menus.

As Figure 8.3 shows, green cuisine takes some getting used to, but it can offer many rewards to your meeting or event. Hall offers his own list of the rewards provided by sustainable catering:

> By purchasing products that are grown, produced, and/or manufactured in our region, we help to sustain our local economy. By donating products to outreach programs for the elderly and less fortunate, we can contribute to social sustainability. By purchasing products that have been raised, grown, or manufactured in a sustainable manner, we can contribute to a sustainable environment and future.
> —*Jeff Hall, Savor. . . San Francisco, interview, August 2010*

Sustainable foods can enhance the event atmosphere, support the local green economy, inspire creativity in chefs and caterers, and reduce the environmental impact caused by unsustainable foods. Some food options, such as vegetarian menus, can drastically reduce costs as well. The greatest benefit of all may be that food that is ethical, local, natural, and seasonal oftentimes just tastes better as well.

For an example of a sustainable menu, see the appendices of this book.

Challenges	Opportunities
Researching the ethical and environmental impact of various foods	Understanding the food supply chain and making it transparent for attendees and stakeholders Making informed decisions on ethical purchasing
Working with small, local food providers who have limited event experience	Featuring rare and unique local foods Supporting the local green economy
Sourcing organic, natural, and seasonal ingredients	Providing wholesome organic cuisine Reducing your environmental impact
Working with caterers to create sustainable menu options	Creating innovative new menu options for attendees Inspiring creativity among chefs

Figure 8.3 Creating Sustainable Menus: Challenges and Opportunities

Presentation and Packaging

Presentation is everything, and the way you garnish, decorate, plate, and serve your food can make a big impact on attendees. Increasingly, caterers and chefs are coming up with creative ways to present foods in a sustainable manner. By minimizing packaging and favoring reusable or compostable plates and cutlery, you can give your food the ultimate sustainable presentation.

The 2010 Big Tent environmental music festival in Fife, Scotland (www.bigtentfestival.co.uk), featured outstanding local Scottish cuisine such as smoked salmon, fresh mussels, and organic beer from the Black Isle Brewery (www.blackislebrewery.com). Food presentation and packaging at an outdoor festival is always difficult, but the organizers created many creative, sustainable solutions, described in Figure 8.4.

In the Head Zone tent, BOE catering impressed diners with its bread bowls, china, and silverware. In addition, attendees could purchase Big Tent Mugs, reusable, bioplastic mugs with the Big Tent logo printed on them. For £4 (about US$6.50), attendees could purchase a mug with a hot or cold drink inside, and mugholders received a discount off all future beverages.

The Big Tent was able to use china and silverware in some instances, but, as with most outdoor festivals, disposables were necessary as well. It purchased cold beer cups made from natural starch, which were fully compostable. Bins for compostable items were provided at nearby waste stations, and stewards were on hand to ensure that these beer cups made it into the compost stream.

Reduce food packaging whenever possible. Instead of millions of tiny packets of ketchup, purchase condiments in bulk and serve them in bulk. Condiments like ketchup, butter, and salad dressing can be served in elegant glass bowls with spoons or knives, or

Food and Drink	Presentation
Red Kite Ale, Yellowhammer IPA, and Blonde beers from the Black Isle Brewery (www.blackislebrewery.com)	Stewards showed attendees how to place compostable plant starch cups from Biopac (www.biopac.co.uk) in compost bins.
Dahl soup in a bread bowl with side salad	Soup was served in a rustic bread bowl (edible bread formed in the shape of a bowl) and salad was served on a china plate with silverware.
Pillars of Hercules (www.pillars.co.uk) organic food tent	Raw vegetables were presented without packaging or in wicker baskets. Hay bales were used for seating.
Puddledub Buffalo Burgers (www .puddledubbuffalo.co.uk), farmed locally in Scotland	Burgers were served on a paper napkin, rather than a plate.

Figure 8.4 Sustainable Catering at The Big Tent (www.bigtentfestival.co.uk)

from refillable bottles. Salt, pepper, and sugar can be purchased in bulk and served in refillable shakers or bowls. Beverages can also be sold in bulk: beer can be purchased in kegs and served over a bar tap, soda can be served from a soda gun, and iced tea can be made with filtered tap water.

Vegware provides compostable food packaging, such as this salad box.
Courtesy of Vegware.

Vegware

While working on a technology project in California, Joe Frankel heard about developments in the world of bioplastics, and he got the idea to create food packaging and catering accessories out of organic, recycled and biodegradable materials. Vegware (www.vegware.com) is now a successful business operating in the United Kingdom, Europe, and the United States, supplying caterers and events with low-impact, eco-friendly supplies made from materials such as cornstarch, wood pulp, and recycled paper.

Frankel attributes his success to a commitment to "Great products with a low environmental impact, clear messaging, excellent customer service and genuine enthusiasm for the industry." As an eco-business, customers also appreciate Vegware's transparency and factual reporting of environmental impacts. "We have a proper understanding of our materials," says Frankel, "and we quantify the benefits with our eco stats, rather than making assertions we can't back up." Vegware's eco stats, available on the home page of its Web site, show that, as of August, in 2010 it diverted 827780.3 kg of potential landfill waste, and saved 38869.6 kg of carbon and 43677.9 kg of virgin material. These numbers will continue to be updated as the year progresses.

The Vegware Web site also explains the manufacturing process, the materials used, and the composting process, shown in Figure 8.5. Frankel believes that transparency and hard data are more useful than making sweeping statements when communicating environmental practices, saying, "We don't impinge on current practice or preach. People are under pressure to improve their environmental impact from all angles, and we offer a simple, effective and economic way to do that."

Vegware provides meetings and events with everything from biodegradable cutlery made from corn and potato to compostable tableware made from cassava starch and plant fibers, from hot cups lined with cornstarch to cold cups made from natural starch. A recent innovation is the Hot Cup Lid, which won Product Innovation at the 2010 Cafe Society Awards and Best Disposables at the Caterer and Hotelkeeper Excellence Awards. "It took a lot of iterations to get the material right," Frankel recalled in our conversation in July 2010. "Something which has the strength, thickness and can take the heat—and is compostable—was not straightfoward," he says. "We are now on the third generation, and they are working really well."

All Vegware products are either compostable or biodegradable. "Commercial composting is becoming more widely available with thousands of tonnes of extra capacity coming online in the UK each year," says Frankel. "Typically the goods are turned into compost, or biogas and top soil, depending on the particular process which is used." Figure 8.6 shows the cradle-to-cradle lifecycle of Vegware products: from soil to plants to products to soil.

Frankel sees a paradigm shift in the way we now look at waste, saying, "The commercial composting industry is coming of age—sure, we need to avoid landfill on a small and crowded island like the UK, but just as important, we should see the mix of food and packaging waste as a *resource*. There are calories and nutrients that can be used."

Vegware is dedicated to making it easier for meeting and event planners to lower their carbon footprints. "Vegware has clear environmental benefits, and minimal cost implication," says Frankel. "A large venue will have the facilities in place to manage waste already, and so it's not impractical to incorporate bins for food or packaging compost."

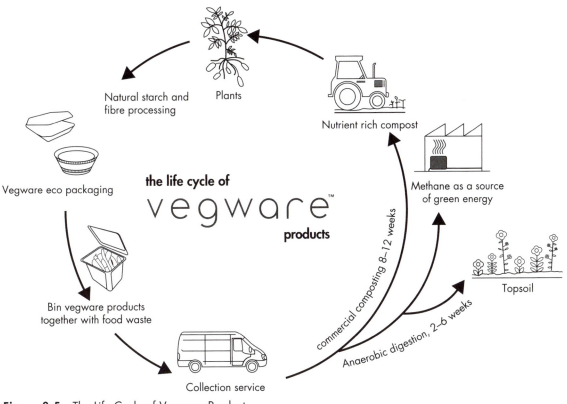

Figure 8.5 The Life Cycle of Vegware Products
Courtesy of Vegware.

■ Water

Bottled water has become immensely popular over the last ten years, and is a staple of most meetings and events. Although convenient, bottled water has a major impact on the environment. According to the Natural Resources Defense Council (www.nrdc.org), in 2006, the equivalent of 2 billion half-liter bottles of water were shipped to U.S. ports, generating thousands of tons of greenhouse gas pollution. Most water bottles are recyclable, but only about 13 percent of them ever get recycled, and in 2005, 2 million tons of plastic water bottles ended up in landfill.

Greener meeting and event pioneers can drastically reduce waste by avoiding bottled water and using tap water instead. Determine the safety of your tap water by contacting the local water company and asking for its latest health and safety report. The Environmental Protection Agency (EPA) provides a guide to safe drinking water online at www.epa.gov/safewater, and a safe drinking water telephone hotline at 1–800–426–4791. You may also try the Environmental Working Group (EWG) National Drinking Water Database at www.ewg.org/tap-water/welcome.

Even if your tap water is 100 percent safe to drink, it may not taste as good as bottled spring water. Consider purchasing water filtration products in order to improve the water

Vegware makes compostable flatware from plant starch.
Courtesy of Vegware.

even further. Look for products certified by NSF International, The Public Health and Safety Company (www.nsf.org) and the Water Quality Association (www.wqa.org).

Portable beverages are necessary and useful at meetings and events. Instead of providing disposable water bottles, try serving filtered tap water in reusable bottles.

Eco-Chic Decor

Candles create an elegant atmosphere at fancy events. Instead of purchasing regular petroleum-based candles, try using candles made from beeswax to limit your environmental impact and impress your attendees. Increasingly, attendees want to see raw, earthy materials like beeswax, organic cotton, recycled paper, and live plants in the event decor.

Five Water Filters

- Kenmore Single Undersink Drinking Water System (www.sears.com)
- Brita (www.brita.com)
- Trojan UV (www.trojanuv.com)
- UV Pure (www.uvpure.com/html/Our Systems/drinking-water.php)
- Kinetico (www.kinetico.com)

Like organic vegetables, the appeal of eco-chic decor is that it is not sleek and stylish, but real, raw, and earthy.

Recycled Materials

There is a certain magic about delivering a product that used to be something completely different, and modern companies working with recycled materials do just that. Meeting and event planners can now source carpets made from used textiles, bags made from industrial waste, and even bowls made from melted vinyl records.

When designing your next meeting or event, consider approaching companies that work with recycled materials. Many of these products create the *wow factor* (as in, "Wow! I'm impressed!") when attendees realize that the product used to be something else.

Bioplastics and Biodegradables

Revolutions in plastics in the twentieth century created a booming industry for inexpensive goods factory-produced with chemicals such as petroleum. Materials such as bakelite, linoleum, polystyrene (Styrofoam), cellophane, and nylon are now

Saffron Winds (www.saffronwinds.com) presented designer handbags made from reused mosquito netting at The Big Tent.

Recycled Products

- Pilot b2p (www.pilot-b2p.com): pens made from recycled water bottles
- Simon Lee Guitars (www.simonleeguitars.com): guitars made from recycled plastics
- Weisenbach Recycled Products (www.recycledproducts.com): pens, bags, and many other accessories made from recycled materials
- Green Toys (www.greentoys.com): toys made from recycled plastic milk jugs
- Green Promotions (www.greenpromotionsltd.com): clipboards made from recycled juice cartons and circuit boards, and other conference and exhibition supplies
- Ecocard (www.eco-card.co.uk): business cards made from recycled paper and wildflower seeds that bloom into flowers when planted
- Saffron Winds (www.saffronwinds.com): beautiful bags made from used mosquito netting

common materials used in everyday life. Although industrial plastics have revolutionized medicine and engineering, leading to many great inventions, the manufacturing of plastics carries a large carbon footprint, and many of these household products are not recyclable.

We are now seeing vast developments in *bioplastics*, or plastics made from plants or organic materials rather than from petroleum. Even products made from regular plastics, such as grocery bags, are increasingly being treated to biodegrade naturally. Biobadge (www.biobadge.com) serves the meeting and event industry with biodegradable name badges, as well as promotional items such as mugs and golf tees. Below are just a few of the many biodegradable products available on the market for greener meeting and event pioneers.

Bioplastic and Biodegradable Buys

- BioBag kitchen bags (www.biobagusa.com)
- Vegware forks, knives, spoons, cups, plates, bowls, napkins, and assorted food packaging (www.vegware.com)
- Biobadge name badges, mugs, golf tees, luggage tags, and pens (www.biobadge.com)
- Ecoparti confetti (www.ecoparti.com)
- White Bio Dove balloons (www.joylantern.com/pshow.asp?ps_id=6)

Greener Giveaways

Giveaways present an exciting challenge for greener meeting and event pioneers. How can exhibitors promote themselves without producing plastic keychains, pens, and paperweights that often go unused? Greener exhibitors can now source products made from recycled, bioplastic, or biodegradable materials to lower the impact of their giveaways. Pens made from water bottles, clipboards made from circuit boards, and recycled paper cards that bloom when planted are all fun and impressive giveaways.

South by Southwest (www.sxsw.com) is a music conference and festival that gives those in the entertainment industry a major opportunity to increase awareness of their brand. It is a tradition for exhibitors to place promotional materials in the "big bag," a reusable canvas bag that attendees receive. Trying to cut down on waste, in 2010 Executive Director Mike Shea put a serious restriction on promotional brochures going in the bags. When we spoke in May 2010, he told me, "We tried to cut down on leaflets, which people don't really value, and encourage people to put in reusable things that have a value, whether it's a CD or a DVD or a water bottle, a cigarette lighter or a bottle opener."

Figure 8.6 provides some examples of promotional giveaways with actual value that attendees are more likely to keep, reuse, and remember the brand by, as well as examples of giveaways with less value attached. When helping exhibitors to go green, Shea emphasizes the importance of setting a policy and sticking to it. Greener meeting and event pioneers may give their exhibitors a list of criteria or suggest giveaways with more value to create more sustainable marketing opportunities.

Eco-Awards

Environmentally friendly trophies or awards are a perfect way to bring out sustainable themes at a greener meeting or event. You can now source awards made from sustainably harvested wood, or from recycled materials. Rivanna Natural Designs (www .rivannadesigns.com) produces beautiful awards that have been used at the IMEX Green Awards ceremony. Using recycled glass, recycled wood, and wood certified by the Forest Stewardship Council (FSC) (www.fsc.org), Rivanna Natural Designs

Less Value	More Value
Keychains	Bottle openers
Toys	Packets of seeds
Paperweights	Fairtrade crafts from the developing world, such as frames made from recycled paper
Candies	Fresh fruit
Promotional flyers	Informative brochures

Figure 8.6 Give Attendees Value

also hires refugees and disadvantaged persons as part of its commitment to social responsibility.

For the Ethical Awards, Seventeen Events commissioned an artistic trophy created by Giraffe Innovation (www.giraffeinnovation.com) titled "Habit." Andrew Williams explains: "They have a humanoid shape and are designed to represent your carbon footprint. If you travel a lot by air or car, your shape will have really big feet. If you have a meat-based diet and eat a lot of imported and processed foods, you would have a really big stomach." Williams believes that incorporating themes of environmentalism and sustainability in award design can be thought provoking. "It's a visual message, as well as something for the winner to take away."

Environmental Invites

The 2009 Green Inaugural Ball was the first high-profile, VIP gala to eschew fancy paper invitations in favor of electronic invitations sent via email, called *evites*. Evites reduce paper waste, limit the carbon emissions of postage, and cut costs. Graphic designers may use programs such as Adobe Photoshop to craft beautiful invitation images that can be emailed as JPEG or PDF attachments, and these evites can link to personalized, interactive websites that function as invitations and previews of the meeting or event.

Still, in many situations, a physical invitation is absolutely necessary. "The whole invitation thing is very difficult," says Williams. "Normally we would recommend electronic invitations, but it can be hard to find an appropriate email address for high level politicians and Royalty, so we do have to rely on physical invitations. Last year the invitations were printed on paper that had flower seeds embedded on it, and guests got their invitations back at the end so that they could plant them and grow flowers. The year before that we had invitations made from crushed, recycled wellington rain boots, which could be used afterward as drinks coasters."

Look for creative ways to make sustainable invitations that will give attendees the *wow* factor. Find unusual recycled materials, or consider using organic inks and papers. As the first impression you make on your attendees, invitations are a perfect opportunity to position your meeting or event as ethical and sustainable.

Sustainable Signage

One major source of waste at meetings, conventions, and exhibitions are disposable signs. Signage is a critical part of any large event taking place across several rooms or sites, and clients typically want signs to be professional and to include their company logo. Greener meeting and event pioneers may reduce waste by creating reusable signs.

For informal events, chalkboards or white boards may function as reusable signs that can be erased and rewritten on to suit any purpose. In more formal situations, professionally printed signs made from recycled paper may be posted on reusable signboards made from recycled or bioplastic materials. Larger conventions and events may wish to consider digital displays that can be programmed to function as interactive, informative electronic signs.

Vintage Victory

Seeking out vintage goods is one of the most fun ways to precycle. Used furniture is often less expensive than new, and can add character and distinction to a meeting or event. Vintage decorations can lend authenticity to an historic event theme, and take your attendees on a nostalgic trip down memory lane. Thrift shops, antique stores, and eBay (www.ebay.com) are great places to find used goods, which can later be sold online or auctioned off to guests. Figure 8.7 gives some nostalgic design ideas that incorporate buying used goods.

Because the manufacturing of new products is one of the largest carbon-emitting activities, one of the greenest things that you can do is simply to buy used products. Rather than buying new lavalamps that have been created in a 1970s style, seek out the originals and impress your attendees with the authenticity of your event design. You may save money by purchasing used, broken antiques, and then refurbishing them to suit the event design. Old church pews can be reupholstered, and broken jukeboxes can be repainted and used as decor.

Up-Cycling

Up-cycling means creating art from waste materials, and can be a creative, interactive addition to any event. Waste Innovations (www.wasteinnovations.com), in Edinburgh, sells stylish earrings made from old vinyl records. Shops like Philadelphia's Indigo Arts (www.indigoarts.com) import developing-world folk art made from recycled soda cans and newspapers. Challenge the attendees of your next meeting to create a piece of art from their empty soda can from lunch, as a team-building activity.

Arlene Rush, Rebecca Jones, Gemma Patterson, and Louise Alexander, students of Event Management at The Queen Margaret University in Edinburgh, Scotland, produced a new event in 2009 based completely on the concept of up-cycling. The Green Fashion Event challenged clothing designers to create high-fashion from reused or recycled materials. The event raised funds for Friends of the Earth Scotland, and promoted reuse. The winning number, a provocative dress made from smashed glass bottles, caught a lot of media interest as well. This event was honored by the Scottish Event Awards with three nominations for the best event in Scotland (Rush, interview, March 2010).

Antiques (Seniors)	1950s and 1960s (Baby Boomers)	1970s (Generation X)	1980s and 1990s (Generation Y)
Old-fashioned popcorn machine	Vinyl records used as trays for drinks or finger foods	Lava Lamps	Retro video games for attendees to play
Church pews as seating	Jukebox	1970s fabrics decorating tables and walls	1980s boomboxes and tape cassettes as decoration

Figure 8.7 Vintage Designs Take You Back in Time

Green Thumb: Sustainable Floristry

The Big Tent featured large, unpainted wooden signs with the word "Scotland" cut out, and live plants growing out of each letter. By using raw materials and live plants, this sign, prepared by Event Scotland (www.eventscotland.org), perfectly captured the event's commitment to a sustainable Scotland. Floral arrangements are a perfect opportunity to showcase your commitment to the environment. Shawna McKinley, project manager at MeetGreen (www.meetgreen.com), often works to deliver sustainable floristry at meetings and events, and says, "There's different sustainability criteria you can use for floral arrangements."

One of these criteria is moving from cut florals to live plants, which can live on after the meeting or event. McKinley says that live plants can be more difficult to source, but that typically less of them are required. "It can take a little bit more time to source," she says. "Typically the live stuff is a bit more expensive because it is less available and incurs shipping costs." McKinley goes on to highlight a client that has successfully fit live plants into the budget, saying, "It has been a good solution for them, because it has caused them to pull back on how much floral they use, as well, so they use less of it."

In addition to live plants, McKinley tends to favor local plants. She works with local florists to source the best, most sustainably harvested flowers, and at a recent event held in San Francisco, she managed to source everything within the Bay Area. This is not possible everywhere, she notes. "You can do that in California in April, but it depends on your location and seasonality, so destination selection comes in there as well," she says.

Cut florals can be donated after the event to hospitals or care homes so that the flowers get maximum use. McKinley believes that this donation element is important. "We had one event that was held in Los Angeles," she recalls, "and down the street from the venue was an extended care facility. We took 22 small floating centerpieces with cut flowers to them to be used at that facility." Floral arrangements can make an enormous impact on hospital patients and the elderly, creating a wonderful legacy for your cradle-to-cradle event design.

Interactive Ideas

In addition to being an event that looks, sounds, smells, and tastes great, greener meetings and events often bring attendees into the design with interactive activities. Whether it is an invitation that can be replanted on the event site, an opportunity to up-cycle event waste into art, or a challenge to measure one's own carbon footprint, interactive ideas can get attendees excited about sustainability.

The Free Store

At the 2010 Capital Fringe Festival (www.capitalfringe.org), I created The Free Store, a books, clothing, and music swap for patrons that promoted reuse and attracted new audiences. With very little promotion, old and new patrons embraced The Free Store enthusiastically, contributing bestselling books and CDs as well as designer clothes. Serving as a cultural meeting place for patrons and nonpatrons to discuss books, music, and Festival shows, The Free Store generated extra foot traffic while serving as tangible evidence of the Festival's commitment to reuse.

Executive Director Julianne Brienza recalls, "The Free Store exposed us to a whole different part of the city. People were bringing things in who didn't know anything about theatre; they came in there and *then* found out about the Festival." Brienza also appreciates that The Free Store stimulated additional online and viral buzz about the Festival: "The Free Store became the hottest thing on the Capital Fringe Twitter."

By creating a book swap, an e-cycling meetup, or a used clothing trade, you can give attendees a valuable opportunity to donate old products and gain new ones. This marketplace of personal items always stimulates discussion and interaction, bringing attendees together in new and meaningful ways.

At The Big Tent, Fife Diet provided a stationary bicycle that powered a blender. Festival-goers got to exercise while blending themselves a rewarding smoothie.

Smoothie Cycle

At the 2010 Big Tent Festival in Fife, Scotland (www.bigtentfestival.co.uk), one attendee was getting tired from bicycling hard. She was rewarded with a delicious fruit smoothie that she herself had helped to make. How? This attendee had been pedaling a stationary bicycle with a nonelectric blender mounted on the front. The gears of the bike were connected to the blades of the blender, meaning that, while riders pedaled, they were simultaneously blending themselves a refreshing smoothie.

The smoothie cycle, provided by Fife Diet (fifediet.co.uk), featured local, organic fruits, and smoothies were served in reusable mugs and glasses. It was the most popular attraction in the food area of the Big Tent, with customers aged from 6 to 60 lining up to burn some calories while blending their own reward. The smoothie cycle saves electricity, encourages exercise, engages with attendees, and promotes healthy eating. Also, smoothies that you blend yourself do seem to taste better.

Cosy Cosy Gameshow

Faced with the challenge to create an interactive game for the 2010 Edinburgh International

Science Festival (www.sciencefestival.co.uk), Science Educator and Performer Matthew Wright created Cosy Cosy Gameshow, a chance for children of all ages to learn about energy conservation and heat insulation. Cosy Cosy Gameshow provides contestants with electric toy houses that expel real heat. Through energy conservation and insulation, they compete to see who can save the most heat. Sponsored by Natural Scotland (www.infoscotland.com/infoscotland/44.html), Cosy Cosy Gameshow features a heat-vision camera that displays onto flat-screen televisions, as well as samples of high-tech insulation materials.

After participating in Cosy Cosy Gameshow as a contestant at The Big Tent in July 2010, I spoke to Wright about his educational concept. "We allow children to enter a TV-style glitzy world which they have only ever watched from the screen and have seldom had a chance to engage in," he said. This entertaining atmosphere engages children in a discussion about environmental issues. "At the beginning of the show, we highlight the fact that it us costs a lot, both economically and environmentally, to have heat escaping

Matthew Wright and Sian Hickson perform in Cosy Cosy Gameshow, an interactive experience which teaches young people about energy conservation, at The Big Tent.

from our homes, but the message is not labored," says Wright. "Many children these days understand the basic environmental message that reducing consumption is necessary if we want to protect natural systems and they seem to be interested in taking this understanding to its next, more practical stage."

Model Greener Event: Seventeen Events

Andrew Williams founded Seventeen Events (www.seventeenevents.co.uk) with his wife after the couple spent a year road-tripping South America. They returned to London determined to make a positive impact on the world without generating waste and pollution, and five years later they are one the UK's hottest sustainable events companies.

"Sustainability for us is about more than just obvious green touches like recycling or organic tea and coffee," Williams told me in May 2010. "It goes to the heart of what makes a successful business, and we don't see our sustainable approach as a gimmick; we take it very seriously. We don't do second-rate—to us, sustainability is synonymous with excellence. That's why we're not called the 'Green Events Company.' We don't believe that sustainability is an optional extra or something you do to win brownie points. It's just a better way of doing business."

Williams believes that this concept of superior events is critical for getting clients on board. "People won't always do this because it's the right thing to do," he warns. "At the end of the day, people will want to have solid reasons for a sustainable approach. It's got to be around the quality of the product, and financial reasons as well. If you can present a green option as being cost effective, that's crucial."

Communicating about sustainable practices is key for an environmentally conscious event such as the Ethical Awards project, which it runs for a national UK newspaper. "It's a very informed audience, and so you want to be very clear about your practices," Williams says. "There's a huge reputation issue for the client in terms of how it's presented. There are a lot of rival press there, and it would be a big story if they spotted any hypocrisy. We have to make sure that every single element, including the food and the staff, are beyond reproach."

Although Seventeen Events delivers the same excellence and sustainability to all clients, it is not always as critical to advertise the sustainable practices as it is at an environmentally conscious event such as the Ethical Awards. "Other clients, frankly, are not as concerned," says Williams, "and so it isn't always appropriate for us to hammer on about all the green stuff, because that could deflect from the actual goal of the event."

Seventeen Events produces the Sustainable Events Summit, a forum that annually gathers the most prolific and innovative meeting and event planners to share their best practices in sustainability. "The feedback has been very positive," says Williams. "We saw that there was a need in the industry for people to get together and discuss the issues around sustainable events, as well as to share best practices. Our starting point has always been that it's got to be practical. Talking heads in a room with no action is of no use. What will be useful tomorrow when we are back in our offices?"

(continued)

(continued)

When asked what advice he would give event planners who want to go green, Williams quotes the enlightenment philosopher Edmund Burke: "No one makes a greater mistake than he who does nothing because he could only do a little." Williams says:

> That is neither an excuse for inaction nor a justification for greenwash—we should all aim to be improving as quickly as possibly and making our actions as transparent as possible. But I believe it serves no one to criticise those who are making small steps—we should be encouraging them to move on to giant leaps, not forcing them back behind the parapet. I find it incredible and unfortunate that so often groups who are doing a little attract greater criticism than those who are doing nothing at all.

Seventeen Events is progressing by leaps and bounds, but through initiatives such as the Sustainable Events Summit, it is also helping its colleagues in the industry take their first small steps toward sustainability.

Summary

Incorporate themes of nature, sustainability, and the environment into your meeting or event design. Sustainable foods may be ethically produced, locally sourced, natural, organic, or seasonal. Greener chefs and caterers take on the exciting challenge of creating sustainable menus in order to deliver outstanding dishes to attendees. Present your foods in a sustainable way by minimizing packaging waste. You may source recycled, bioplastic, or biodegradable products in order to limit disposable decorations. Source giveaways, awards, invitations and signage made from these materials, and work to ensure these items are reusable. Source live, local plants for sustainable floral arrangements, and incorporate interactive ideas into the event design to engage attendees with your sustainable themes.

Key Terms and Definitions

- **Greenwash**: painting something green without actually making it environmentally friendly.
- **Permaculture**: an approach to designing human settlements that mimic the relationships found in natural ecologies.
- **Biomimicry**: the examination of nature to serve human purposes.
- **Cradle to cradle**: the concept of giving products an ongoing lifecycle so that their disposal generates future products.

- **Recombinant bovine somatotropin (rBST)**: a controversial synthetic growth hormone for cows.
- **Food miles**: the distance food travels.
- **Free range**: farm animals that have had access to the outside.
- **Cage free**: farm animals that are not kept in cages.
- **Organic**: foods prepared without chemicals.
- **Wow factor**: aspects of meetings or events that especially impress or surprise attendees.
- **Bioplastics**: plastics made from plants or organic materials rather than from chemicals.
- **Evites**: electronic invitations sent via email.
- **Up-cycling**: transforming waste materials into art.

Blue Sky Thinking

You have been hired to organize a gala dinner and awards presentation in New Orleans, Louisiana, celebrating the major donors, government officials, and volunteers who have worked to mitigate the 2010 BP gulf oil spill. Environmental sensibilities are very important at this high-profile event. What themes relating to New Orleans and sustainability can you bring out in your event design? How will you reflect sustainability in the decor, flowers, invitations, and awards design? Create a three-course menu for the gala dinner that includes an appetizer, a main course, and a dessert. Now create a designer cocktail that features sustainable ingredients. How will you present these foods and drinks in a sustainable manner? For extra credit, how will you ensure that your local ingredients are not contaminated by the oil spill?

Renewable Resources

Eat the Seasons: www.eattheseasons.com
Food, Inc, a film by Robert Kenner: www.foodincmovie.com
Schlosser, Eric (2002). *Fast Food Nation*. New York: Harper Perennial.
Walton, Stewart (2000). *Eco Deco: Chic Ecological Design Using Recycled Materials*.

Gerding Theatre at the Armory, home to Oregon's Portland Center Stage, is a successful LEED-certified event venue.
Courtesy of Portland Center Stage.

CHAPTER 9

Greener Hotels, Venues, and Vendors

"Organic buildings are the strength and lightness of the spiders' spinning, buildings qualified by light, bred by native character to environment, married to the ground."

—*Frank Lloyd Wright, Architect (1867–1959)*

In this chapter, you will learn:

1. How LEED-certified buildings can host successful greener meetings and events

2. How to begin your greening process with your own office

3. How the hospitality industry is working to provide greener hotels

4. How sustainable convention centers, sports arenas, and theaters can support greener meetings and events

5. How to bring exhibitors at conferences and tradeshows into the greening process

6. How vendors of lighting, sound, special effects, linens, and other goods and services can support sustainable meetings and events

As CEO of the International Congress and Convention Association (ICCA) (www.iccaworld
.com), Martin Sirk has toured new and old venues for meetings and events around the
world. When we spoke in September 2010, he said, "New venues are aiming for best
sustainable building standard qualifications to market themselves as sustainable from the
outset as part of their strategy. Existing buildings are retro-fitting environmental improvements, implementing staff feedback processes and including this information in their

collateral." One thing is clear. According to Sirk, when it comes to venues for meetings and events, "Sustainability is now on everyone's agenda."

One of the forces behind this sustainable agenda is the United States Green Building Council (USGBC) (www.usgbc.org), an important organization in the world of architecture and the built environment. The USGBC works to promote sustainable building practices through its Leadership in Energy & Environmental Design (LEED) program, which certifies sustainable architecture. Major buildings such as Washington Nationals Stadium in Washington, DC, have pursued LEED certification to show their commitment to sustainability. LEED criteria for sustainability includes water and energy efficiency, sustainable resources, waste management, indoor air quality, transit access, and innovation, as described in Figure 9.1.

Category	Description
Sustainable sites	Minimized ecosystem and waterway impact Regionally appropriate landscaping Smart transportation choices
Water efficiency	Efficient appliances, fixtures, and fittings Water-wise outdoor landscaping
Energy and atmosphere	Energy use monitored Energy efficient strategies Energy efficient appliances, systems, and lighting Renewable energy
Materials and resources	Sustainably grown, harvested, produced, and transported products and materials Reduced waste production Reuse and recycling strategies
Indoor environmental quality	Improved indoor air Access to natural daylight Improved acoustics
Locations and linkages	Built away from environmentally sensitive places Infill, previously developed sites Sites near existing infrastructure, community resources, and transit Access to open space for outdoor activity
Awareness and education	Educational resources available Sustainable features clearly communicated
Innovation in design	New and innovative technologies and strategies LEED-accredited professional involved Holistic, integrated approach to the design and construction phase
Regional priority	Meets environmental concerns identified by regional LEED council

Figure 9.1 LEED Categories of Sustainable Architecture

More and more hotels, convention centers, meeting facilities, and sports and entertainment venues are pursuing LEED certification. Architects are featuring sustainable technologies in new buildings and using environmental strategies to retrofit existing structures. Greener meeting and event pioneers can utilize these new facilities to produce spectacular events. Similarly, greener vendors are providing environmental alternatives to standard technical equipment hire and services. Increasingly, greener meetings and events feature outstanding sustainable venues and vendors.

Environmental Offices

Many green business pioneers suggest looking at your own office as a starting point before attempting to green the entire business. Mike Shea, executive director of South by Southwest (SXSW) (www.sxsw.com), says, "The first thing to do is to get your own house in order." For SXSW, that meant monitoring and measuring office travel and electricity. "Our first step was to measure our own office and travel processes and calculate our own carbon footprint," Shea told me in May 2010. "Once you get that underway, then you can look at the bigger picture in greening up your event."

The same criteria for greener hotels and venues holds true for office buildings. Use water and energy efficiently, and create a waste management program. Look for office locations with sensible transit routes, such as nearby bus or subway stations. Consider renovations such as cavity wall insulation, green roofs, or even renewable energy projects that meet LEED criteria. SXSW installed solar PV panels in its office and has been counting the savings ever since.

Seventeen Events (www.seventeenevents.co.uk) is a hip, young, sustainable-events company based in London. Not only does it choose outstanding green venues, but it also has one of London's coolest eco-offices. Housed in East London, Container City is a community of offices and residential units built primarily from used shipping containers. These containers are the ultimate reused building material: strong, industrial units big enough to create entire walls, ceilings, or even stand-alone rooms.

Whether you find an eco-office park like Container City, install solar panels like SXSW, or merely begin energy efficiency and recycling programs, you can make a big statement with a greener office. Sustainability starts at home, so use your office as a testing ground for initiatives you might later implement at meetings or events.

Greener Hotels

In St Andrews, Scotland, eco-conscious guests of the Fairmont Hotel (www.fairmont .com/standrews) can take a short shuttle to their accommodation without worrying about wasting any gas. The shuttle is powered by used cooking oil, recovered from the hotel kitchens and converted into biodiesel with the aid of a Green Fuels Bio-Pod.

"Being responsible stewards of the communities in which we operate has always been an important part of Fairmont's mission," says Sarah Dayboll, manager of environmental affairs for Fairmont. In our conversation in September 2010, she explained that the company took a proactive approach in 1990 with the launch of its industry-leading Green Partnership program, a comprehensive commitment to reducing its impact on the environment. "From this promise, Fairmont's Green Partnership program grew to focus on improvements in the areas of waste management, energy and water conservation, climate change, and innovative community outreach programs involving local groups and partnerships—a path Fairmont continues upon to this day."

Dayboll says that Fairmont has pledged to reduce operational carbon emissions from its existing portfolio of hotels by 20 percent below 2006 levels by 2013, while also ensuring that new properties strive to reduce their carbon emissions through the implementation of a new Energy and Carbon Management program. "We expect to reduce our emissions through improved energy efficiency, increased conversion to renewable energy supply, and promoting conservation practices among our colleagues."

The Bio-Pod at St Andrews is just one of Fairmont's many Eco-Innovations Signature Projects; other initiatives include companywide energy and water conservation, responsible purchasing, sustainable catering, and the Greening Our Greens Golf Program. Fairmont describes these commitments in their Environmental Policy, presented here in Figure 9.2 as a model policy for any greener hotel.

Our Commitment

Fairmont Hotels & Resorts is committed to environmental protection and sustainability guided by our very own Green Partnership Program. The Partnership, a company-wide stewardship program, strives to minimize our properties' operational impact on the environment through resource conservation and best practices.

In delivering this commitment, all of our Fairmont Hotels & Resort colleagues will endeavor to:

- Work diligently to minimize our waste stream and conserve natural resources, particularly through energy and water conservation.
- Value the natural and cultural heritage of our properties, allowing us to give our guests an authentically local experience.
- Comply with all applicable environmental legislation and strive to follow best environmental practices.
- Make environmental considerations an important aspect of decision-making
- Review the objectives of our Green Partnership Program on a periodic basis
- Build local partnerships in the communities where we do business. These partnerships allow us to share our stewardship message, effect positive environmental change, and raise awareness for our guests and colleagues.
- Promise to consider the opinions and feedback of our guests when examining our environmental programs and procedures.
- Identify areas for improvement and innovation at the property level and support the efforts of the Green Teams at each of our properties.

Figure 9.2 Fairmont Hotels Environmental Policy (www.fairmont.com)

By enacting the principles of its Environmental Policy, Fairmont has produced some startling results. The Fairmont Southampton installed a one-million-gallon storage tank and a *reverse osmosis (RO) plant* that collects, treats, and stores rainwater, producing 250,000 gallons of water per week. As a result of replacing 4,440 light bulbs with energy efficient models, The Fairmont Sonoma Mission Inn & Spa saved $61,000 and over 203,000 kWh of energy. This same hotel constructed *worm bins*, composters using live worms to divert organic waste and supply fertilizer, which divert about 132 pounds of organic waste each week.

Environmental initiatives are spreading across the hospitality industry, thanks in part to "Green" Hotels Association® (www.greenhotels.com), which John Graham, president and CEO of ASAE & The Center for Association Leadership (www.asaecenter.org), described to me in May 2010 as, "a clearinghouse, eco-vendor and educator for hotels interested in saving money, supporting corporate goals, and lightening environmental footprints." Hotels affiliated with "Green" Hotels Association® are creating bold strategies for sustainable hospitality management, including the following innovations:

One of the main strategies for greener hotels is to reduce excessive laundry. For over 16 years, "Green" Hotels Association® has provided educational towel rack hangers and sheet changing cards that ask guests to consider using their linens more than once. Importantly, this communication, now found in thousands of hotel rooms around

Innovations from "Green" Hotels Association®

- A Toronto hotel is recycling stained table-cloths into napkins, chef's aprons, and neckties.
- Bicycles are being loaned or rented to guests.
- Coins or chips are being used for car parking and coat checking instead of paper tickets.
- Hotels are making cloth laundry bags from retired sheets.
- Mowed landscaping is being replaced by ground cover. Lawnmowers are used less, so air pollution and noise are reduced.
- A Florida hotel bought a mulcher to chop up its garden clippings and create its own mulch. The mulcher paid for itself in three months.

- A Wisconsin bed and breakfast has installed beautiful blue floor tile made from recycled automobile windshields.
- Chief engineers have found that toilet tank fill diverters in older toilets save about three-fourths of a gallon of water per flush.
- A Pennsylvania property has a 400-foot garden and produces organically grown vegetables for its restaurant.
- Restaurants and bars in hotels are using daylight exclusively for as much of each day as possible.
- Solar energy is lighting signage and heating water for hotels in tropical areas.

And more! Check out www.greenhotels.com.

the world, brings guests into the process and allows them to choose their own level of participation. "Green" Hotels Association® says that at least 70 percent of guests typically choose to participate, saving around 5 percent on utilities.

When I spoke with her in September 2010, Patricia Griffin, president and founder of "Green" Hotels Association®, told me she came up with the towel card idea when she saw a sign on the wall of a German hotel bath asking guests to reuse towels. "It was really an epiphany," she remembers. "When I got home, I came up with my version of the card, had them printed and sent them to 220 Houston hotels. The very first day anyone could have gotten my card, I got an order."

Aside from efficient laundry services for towels, there are many other ways to reduce an environmental impact in hotel bathrooms. First and foremost, greener hotels can provide greener toiletries, or organic toiletries packaged in a sustainable manner. Source local organic toiletry products (soap, shampoo, etc.) and buy them in bulk, to be presented in refillable, nondisposable containers. "Organic bed and bath linens and natural amenities are a pleasure to use," says Griffin. "Guests understand that a green hotel stay is a healthier hotel stay."

As with toiletries, reusable materials are critical for all aspects of hotels, in order to reduce waste. When reusable materials are not possible, source recyclable or biodegradable materials and divert them from the landfill stream into recycling or compost. When purchasing new products such as linens or staff uniforms, look for recycled or environmentally friendly materials.

Fairmont prides itself on the wide range of sustainable activities on offer that present guests with the opportunity to experience the destination and give back to the community. Dayboll says, "Providing guests with first-hand experiences allows for a greater understanding of the local destination, increasing their sense of place and ability to connect to the people and places they are directly interacting with." These experiences include sustainable dinners, learning about endangered species, sightseeing trips to nearby world heritage sites, hikes through nature reserves, or even volunteering for local causes.

Fairmont embarked on its first green travel campaign in 2008, and are now offering "H_2O" packages, with activities focused on water conservation. "We truly understand the need to provide our guests with local, enriching experiences," says Dayboll, "and we continuously look to offer new and innovative opportunities."

Greener Hotel Toiletries

- Reusable, refillable containers
- Packaging made from recycled, bioplastic, or biodegradable materials
- Organic shampoo, conditioner, soap, toothpaste, etc.
- Bioplastic trash bags
- Products sourced locally when possible
- Buying in bulk to avoid packaging waste

Greener hotels present guests with sustainable options, making it easy for them to make environmental choices. Griffin has found that, "Guests love being able to make a difference by making choices offered to them by smart green hoteliers. That's the reason linen programs are so successful at hotels." By providing environmental activities, eco-friendly toiletries, energy saving options, recycling, and other guest services, hotels can provide exceptional, sustainable guest experiences. Figure 9.3 presents some sustainable guest services that greener hotels can offer.

As president and CEO of ASAE & The Center for Association Leadership, John Graham has followed the progress of several sustainable hospitality organizations. In our May 2010 discussion, he said, "Green Keys (www.greenkeyglobal.com) was created as part of an ECOmmodation Rating Program of the Hotel Association of Canada. This is a graduated rating system that shares the results of an environmental audit through awarding one to five 'green keys.' The audit also informs facilities how to 'unlock' more opportunities, such as identifying more energy saving options or training staff about new sustainability practices."

Similarly, Graham has seen the growth of Audubon International's Green Leaf Program (greenleaf.auduboninternational.org). "Like Green Keys, this Canadian certification program uses a one to five rating system to draw attention to hotels and resorts with high environmental performance," says Graham. "Hotels receive one leaf for crafting and

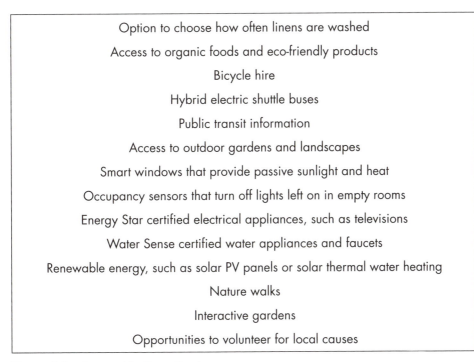

Option to choose how often linens are washed

Access to organic foods and eco-friendly products

Bicycle hire

Hybrid electric shuttle buses

Public transit information

Access to outdoor gardens and landscapes

Smart windows that provide passive sunlight and heat

Occupancy sensors that turn off lights left on in empty rooms

Energy Star certified electrical appliances, such as televisions

Water Sense certified water appliances and faucets

Renewable energy, such as solar PV panels or solar thermal water heating

Nature walks

Interactive gardens

Opportunities to volunteer for local causes

Figure 9.3   Sustainable Guest Services

committing to a set of environmental policies and principles, while the remaining leaves reflect a facility's progress toward its execution."

Doubletree hotels (www.doubletree.com) have received recognition and certification from a wide spectrum of third-party sustainable hospitality organizations, including Energy Star (www.energystar.gov), Green Seal (www.greenseal.org), Green Globe (www.greenglobe.com), Green Keys (www.greenkeyglobal.com), Costa Rica CST (www.turismo-sostenible.co.cr), and "Green" Hotels Association®. Additionally, Doubletree annually gives an Environmental CARE Award to a Doubletree hotel with outstanding environmental stewardship.

One winner of this Environmental CARE Award is the Doubletree Portland (www.doubletreegreen.com), a remarkably green hotel that actually created a carbon calculator for guests and events, specific to the hospitality industry, available on its Web site. Doubletree Portland is one of America's greenest hotels, and in its 2007–2008 Sustainability Report, it listed the following achievements outlined below:

In addition to these achievements, Doubletree Portland provides a wide range of sustainable services for meetings and events. Similarly, Fairmont has created Eco-Meet, a special program to support sustainable meetings, conferences and events. Dayboll explains, "In recent years, as environmental awareness has grown exponentially, planners have also looked to minimize their environmental footprint as a way to enhance their meetings and events and bring people together."

> With Eco-Meet, planners can work with Fairmont staff to tailor aspects of this unique program to whatever their clients and attendees value most. Whether it's disposable-free food and beverage services, gold standard carbon offsetting or innovative eco-inspired meeting breaks, organizers can ensure their meeting or conference is an environmental success.
>
> —*Sarah Dayboll, Fairmont, interview, September 2010*

Doubletree Portland Green Achievements

- Waste disposal reduced by 67 percent since 1996
- 17 tons of kitchen waste diverted from landfill to compost each month on average
- Reduced office paper purchasing by 20 percent annually with employee paper-saving program
- Reduced water usage by 15 percent
- Reduced energy consumption by 32 percent
- Employees receive mass transit subsidies, saving 9,500 gallons of gas per year since 1999

- Propertywide recycling program
- Comprehensive environmental purchasing policy
- 900,000 kWh of electricity purchased from renewable power sources
- 65 percent of food products purchased from within 500-mile region

(www.doubletreegreen.com)

Category	Sustainable Initiatives
Eco-accommodation	Energy and water efficiency Waste management and recycling
Eco-cuisine	Local, organic foods Vegetarian options Food waste composting Food redistribution programs
Eco-service	Eliminating disposables Recycling stations in all meeting rooms White boards used instead of flip charts Option to purchase Renewable Energy Certificates (RECs)
Eco-programming	Walking tours or outdoor activities Education regarding local environmental and heritage issues Participation in environmental conservation or species protection initiatives

Figure 9.4   Eco-Meet Program at Fairmont Hotels (www.fairmontmeetings.com)

Fairmont's Eco-Meet program provides meeting and conference planners with sustainable initiatives in the categories of eco-accommodation, eco-cuisine, eco-service and eco-programming. Figure 9.4 describes some of these initiatives.

In 2009, Fairmont expanded its program to include Meetings that Matter. "Meetings that Matter gives planners an opportunity to make a positive contribution when booking an event with Fairmont," says Dayboll. "Planners receive a 10 percent credit, which can be donated to a charity of choice. No matter which charity they choose—one that suits their corporate social responsibility mandate or one that supports the local community or one of Fairmont's charity partners—one thing is certain: a "meaningful meeting" is an easy way for a group to make a positive impact on the local destination."

For the past few years Fairmont has conducted guest feedback surveys through its President's Club members to gauge awareness of environmental programming. It found that 25 percent of respondents say their companies look to incorporate green meeting options into events, and 60 percent say a hotel's green policies influence their decision on where to stay. "Guest reactions have been very positive," says Dayboll. "They come to expect sustainability from us as a new minimum standard—they definitely pay attention and let us know when we need to do more."

Greener Venues

Thanks to its LEED certification program, the USGBC (www.usgbc.org) is ushering in a new era of sustainable architecture, and you can now choose to hold your next meeting or event in one of many hotels, conference centers, exhibition halls, theaters, and sports arenas with sustainable credentials. Even venues without the means to pursue LEED certification can take simple steps to greening their operations.

Convention Centers

For those in the meeting, conference, tradeshow, and exhibition industries, a huge variety of convention centers to suit various purposes are now available around the world. Seek out convention centers with environmental practices or work with existing buildings to go greener.

For major international conventions, choosing a central location with efficient transport links is crucial. As noted in Chapter 5, efficient transit links are critical for IMEX (www.imex-frankfurt.com), a major exhibition for the destination travel industry. Not only is Frankfurt, Germany, central and widely accessible by train, Messe Frankfurt (www.messefrankfurt.com), but IMEX's convention center host, has a number of outstanding sustainable services. One of these services is the option for clients to use hydroelectric power. Carina Bauer, CEO of IMEX, told me in May 2010 that she appreciates this option, saying, "It's slightly more expensive but still very doable."

Location is also a key to the sustainable success of the Moscone Center (www.moscone.com), managed by SMG (www.smgworld.com), which is situated in the heart of downtown San Francisco and surrounded by the 87-acre Yerba Buena Gardens District. Kathleen Hennesey, recycling manager, explains that Moscone's location reduces car travel, saying, "More than two-thirds of San Francisco's 35,000 hotel rooms are within a short walking distance of the Moscone Center." Hennesey sees Moscone's location as a unique selling point. "Sitting squarely in the heart of a great city, the Moscone Center anchors a thriving commercial and residential neighborhood. The complexity of this urban fabric offers daily opportunities to participate in this microcosm of life in San Francisco, as well as the challenges of operating in a dense and layered environment."

The Moscone Center also has some of the longest-standing environmental practices among American convention centers. Hennesey explains, "Moscone's recycling program began in 1998 and was a first of its kind among major U.S. convention centers. In 1996, consultants conducted an audit of Moscone Center's wastestream, and since then information has been tracked and reported." Hennesey sees this measurement as a critical aspect of a sustainable convention center: "One cannot manage what one does not track."

Hennesey works hard to support San Francisco's ambitious waste reduction goals, saying, "As one of the largest commercial generators in San Francisco, SMG recognizes the responsibility it has to help the City and County of San Francisco achieve its goal of 75 percent diversion by the end of 2010. That goal necessitates the increased capture of materials for diversion, whether through donation, reuse, recycling, or composting."

Hennesey is intimately aware of municipal waste issues:

San Francisco's agreement with the Altamont Landfill in Alameda County provides for waste disposal of up to 15 million tons. At the end of 2007, nearly 12 million tons of this contract capacity had been used by San Francisco, leaving about three million tons of capacity remaining. At the current disposal rate at the Altamont Landfill, San Francisco has until 2013 left on the current landfill contract. Increased diversion will extend the life of this landfill contract, with its very low disposal costs, which greatly benefits San Francisco residents and businesses financially.

Moscone's success as a sustainable convention center is, in part, thanks to state and local legislative mandates, exceedingly high commercial garbage rates, and strong access to recycling markets. California's AB 2176 requires the largest venues and events to develop waste reduction plans and annually report progress to their local government," she says, "and San Francisco's Board of Supervisors passed a resolution in support of diverting 75 percent of the city and county's waste stream by the end of 2010. However, markets for organic materials and many types of plastics have continued to expand and provide new program opportunities.

—Kathleen Hennesey, Moscone Center, interview, July 2010

As convention centers are typically a large force in their local economies, bringing in tourism and stimulating the economic engine, they also have a sizable environmental impact. Sustainable convention centers can engage in community issues and support municipal goals to reduce waste and carbon emissions. Figure 9.5 demonstrates some of the best practices of greener convention centers.

Exhibition managers should cultivate strong relationships with their convention centers to get the most sustainable experience possible. For its new exhibition in Las Vegas, IMEX started planning far in advance to ensure that its environmental needs would be met. Bauer says, "Because we don't know the venue as well and what they can do, we've hired an environmental consultant to help us with the suppliers out there. I do think that how you work with the suppliers and the venue is crucial."

Connects with local culture and politics

Central location, widely accessible by train

Working toward municipal environmental goals, such as waste reduction

Educates exhibitors on sustainability

Staff dedicated to sustainability

Renewable energy options

Donation program in place to redistribute food or other materials

Recycling program

Willingness to work with clients to achieve sustainability goals

Figure 9.5 Features of Greener Convention Centers

Green Arenas

Residents of the District of Columbia were thrilled to receive their own Major League Baseball (MLB) team, The Washington Nationals (www.nationals.com), in 2005, but they were divided on whether to build a new stadium. Such a major construction project could divert public funding at a time when DC's public schools badly needed it. Any new stadium would have to be ethically and sustainably built, and bring considerable value to the District.

Nationals Stadium, opened in 2008, was the first ever MLB stadium to earn LEED certification. Located near Navy Yard Metro Station, the stadium is easily reached by public transportation. Car parking is limited, but bicycle parking is plentiful, and a bike valet service is provided on game days. A 6,300-square-foot green roof, screens that capture solid materials, and large sand filters help to filter and improve storm water and wash water entering the nearby Anacostia River.

With low-flow faucets, efficient field lighting and an LED scoreboard, the park uses 15 percent less energy and 35 percent less water than an equivalent stadium. Additionally, 83 percent of construction waste was diverted from landfill. DC Mayor Adrian Fenty said, "Every resident of the District of Columbia should be proud that we have not only the greatest ballpark in the country but also the greenest" ("A Grand Slam for Washington, DC" 2008).

Ask your local sports or music arena if they have any environmental policies, then work with them to meet the needs of your sustainable meeting, event, concert, or sports event. You may help them find simple ways to save money by using less water and electricity. You might also improve attendee experience by reducing disposables, creating a recycling program or serving organic foods. Figure 9.6 provides a graduated list of sustainable practices at arena events, starting with the bare minimum and moving up in commitment level. Truly sustainable arenas can really hit a home run with their next event.

Green Theaters

As theater is often on the cutting edge of culture, modern performing arts centers are increasingly positioning themselves on the cutting edge of sustainable architecture. London's Arcola Theatre (www.arcolatheatre.com), for instance, uses a *hydrogen fuel cell*, a device that generates electricity by combining hydrogen and oxygen, to power its productions. In 2007, this theater took the extraordinary step of forming an energy company, Arcola Energy (www.arcolaenergy.com), which manages the sustainability initiatives of the theatre company and also sells and promotes renewable energy and energy efficient devices.

Bryan Raven, managing director of White Light Ltd (www.whitelight.ltd.uk), a leading theatrical lighting supplier, supports Arcola Theatre with equipment and is impressed at their energy efficiency:

> With their low power requirements, there is a finite amount of kit they need, and as long as the lighting designer is flexible, we are normally able to find enough spare equipment to help them out. Champions such as Arcola deserve as much support as they can get.
>
> —*Brian Raven, White Light Ltd, interview, August 2010*

Commitment Level	Sustainable Practice
First Base	Clear all litter. Only turn on lights and air conditioning in spaces that are being used. Only turn on field lights, jumbotrons, and scoreboards when in use, and turn them off promptly afterward. Use organic cleaning products.
Second Base	Use recyclable or biodegradable materials, and provide recycling and compost streams. Serve filtered tap water instead of bottled water. Source beer from local microbreweries. Source local and/or organic foods. Encourage attendees to bike, walk, or use public transportation to get to the field.
Third Base	Eliminate disposables. Purchase Energy Star devices and Water Sense appliances. Engage your attendees with optional exercise activities to bring them into the game!
Home Run!	Consider engaging attendees in a stationary biking activity on the field that provides pedal power for sound, lights, or digital displays.

Figure 9.6   Home Run Events at Sustainable Arenas

In 2008, The Theatres Trust (www.theatrestrust.org.uk) and The Mayor of London (www.london.gov.uk) unveiled Green Theatre, a step-by-step guide to producing theater and operating theatrical venues sustainably. Additionally, The Theatres Trust delivered a carbon calculator specifically for theater producers, available at www.theatrestrust.org.uk/events/green-theatre, and it has recently announced a program called Ecovenue (www.theatrestrust.org.uk/resources/ecovenue), which will provide sustainable advice and support to 48 London theaters.

On October 1, 2006, Portland Center Stage (PCS) (www.pcs.org) opened its brand new performing arts center, Gerding Theater at the Armory. Built in a repurposed nineteenth-century Armory in downtown Portland, Oregon, using 25 percent recycled materials and 45 percent regionally manufactured materials, Gerding Theater diverted over 95 percent of construction waste away from landfills and is LEED certified by the USGBC (www.usgbc.org).

Host to a wide range of arts performances and corporate events, PCS features a 10,000-gallon underground cistern, which harvests rainwater for reuse in the building's toilets. Luckily, the PCS performance season coincides with Portland's peak rainy season. Sustainable features also include cavities beneath floors to improve air circulation, skylights

The Baldacchino Gypsy Tent Bar at the Capital Fringe Festival featured psychadelic walls made from reused doors.

to provide sunlight and fresh air, hot water tubes embedded in cement floors providing radiant heat in lobbies, *chilled beams* (efficient cooling systems using small fans and tubes of chilled water), and recycling systems.

Responsible for creating several new impromptu theater venues each summer, Capital Fringe (www.capitalfringe.org) Festival Director Scot McKenzie collects as much reused building material as possible, much of which comes from Maryland's Community Forklift (www.communityforklift.com) at a discount price in return for sponsorship. In 2008, McKenzie created the Baldacchino Gypsy Bar, a tented, outdoor cabaret venue, using over 50 former household doors to create walls. Church pews, donated freely from a former congregation, became the most popular seats in the theater.

More than just reusing doors and church pews, McKenzie also recycled entire buildings, staging sold-out performances in former neglected buildings in downtown Washington, DC. The repurposing of neglected sites for new sustainable activity is a criterion for LEED certification, but McKenzie sees it as simply the right thing to do. "Some people want everything to be brand new," McKenzie says, "but they miss out on what's all around them. There are so many good used materials going to waste."

Outdoor Events

Mother Nature is the greenest venue of all, but she also requires the most care. Outdoor meetings and events have the greatest opportunity to bring attendees in touch with nature, but simultaneously the greatest responsibility to protect their environment. There are many ways to make outdoor events even greener.

Sustainable Landscapes for Outdoor Events

- Use rainwater harvesting techniques (as described in Chapter 7) to reuse rainwater.
- Keep human activity at a safe enough distance from trees to protect their roots.
- Use trees, at a safe distance, to shade outdoor air-conditioning units, generators or coolers.
- Restrict human activity near water sources.
- Install floorboards and walkways to protect the earth.
- Seed and regrow grass after the event.

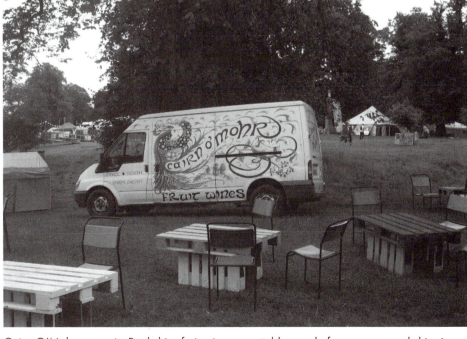

Cairn O'Mohr serves its Perthshire fruit wines over tables made from repurposed shipping palettes at The Big Tent.

Pillars Organic Cafe used hay bales as furniture at The Big Tent.

Sustainable Furniture

Furniture can make just as spectacular an impression on attendees as the venue itself. Consider finding special antique furniture for key areas, such as on stages, to show reuse. For larger allocations, such as hundreds of chairs, look for sustainable materials, such as wood, instead of plastic. Be innovative: At The Big Tent (www.bigtentfestival.co.uk) environmental music festival in Fife, Scotland, Cairn O' Mohr Fruit Wines (cairnomohr .homestead.com) made picnic tables from used wood shipping palettes. At South by Southwest (SXSW) (www.sxsw.com), attendees can sit on chairs made from reused street signs while charging their phones in the SolarPump (www.soldesignlab.com).

Ethical Art

Owners of large hotels, convention centers, theaters, and arenas will understandably wish to decorate these grandiose buildings with beautiful artworks. Hoteliers may wish to hang smaller artworks in individual rooms, whereas convention centers may require a large outdoor sculpture to make a powerful statement and to draw focus. By choosing to display art in your venue, you are not only supporting the arts, you are also enhancing the quality of life for the public who get to enjoy the art. Public artworks may not always be to everyone's taste, but they are sure to stimulate public interest and discussion.

Once you have decided to display art, you may wish to consider ways in which this art can support social causes or sustainability goals. For instance, by commissioning artworks from developing countries, you can support struggling economies and raise awareness of the developing world. You may also obtain these artworks at an inexpensive rate (compared to works from more established artists), although it is important to pay a fair price, making a meaningful investment in the artist's community if possible.

Diners at the South African restaurant chain Nando's (www.nandos.com) can experience walls full of beautiful, lush artworks made by South African artists. Nando's sponsors these artists to create works, providing tuition and recognition for persons who otherwise may not have these opportunities. Works such as these from the developing world might provide an affordable alternative to generic art placed in hotel suites or meeting rooms.

Alternatively, you may wish to find a local artist and either commission or purchase a piece with some local resonance. Not only will you be supporting local artists, but you might find a work that touches on local themes, engages residents in discussion or promotes your region as a destination. Cow Parade (www.cowparade.com) is the largest public art event in the world. Since 1999, it has commissioned local artists, from the amateur to the famous, to paint life-size cow sculptures and has placed them around over 50 major cities, including Chicago, New York, London, and Tokyo. These artworks often feature local themes. You might be one of the over 100 million people who have seen one of these painted cows on a city block.

Environmental art, or art using organic materials and/or engaging with the natural world, is a wonderful way to reconnect with nature. Consider artworks made from sustainable materials or touching on environmental themes. Robert Smithson's Spiral Jetty (www.diaart.org/sites/main/spiraljetty) is one of the most famous original works of environmental art. The artist used local black basalt rocks to create a 1,500-foot-long coil of earth in Utah's Great Salt Lake.

Sarah Hall (www.sarahhallstudio.com) is a Canadian stained-glass artist who incorporates solar PV panels into her glass art creations. By embedding the PV cells between two panes of glass with high light transmittance that have been heat-strengthened, Hall creates beautiful works of public art that not only utilize passive sunlight to provide heat and light but also generate active solar power.

Eco-Friendly Exhibitions

Exhibitions and tradeshows face the enormous task of managing tens, often hundreds, of private exhibitors. Each exhibitor works independently, registering, constructing, and shipping a display booth, traveling and operating the booth at the exhibition. Companies not used to exhibiting might be unaware of best practices in exhibitions and need guidance in order to operate a successful display booth. You can help your exhibitors to create sustainable, spectacular booths, by setting out guidelines for them.

Figure 9.7 offers suggestions for how exhibitors may construct, ship, operate, and travel with display booths in a sustainable manner. The key is to make it easy for your exhibitors to make sustainable choices—for instance, by pointing them toward local sustainable businesses. Furnish them with the information and resources they need to make sustainable, spectacular displays.

Kimberly Lewis, vice president of events for USGBC created a set of exhibitor guidelines in 2009 for GreenBuild (www.greenbuildexpo.org), the annual USGBC convention. These guidelines offer suggestions such as refurbishing existing booths rather than buying a new one each year. "The USGBC aims to demonstrate leadership in sustainable trade show practices and uphold Greenbuild's reputation as one of the greenest trade shows in the world," says Lewis. "As part of this, USGBC requires all Greenbuild exhibitors to meet the Greenbuild Mandatory Exhibition Green Guidelines (GMEGG) to be eligible to exhibit the following year."

GMEGG was developed by USGBC to establish a baseline measurement and gain an understanding of current exhibition practices at Greenbuild, while requiring minimum compliance on five basic criteria. GMEGG will be used by USGBC to develop best practices for the Greenbuild exhibit hall, in order to help Greenbuild exhibitors build, operate, and maintain their booths more sustainably.

USGBC is collecting data and measuring compliance on the following areas of exhibition: indoor air quality, booth flooring, booth graphics and signage, communications and collateral, and shipping materials. "It's about helping your exhibitors understand and be a part of your goals and objectives," Lewis explains. "We worked so much on ourselves inwardly that it was time to open up and bring our attendees and exhibitors into that process."

> We've been able to tell some really strong stories about what our exhibitors are doing. We are helping to educate not just attendees, but also suppliers, partners and exhibitors. They want to be better, and they want to tell their story as well. That's been a huge legacy for us.
> —*Kimberly Lewis, U.S. Green Building Council, interview, May 2010*

Carina Bauer is CEO of IMEX, a major international exhibition for meeting, tourism and destination management professionals. Like Lewis, she has worked over the past several years to share with exhibitors IMEX's commitment to sustainability. As part of their annual Green Awards, given in conjunction with the Green Meeting Industry Council (GMIC) (www.greenmeetings.info), IMEX distributes a Green Exhibitor Award (www.imex-frankfurt.com/greenexhaward.html), which recognizes outstanding sustainable practice in exhibitors. "It really makes an impact on the way they think about what they do at the show," says Bauer. "It's very important in changing the way people think about exhibiting."

Bauer says that Visit London (www.visitlondon.com), winner of the 2007 Green Exhibitor Award, worked very closely with its stand designer to source sustainable materials, but that it also approached its entire operation with a sustainable mindset. "They looked at everything, including how many staff to take from London," recalls Bauer. "There is a long way to go for everybody to get to that stage."

Area	Action
Construction	Consider refurbishing existing booths instead of purchasing new ones every year. When purchasing new, look for booths that can be reused in future exhibitions. Look for booths made from recycled materials. Look for collapsible booths for easier shipping.
Signage	Chalkboards and whiteboards are reusable and allow for quick changes. Electronic displays are reusable and can produce in-depth, interactive information. Consider recycled paper with organic inks. Avoid unnecessary lamination, so that paper may be recycled.
Handouts	Consider fair trade crafts instead of plastic toys. Look for products made from recycled materials, such as pens made from water bottles (www.pilot.com). Only give items with actual value, such as pens and pencils instead of plastic toys. Fresh fruit or seed packets are a wonderful alternative to candy or soda. Reduce excess promotional paper handouts. Attendees generally want to take away informational materials instead of advertisements. Do not overprint brochures. Print brochures so that they can be reused at future exhibitions. Avoid individually wrapped goods with excess plastic packaging. Have a plan for recycling or reusing excess materials.
Operation	Minimize the amount of unnecessary electronic devices. Use Energy Star approved electronic devices. Use efficient lighting such as CFLs or LEDs. Plug electronic devices into a control strip, and turn off before and after use. Consider providing recycling facilities. If you are the only booth with these facilities, attendees will all come to you. Use reusable bags and containers.
Shipping	Consider assembling your booth near to the exhibition location to avoid long-distance shipping. Consider purchasing booth accessories such as signage or electronics near to the exhibition location. Purchase handouts locally. Source local print suppliers. Minimize excess packaging. Avoid plastic wrap. Look for recycled, bioplastic, or biodegradable packaging materials. Do not use polystyrene blocks or pellets to cushion packages. Instead, use cardboard or air-filled plastic.
Travel	Consider train or bus travel before plane or car. When in the exhibition location, use public transportation or walking instead of rental car or taxi. Look for a hotel close to the exhibition center to avoid excess transportation. Travel in groups, instead of individually.

Figure 9.7 Exhibition Booth Green Guidelines

How "Visit London" Won the IMEX Green Exhibitor Award

(www.imex-frankfurt.com/greenexhaward
.html)

- Worked closely with Protean Design and in-house 'green unit' Future London
- Used innovative acrylics and PETG plastic plus di-bonded aluminum frames
- 100 percent of the construction materials recyclable
- Compact design reduced shipping and storage requirements
- Documented event environmental policy, including a "lifecycle audit"
- Reduced printed materials by providing information on a USB
- Bottled water was supplied by Belu (www .belu.org), funding clean water projects worldwide
- Carbon offset program accounted for both staff and freight travel

IMEX also recognizes the more basic sustainable practices among all exhibitors. "We introduced something called the IMEX Green Team," Bauer says, "where if exhibitors do two out of three tasks, they receive a green ribbon." Small as they were, these green ribbons gave great visibility to the sustainable agenda of IMEX. "It promoted the fact that they should not throw away their brochures at the end, or perhaps not bring them at all; bring USB sticks."

Like Lewis, Bauer strives to make it easier for exhibitors to make sustainable choices. "We highlight the greenest products in the exhibitor manual with a little symbol," she says. Sustainable practices don't always catch on immediately, but Bauer believes it is important to maintain awareness, saying, "It's up and down with certain things and it's an ongoing process."

In some situations, penalties can be more effective than rewards. Kevin Danaher is executive producer of Green Festival (www.greenfestivals.org), which, as America's largest green economy road show, takes its sustainable policies seriously. He told me in May 2010 that he expects exhibitors to act responsibly as well: "We tell them, 'If you leave any trash behind, you're fined $75.'" These regulations can help to ensure full participation.

Greener Vendors

A meeting or event manager can tell you that any event is only as strong as its *vendors*, or the companies that provide goods or services such as tent rentals, linen hire, or sound and lighting equipment. In today's competitive market, more and more vendors are using modern sustainable practices to sustain their businesses and get an advantage. Greener meeting and event pioneers can seek out these greener vendors, or work with existing vendors to achieve sustainable goals.

Shawna McKinley, project manager for MeetGreen (www.meetgreen.com), took the events team at Oracle (www.oracle.com) through a comprehensive greening process. She said, "Once the internal team members have clarity and direction, it's usually a case of 'How do you influence the vendor pool, the supply chain, and get them on board?'" McKinley notes that, although many vendors already have their own excellent sustainable policies, "Sometimes they are not as bought-in." Once Oracle had set sustainable policies and trained its staff, McKinley helped bring vendors into the green agenda.

> They cast the invitation open to the vendor team to say, 'We want you involved in this as well. We know you're doing stuff, that's great. Thank you. What can you do in addition to that to take us to the next level?' That's what they did straight through their 2009 event cycle.
> —*Shawna McKinley, MeetGreen, interview, May 2010*

Hennesey acknowledges that the sustainable success of the Moscone Center is, in part, thanks to outstanding contractors:

> The three main Exhibition Service companies and the Exhibitor Appointed Contractors have been receptive to our sustainable programs since we started in 1998, and have shown good faith efforts to comply with our expanding programs and convey procedural information to their workers. It takes partnership and communication to produce success.
> —*Kathleen Hennesey, Moscone Center, interview, July 2010*

You, too, can pursue the very best sustainable practices from sound, light or other vendors or contractors.

Green Light

The theatrical lighting industry is leading the way in energy efficiency with innovative new products and strategies. Bryan Raven, managing director of White Light Ltd, says that this is partly due to increased client demand. "The first people to ask about the environmental aspects of our services were the corporate bodies, such as banks, to whom we supply technical services for parties and corporate events," says Raven. "Theater has been slower to respond, but they also had less to change, as a lot of theatrical working practices are sustainable for economic reasons."

Raven has enacted several strategies to improve energy efficiency and reduce waste in White Light's operations, including the White Light Green Guide, a comprehensive document available online (www.whitelight.ltd.uk), which advises event managers how to use lights efficiently and effectively. When we met in August 2010, Raven explained that the Green Guide offers easy-to-understand advice, such as sourcing gear locally, only ordering what you need, and making sure you switch it off when you don't need it. Raven sees these basic principles ignored quite a lot. "So many times you walk past lights at festivals that are on during daylight hours."

In addition to new, energy-efficient technology, Raven also believes in reusing old equipment, although he acknowledges the challenges, saying, "We have older fixtures that

- Keep lights switched off until 35 minutes before the show.
- Treat lighting instruments with care to preserve their long-term use.
- When testing, fade lights up and down; switching quickly from off to full reduces the life of the bulb.
- Use the fewest number of lights possible to achieve the desired effect.
- When daylight is available, use it to reduce electric lighting.
- Reuse the number of lights needed whenever possible. For instance, instead of using different lights for scene changes, use the show lights on a dim setting.
- Use LEDs whenever possible for theatrical lighting.
- Use CFLs whenever possible for operational lighting.
- Consider renewable energy to power the lighting rig.
- Keep and reuse color fills and gobos, or donate them to local theater or art group.
- Avoid high-wattage special lights if smaller lights could have the same effect.
- Turn lighting instruments off after their last cue, not after the show is over.

Figure 9.8   Sustainable Lighting Tips

work perfectly well, but are expensive to use because of replacement lamp costs, or the spare parts may be difficult to get hold of, or the unit is simply unreliable." He compares these older lighting instruments with older cars, saying, "There comes a point where they are too expensive to run and too unreliable to use."

Because it is so visible, theatrical lighting is often singled out as a major carbon emitter, but Raven reminds venue managers that standard building operations typically use more energy. "Lighting is seen as the biggest culprit for carbon use in a theater, whereas the truth is that it is air-conditioning and heating," Raven says. "In most theatres, the freezers for the ice cream use more electricity than the onstage lighting rig, mainly because it is only used for a couple of hours per day."

White Light's Green Guide can help ensure that lighting remains one of the most efficient aspects of any meeting or event. Figure 9.8 provides some easy-to-follow tips on how to keep your lighting display as sustainable as possible.

■ Light Emitting Diodes (LEDs)

LEDs or *light emitting diodes* are perhaps today's biggest innovation in energy-efficient lighting. According to Raven, "LEDs are a form of producing light using very little power compared to traditional tungsten or discharge lighting sources." He numbers the many benefits of LEDs, saying, "They have a low cost of ownership, as they have a lamp life measured in thousands of hours not hundreds of hours. They also produce very little heat, so the mechanical side of the equipment lasts longer, and you also don't need as much air conditioning!"

There are those who prefer the quality of light and focusing abilities produced by traditional tungsten lamps, and Raven does not begrudge them this point. "The tungsten light bulb is much maligned," he says. "In performance situations where you need to control the intensity constantly for various lighting states, the tungsten source is the most efficient type of lamp, as it only draws electricity when it is emitting light. Other forms of lighting often draw the same amount of power, whether they are on or not."

However, as manufacturers continue to innovate, LEDs are becoming increasingly versatile and accessible. Raven sees a shift toward LEDs, saying, "As the quality of the light from LED sources improves, this low-energy technology is increasingly replacing more power-hungry equipment." LEDs are available in the United States from Color Kinetics (www.colorkinetics.com). The LED lights used at the 2009 Super Bowl required only 290 watts per fixture, compared to the 1,600 watts a standard fixture requires (Klingler 2009). Nila Lighting System (nila.tv) for film and television uses 50 percent to 75 percent less electricity than traditional lighting systems.

Innovative companies such as White Light are keeping the lighting industry at the forefront of sustainable events, as they continue to provide some of the most efficient and sustainable vendor services available. Look out for new developments in LED technology,

Brazil! Brazil! performs with LED lighting at The Big Tent.

as well as new efficient devices such as *plasma lamps*, or electrodeless lamps energized by radio frequency power.

■ Mirrors

Mirrors are a simple and often overlooked invention when it comes to lighting efficiency. Quite simply, mirrors reflect and multiply light sources. Incorporating mirrors into the event decor can increase the sense of space in a room while providing a glittering complement to the lighting design. Place mirrors strategically to maximize their reflection of lighting sources, while taking care to not reflect light into attendees' eyes.

Light reflectors are mirrors positioned to reflect passive sunlight into a room. Queen Margaret University's (www.qmu.ac.uk) new sustainable campus in Edinburgh features a transparent sunroof and light reflectors, which bounce sunlight into the central atrium. With enough sunlight and reflectors, you may not need electric lights at all. Additionally, some energy-efficient lighting fixtures use mirrored reflectors to maximize luminescence.

Sustainable Sounds

Sound gear can be just as energy intensive as a lighting rig, especially at any event featuring music. Make sure that you are using sound equipment efficiently to save costs and energy. The first step might be to choose a venue with excellent acoustics, which will thus require less amplification. Once you have the best possible space for sound projection and resonance, use speakers of a size appropriate to the desired volume. Figure 9.9 provides some "sound advice" regarding sustainability.

The UK music industry is making great strides toward sustainability, thanks partly to Julie's Bicycle (www.juliesbicycle.com) and the Office of the Mayor of London

---

- Choose a venue with great acoustics, so that minimal amplification will be required.
- Keep speakers and sound equipment switched off until 35 minutes before the show.
- Handle sound equipment, microphones, and cords with care to preserve their long-term use.
- Use the fewest number of microphones possible to achieve the desired sound.
- Reuse microphones during a show whenever possible.
- Do not use unnecessarily large speakers and amplifiers; match the equipment size to the desired loudness.
- Sound insulation in recording studios can also function as heating insulation.
- Sound technicians use new batteries every time a wireless mic is used. Donate these used batteries to a local group.

Figure 9.9 Sound Advice

(www.london.gov.uk), who collaborated on Green Music, a report on sustainability in the UK music industry. Available at www.juliesbicycle.com/green-music-guide, Green Music showcases the best practices in the music industry while also highlighting areas in need of improvement.

Green Music estimates that London music venues produced 112,500 tonnes of carbon emissions in 2008, but that energy efficiency and waste reduction could reduce this number by 20 percent in 2025. Towards this goal, The Academy Music Group (www .academy-music-group.co.uk) is measuring energy use in its O2 Academy Brixton, O2 Academy Shepherds Bush Empire, and O2 Academy Islington venues, and creating custom-tailored energy reduction plans. The Royal Albert Hall (www.royalalberthall.com) is piloting new software that tracks energy efficiency within a building.

One triumph of the UK music industry is The Premises (www.premisesstudios.com), Europe's first solar-powered recording studio. A new roof and solar PV system cost The Premises £20,000 in 2006, but government subsidies mean that it will soon recoup this investment and be able to sell excess power back to their energy supplier at a profit. Smarter sound insulation eliminated the need for heating, and the solar PV system has raised the profile of The Premises immensely, making it one of the UK's most sought-after recording studios.

Special Effects

Nothing is more high-impact than pyrotechnics, lasers, confetti canons, or other theatrical special effects used at a special event. Greener event pioneers can find innovative ways to make sure these high-impact effects have a low impact on the environment. Make sure you are getting the most "bang for your buck," and use special effects sustainably and efficiently, as described in Figure 9.10.

Rock concerts are notoriously heavy on special effects, whether it's pyrotechnics, laser shows, or flying set pieces, but in 2008, Radiohead (www.radiohead.com/deadairspace)

- Keep special effects switched off until 35 minutes before the show.
- Turn effects off after they are used, not after the show is over.
- Position hazers and smoke machines strategically so that no haze or smoke is wasted on invisible or backstage areas.
- Do not overuse pyrotechnics: use them strategically so that they have maximum impact.
- Collect melted water from ice sculptures for reuse.
- Source biodegradable confetti and bioplastic balloons.
- Use sustainable materials whenever possible.
- Collect and reuse balloons and confetti when possible.

Figure 9.10   Efficient Effects

wanted to make sure its world tour was both spectacular and energy efficient. It created a dazzling lighting rig and multimedia set design that exclusively used LEDs, producing vast savings of energy and money. According to i-Pix (www.i-pix.uk.com), the lighting supplier, Radiohead's 2008–2009 world tour used instruments called BB7s, seven-cell high-powered homogenized 10 degree RGB lightsources, as well as floor-mounted i-Pix Satellites with holographic film to light the band. This high-tech, high-impact rock show ended up being low energy and low cost.

Greener Venue: Melbourne Convention and Exhibition Centre

Opened in 2009, the Melbourne Convention and Exhibition Centre (MCEC, www.mcec.com.au) is the only 6 Star Green Star environmentally rated convention centre in the world, and a quick tour of the building reveals the sustainable technologies that earned it this accolade from the Green Building Council of Australia:

- Solar panels provide 100 percent of public amenity hot water requirements.
- An 18-meter glass façade with spectrally selective glass allows for a high degree of diffused natural light, reducing the need for artificial light.
- Electric indoor lighting is conserved by the use of occupancy sensors, local switching, and daylight sensors.
- Low-level air delivery and high-level air exhaust provides excellent air change effectiveness at low energy consumption.
- Radiant slab heating and cooling provides energy-efficient thermal comfort and reduces air conditioning requirements.
- Carpets, paints, adhesives, and sealants are low in volatile organic compounds (VOCs) to enhance indoor air quality.
- Materials and components have a high recycled content and minimal polyvinyl chloride (PVC) content.
- Only 56 Australian Eucalyptus Maculata (spotted gum) trees from a sustainable

source were used to cover 8,500 square meters of timber veneer paneling in the plenary, foyer, and grand banquet rooms.

In our May 2010 discussion, Leigh Harry, CEO of MCEC, told me, "The design of the MCEC allows high levels of natural light into the foyer spaces and an intuitive air conditioning system ensures high-quality indoor air." Harry added, "These conditions provide a comfortable environment for all visitors to the centre."

The MCEC also has the first privately funded black water treatment plant in a public building in Australia. "The plant treats wastewater, rainwater and storm water to Grade A quality for reuse in the building," Harry explains, "reducing the flow to the sewerage system, while reducing the MCEC's reliance on potable water."

In addition to the sustainable technologies engineered into the building, the staff provides many green services, custom-tailored to the events being hosted. "We offer a full range of environmentally friendly practices in relation to the operation of the building, catering and other services," says Harry. Some of these services include:

- Providing multiple streams for waste management, including full composting facilities for food waste

Linens

Pressed white tablecloths are a staple of any fancy dinner, but greener attendees might prefer a more earthy fabric made from undyed, organic cotton. Environmentally conscious attendees prefer raw, organic materials in their linens. Some patrons may even appreciate reused fabrics, such as those sourced from discarded textiles. The 2009 Green Inaugural Ball famously presented a green carpet made from recycled textiles instead of a standard red carpet.

- A closed-loop recycling system on site that clients can use free of charge
- Calculating the amount of waste produced for specific events to help event organizers calculate the amount of waste going to landfill
- Offering clients green power for their event, where equivalent power usage is purchased from a renewable energy source
- A sustainable food menu using products supplied by local Victorian producers specifically tailored for each event

The MCEC even provides clients with a whole host of green information and a green event checklist on how to incorporate green solutions into their events. Harry explains that the MCEC seeks to support each client's unique sustainability needs, saying, "We take environmental issues seriously and are committed to providing sustainable options for all events taking place in the center."

A team of dedicated MCEC employees— aptly named the M Green Team—was created to implement fresh initiatives and new strategies to continue to benchmark and progress MCEC's environmental performance.

The M Green team reflects the center's commitment to an environmentally sustainable business and industry, and they work hard to ensure every aspect of our operation is conducted in an environmentally conscious manner. Our environmental initiatives have been well received by all of our stakeholders, clients and delegates. Sustainability is often high on the agenda for event organizers and the services provided at the MCEC can fulfill many of their sustainable event requirements.

—*Leigh Harry, MCEC, interview,*
May 2010

An online resource, the M Green micro-site (www.mcec.com.au/mgreen.html), offers visitors a glimpse inside the MCEC and showcases its green design and operations. "The micro-site features environmental strategies that have already been implemented at the MCEC and the initiatives that continue to benchmark the MCEC's environmental performance," says Harry.

The MCEC also operates a Green Office Program to promote recycling in the workplace. "Promotional materials are produced using recycled and vegetable inks, toner cartridges are recycled and electronic resources are utilized wherever possible," says Harry. "We have also installed new state-of-the art printers that use less power and toner than previous devices," he adds.

Leigh Harry and the team at MCEC truly believe that sustainable events make for superior experiences. "The MCEC's innovative sustainable design and operational features ensure that the comfort of delegates and the protection of the environment go hand-in-hand," he says. It is this superior experience coupled with sustainable practice that brings clients back to the MCEC again and again.

The way linens are treated also matters. Wash used linens at low temperatures, in full loads of laundry and with organic cleaning solution. Air dry if possible. This environmental approach to laundry may take some getting used to, but can save money in the long term and impress environmentally conscious attendees along the way.

Fairmont hotels have several innovative strategies for sustainable laundry systems. The Fairmont Kea Lani in Hawaii has a wastewater recycling facility that is capable of recycling 75 percent of all laundry water. In Toronto, Canada, The Fairmont Royal York installed a commercial water softener that reduces water use in the laundry to one wash and one rinse per cycle. This system saves 476,000 liters of water each day, or enough water to supply 500 homes.

Summary

Sustainable architecture and building management is on the rise, thanks to the U.S. Green Building Council's LEED certification system. Begin by greening your own office, reducing waste, and finding efficiencies in the energy and water systems. Greener hotels use water and energy efficiently and provide outstanding sustainable services for eco-conscious guests and meeting attendees. Greener arenas and performing arts centers can follow LEED guidelines to reduce waste, use water and energy efficiently, and provide a more sustainable audience experience. Exhibition managers must reach out to exhibitors to find sustainable solutions to display booths, travel, and handouts. Lighting suppliers can provide efficient lighting arrays as well as low-energy lights such as LEDs. Work with all vendors, including sound, special effects, and linens, to minimize waste and use water and energy efficiently.

Key Terms and Definitions

- **Leadership in Energy and Environmental Design (LEED)**: U.S. Green Building Council certification for sustainable architecture.
- **Reverse osmosis (RO) plant**: rainwater harvesting device that collects, treats, and stores storm water.
- **Worm bins**: composters using live worms to divert organic waste and supply fertilizer.
- **Chilled beams**: efficient cooling systems using small fans and tubes of chilled water.
- **Environmental art**: art using organic materials and/or engaging with the natural world.
- **Vendors**: companies that provide goods or services to meetings and events.

- **Light-emitting diodes (LEDs)**: a form of producing light using very little power compared to traditional tungsten or discharge lighting sources.
- **Plasma lamps**: electrodeless lamps energized by radio frequency power.
- **Hydrogen fuel cell**: a device that generates electricity by combining hydrogen and oxygen.

Blue Sky Thinking

You are exhibiting at IMEX 2012 (www.imex-frankfurt.com) and want to win the Green Exhibitor Award. Choose a tourist bureau, such as Visit Scotland (www.visitscotland .com), Go Hawaii (www.gohawaii.com), or Australia (www.australia.com) to represent, and design a sustainable display booth that will showcase your destination as a premier ecotourist spot. Your booth should incorporate the local culture of your destination but also feature the sustainable ecotourist activities on offer. How will you construct your booth in an environmentally friendly way, showing water and energy efficiency and waste reduction? How will your travel and accommodation reduce your carbon footprint? Write a plan for your sustainable exhibition booth that includes construction, operation, travel, handouts, and educational content.

Renewable Resources

Community Forklift (www.communityforklift.com)
Ecolab (www.ecolab.com): provider of sustainable building maintenance services
Green Theater Initiative (www.greentheaters.org)
Julie's Bicycle (www.juliesbicycle.com)
The ReUse People (thereusepeople.org)

PART THREE

Education

At The Big Tent, Scottish Youth Parliament inspires young people to "Picture The Change" they want to see in politics by stepping inside a giant picture frame.

CHAPTER 10

Social Sustainability

"I want to work for a company that contributes to and is part of the community. I want something not just to invest in. I want something to believe in."

—*Dame Anita Roddick, Founder of The Body Shop (1942–2007)*

In this chapter, you will learn:

1. How meetings and events may contribute to social well-being

2. How corporate social responsibility (CSR) commitments can provide volunteer, financial, or in-kind support to social causes

3. How to maintain a happy, healthy workforce through sustainable human resources

4. How to meet standards for equality and accessibility

5. How to make your meeting or event a welcoming environment for all persons

6. How to source local goods and services

7. How to create a legacy of positive social impacts in areas such as health, ecosystem, and urban regeneration

---

There is a rich debate about whether a meeting or event can ever be completely *carbon neutral*, having zero carbon emissions. When you factor in staff, stakeholder, and attendee travel; shipping costs; and energy and water use, there are invariably at least a few carbon emissions that can be offset but not eliminated. Knowing that even the greenest meetings and events will have at least some small environmental impact, professionals can ensure a positive legacy through socially responsible programs and charities.

As president and CEO of the Professional Convention Management Association (PCMA) (www.pcma.org), which represents over 6,000 meeting industry professionals, Deborah Sexton knows the pressure to go green. "Meetings are here to stay and environmental issues are here to stay," she says. "Do meetings leave a footprint? Yes. Do meetings also deliver something very valuable for the attendees, the host destinations, the economy and the world? Yes."

> It is incumbent upon us as an industry to minimize our footprint and promote how meetings can reduce the impact we have. Simultaneously, many meetings – and I hope more and more – are doing a wide variety of things to give back to the communities in which we meet.
> —*Deborah Sexton, Professional Convention Management Association (PCMA), interview, July 2010*

Meetings and events may give back to their communities through social sustainability programs, including volunteerism, donation, and policies of equality, accessibility, and fair trade. These programs are rooted in the modern philosophy of corporate social responsibility.

Corporate Social Responsibility

As discussed in Chapter 1, *corporate social responsibility* (CSR) is a theory promoting ethical and charitable corporate behavior. In 2008, the American Society of Association Executives (ASAE) (www.asaecenter.com) held The Global Summit on Social Responsibility, which connected association leaders from over 19 sites across the world and online to discuss CSR. John Graham, president and CEO of ASAE, recalled in May 2010, "It was truly a global experience and we made some very important commitments to be more socially responsible. A number of different projects emerged during the event with commitments to further explore each idea following the Summit."

One of the most important outcomes of the Summit was the Global Principles for Socially Responsible Associations & Nonprofits (ASAE 2010). Graham explains, "The principles outline social responsibility guidelines for organizations to adopt and implement in their daily operations in areas related to association and nonprofit management." Below are some of the areas promoted by these principles.

These principles were designed to complement the United Nations Global Compact, a universally vetted set of goals addressing many of the world's most challenging problems, and ASAE staff have even met with the top leaders of the United Nations and presented the principles. "We plan to continue the discussion on how the association and nonprofit

Global Principles for Socially Responsible Associations and Nonprofits (Featured Areas)

- Advocacy
- Leadership
- Ethics
- Diversity
- Self-regulation

- Human rights
- Philanthropy and community service
- Environmental and economic sustainability

Source: ASAE 2010.

community can play a bigger role in advancing social responsibility along with the United Nations," says Graham.

Graham describes the response from ASAE members and guests who participated in the Summit as "overwhelming," saying, "Everyone is very excited about our efforts and we are looking forward to taking the next steps. Since the Summit, we have been working continuously to carry on the momentum from the event and the aspirations of our members and friends who participated in this important endeavor."

> Associations are some of the most prominent champions of social responsibility. We help our members, as well as industry partners and for-profits, in increasing their knowledge of social responsibility and of their immediate and long-term benefits not only to the environment but also to our businesses and local communities.
>
> —*John Graham, ASAE, interview, May 2010*

Graham hopes the Global Principles of Socially Responsible Associations and Nonprofits inspire other organizations to adopt them in their daily work, saying, "We encourage associations and nonprofit organizations to sign onto the principles as part of a commitment to using social responsibility as a business driver and as a vital tool for positive environmental, economic, and social change."

Volunteerism

One of the most visible ways that a company might support CSR is through volunteering for a social cause. Company meetings and events can gather a large workforce together and put their skills toward a charitable cause, such as creating an urban garden, serving at a homeless shelter, or constructing low-income housing. Importantly, the act of volunteering has the power to benefit not just the community but also the employees who volunteer, as it provides them with a positive, inspirational experience.

Habitat for Humanity (www.habitat.org) offers groups of employees and colleagues the chance to participate in sustained volunteer programs, building housing in impov-

Staff of the Edinburgh International Conference Centre plant trees in the Scottish Borders. *Courtesy of the Edinburgh International Conference Centre.*

erished areas. Office workers might jump at the chance to work outside for a change. Whether they show off their carpentry skills or simply learn how to paint a fence, building a house with Habitat for Humanity can be an inspirational experience.

Volunteering does not need to entail physical labor. Lawyers often work pro bono for artistic and nonprofit organizations, offering their expert counsel for those who otherwise could not afford it. Volunteer Lawyers for the Arts (www.vlany.org) is a New York–based collective of attorneys who provide pro bono guidance for arts organizations. The arts organizations receive free legal counsel, and the lawyers get the chance to work with artists and support the cultural growth of their region.

Philanthropy

The act of charitable aid or donation, otherwise known as *philanthropy*, is one of the strongest ways that a meeting or event can support CSR initiatives. There are many diverse strategies for raising funds or support for charitable causes through meetings and events. Indeed, the drive to do good is one of the oldest and strongest motivations for gatherings of any kind. Consider philanthropic support for charitable or nonprofit organizations either through financial or in-kind assistance.

Choosing the right charity is of the utmost importance. Research nonprofit organizations in your region that are somehow connected to your business, staff, and stakeholders. Event professionals in Washington, DC, can access the Catalogue for Philanthropy (www .catalogueforphilanthropy-dc.org), a guide to smaller, accredited nonprofit organizations. Look for smaller, but well-managed charities, where your support can make the biggest difference in your region.

■ Financial

At a recent meeting in Dallas, Texas, the PCMA Education Foundation's Annual Giving Campaign fundraiser benefited "Keep Dallas Beautiful." Deborah Sexton says, "Funds raised all throughout 2010 will go to building and stocking a community tool shed, providing the resources to help clean up and keep the Dallas environment clean and healthy for all, especially in disadvantaged communities." Sexton admires those greener meeting and event planners who go above and beyond by supporting environmental or charitable causes through financial philanthropy.

> We all can make a difference by greening our meetings and giving back to the communities in which we meet.
>
> —*Deborah Sexton, PCMA, interview, May 2010*

Meetings and events are the perfect tools for raising financial support for charities, and fundraising galas are one of this industry's most iconic styles of events. *Fundraising*, or *charity galas*, invite wealthy persons to donate to a charity and attend a formal evening of quality food and entertainment. At their May 2010 Waterloo Ball, which featured pop artist Billy Ocean and an auction with prizes donated by corporate sponsors, The Lord's Taverners (www.lordstaverners.org) raised £150,000 for children in Northern Ireland. Figure 10.1 describes the most common strategies for fundraising at meetings and events, along with environmentally friendly ideas for improving these strategies.

Auctions and raffles are popular mechanisms for raising funds, but they only work if the funds raised exceed the costs of the prizes. Seek out donations from corporate or private sponsors or stakeholders with the means to contribute goods or services. Many commercial enterprises, including restaurants, sports teams, theaters, and hotels, will donate a free meal, free tickets, or a free night's stay as a way of promoting their business. Seek out greener businesses to create sustainable partnerships. Figure 10.2 provides examples of environmentally friendly prizes that may be sought for charity events.

Through auctions, raffles, charity events, purchase-point donations, and cash-box donations, meetings and events can raise funds for charitable causes to improve social issues in their region. Any donation, no matter how small, can make a big impact in the lives of those less fortunate.

Strategy	Standard Description	Greener Ideas
Charity Gala	Guests donate to attend a prestigious gala, attended by prominent figures and featuring a gourmet meal, full bar, and entertainment.	Greener galas feature organic foods, energy-efficient lighting, and fewer transportation emissions.
Raffle	Attendees purchase raffle tickets to win items that have been donated.	Raffle organic, sustainable prizes and recycle raffle tickets.
Silent auction	Donated products or services are beautifully presented, along with a ballot form where attendees write the amount they are willing to bid for these items. After a decided deadline, the highest bidders win.	Auction sustainable prizes and decorate auction table with live plants.
Live auction	Donated products or services are presented by an auctioneer for attendees to bid on as part of a live crowd, often using personalized bidding signs.	Reuse bidding signs.
Purchase-point donation	Attendees are invited to add a charitable donation at the point of purchase. For instance, when registering for a conference online, the user may be asked if he/she would like to donate $5 to a nominated charity.	Use online, paperless registration and donation.
Cash donation box	Secure display box with educational signage allows attendees to donate cash during the event experience.	Create a beautiful display featuring organic materials or live plants that will attract attendees.

Figure 10.1 Event Fundraising Strategies

■ In-Kind Support

Supporting a charity by donating goods and/or services, rather than funds, is called *in-kind support*. Food redistribution programs, as undertaken by the National Football League (NFL) and San Francisco's Moscone Center (www.moscone.com), are an excellent way to support local schools, hospitals, and other social services in-kind. Owners of extra-technical equipment might choose to loan it to a local theater company. Convention centers or sports arenas often rent out their facilities to registered charities at a reduced rate.

Consider any surplus assets that you have available, such as extra tables, chairs, linens, or even tents. You can support a chosen charity by loaning them these goods for free or at a reduced rate, to be used at their next charity event. You may receive publicity, and attract new clients.

Type of Prize	Examples
Goods	Local gourmet foods
	Fine organic wines
	Signed books, CDs, or memorabilia
	Free magazine subscriptions
Experiences	Dinner for two at a fancy organic restaurant
	Free night's stay at a four-star greener hotel
	Lunch at an organic restaurant with a celebrity
Packages	Two complimentary tickets to a Broadway show, preshow drinks, and a backstage tour to meet the cast.
	VIP box seats to a sporting event, including complimentary drinks and a signed jersey.
	Vacation package, including train tickets, stay at a greener hotel, dinner at an organic restaurant, tickets to a show, and a bicycle tour.

Figure 10.2   Greener Prizes for Charity Auctions and Raffles

Carbon Offsetting

Some meetings and events use the data from their carbon footprint calculations or their eco-budgets to pinpoint their carbon emissions, and then offset them with the appropriate number of trees planted, or dollars contributed toward environmental charities. *Native*Energy (www.nativeenergy.com) is a company that offsets the carbon emissions from many events and conferences. By contributing toward environmental causes, *Native*Energy can offset the emissions resulting from heating, cooling, and lighting at event venues, as well as emissions from speaker travel and hotel accommodations. It also enables attendees to purchase their own offsets to address their travel to and from meetings and events.

"Any company that is engaged in sustainable business practices eventually has to address the impact of its energy use and business practices on the global climate," said Thomas Rawls, vice president of sales and marketing for *Native*Energy, in our discussion in September 2010. Rawls advocates for companies to minimize their environmental impacts as much as possible, but knows that any modern enterprise will still have a carbon footprint. "Companies that are serious about being sustainable understand the value carbon offsets as a tool to reduce the overall environmental consequences of their business practices."

Rawls says that companies that buy offsets understand that they are an effective tool to address climate change, and also that offset projects can bring other environmental benefits, such as the improvement of water quality in the case of farm methane projects. "In addition," he says, "*Native*Energy's innovative projects promote sustainable economic development in small towns, rural communities, and on tribal lands."

When purchasing *carbon credits*, the financial units in which carbon offsetting is measured, greener meeting and event pioneers should seek meaningful and relevant offsetting projects, locally if possible. Figure 10.3 describes some of the varied projects supported by a few industry-certified carbon offsetting companies.

Over the past few years, Rawls has seen buyers of carbon offsets become more sophisticated in their purchases, insisting on real and permanent reductions that are produced by projects that have been reviewed and certified to the leading offset standards. "This increased reliance on standards developed by independent environmental and policy leaders provides a solid foundation for offsets, which has led to increased confidence among buyers," he says.

Rawls believes that carbon offsetting should be done in tandem with more efficient and sustainable operations, saying, "By operating more efficiently and offsetting emissions that cannot be eliminated, buyers are taking powerful actions. Offset projects create reductions in greenhouse gas emissions that are not regulated and otherwise would drive further warming."

For many of the companies with whom *Native*Energy works, sustainability in general and offsetting emissions in particular are simply part of who they are. "Corporate responsibility is part of their DNA," says Rawls. "Increasingly, companies recognize that consumers expect firms to behave ethically. Environmental and social responsibility is a requirement for business success, and the use of offsets is one of many tools available to companies to develop a coherent and effective approach to greater responsibility."

Provider	Sample Project
Native Energy (www.nativeenergy.com)	Purchasing new separating equipment for composting manure and reducing methane emissions at the Laurelbrook Farm in East Canaan, Connecticut
TerraPass (www.terrapass.com)	Converting methane emissions into electricity at the City of Charleston Landfill in West Virginia
Carbonfund.org (www.carbonfund.org)	Supporting the Bajaj Finserv Wind Project to provide renewable energy in India
The Carbon Neutral Company (www.carbonneutral.com)	Replacing heavy oil with renewable biomass to power three ceramic brick manufacturing facilities in Rio de Janeiro, Brazil
Climate Care (www.jpmorganclimatecare.com)	Installing a new high pressure biomass boiler for steam generation at La Providencia Sugar Mill in Argentin

Figure 10.3 Carbon Offsetting Projects

Human Resources

Rather than channel your CSR initiatives to distant developing countries through carbon offsetting, try improving the social sustainability of your own workplace through better human resource (HR) management. Begin by ensuring that you comply with government regulations for a safe and productive working environment. In the United States, contact the Department of Labor (DOL) (www.dol.gov) to assess your HR policies.

Make sure that your workplace is a healthy, happy environment. Consider exercise initiatives, such as a free or discounted gym membership or optional morning yoga classes in a large conference room. Add live plants, or even a vegetable garden if space is available. Make sure that reusable mugs, plateware, and cutlery are available in the staff kitchen, and use local, organic foods for staff meetings. Consider providing fresh fruit and educating staff on advice for healthy living.

Switching to organic, environmentally friendly cleaning products can really improve the work experience of your maintenance and janitorial staff. Kimberley Lewis, vice president for events at the U.S. Green Building Council (USGBC) (www.usgbc.gov), told me in May 2010, "When you think about operations and maintenance and green cleaning products, you're thinking about your employees who have to clean with those toxins. Sourcing green cleaning products shows that you care about your employees and their health."

Many greener employers are encouraging staff to walk, cycle, or use public transport to get to and from work and meetings. Consider providing a secure bike rack and discounts at a local bike shop. At their new sustainable campus, Queen Margaret University (www.qmu.ac.uk) in Edinburgh, Scotland, provides an enormous bike rack for staff and students, which is prominently displayed and nearly always full of bikes. They also provide a free locker room and showers for these academic athletes.

One of President Obama's most exciting initiatives is Green Jobs (www.dol.gov/dol/green), which promotes environmental jobs that contribute to the green economy. In the United Kingdom, *The Sunday Times* annually ranks the greenest companies, and in 2009, ranked Forster, The National Magazine Company, and MediaCom in the top ten ("Best Green Companies 2009"). Figure 10.4 showcases some of the outstanding sustainable HR initiatives on offer at these companies.

Patricia Griffin, president and founder of the "Green" Hotels Association® (www.greenhotels.com), has seen environmental programs inspire staff to excellence. "The green programs create wonderful camaraderie among staff," she says, "which means enthusiastic staff." Providing office gardens and shower rooms are great ways to share sustainable rewards with employees. As part of its Green to Gold campaign, the DOL is recognizing companies that promote green job growth (http://www.dol.gov/dol/green/greengoldsafe.htm).

Equality

One of the most important aspects of social sustainability is the principle of equality. Conduct a thorough audit of your hiring, contracting, and other business practices to

Company	Green HR Initiatives
Forster (www.forster.co.uk): Communications agency	Employees earn five minutes of vacation time for every trip to and from work made by foot or bike. Provide route maps and organizes bicycling confidence sessions. Give staff hot water bottles and sweaters in winter to reduce heat energy.
The National Magazine Company (www.natmags.co.uk): Magazine publisher	Awards up to £200 for best green ideas. Cavity wall insulation keeps staff warm. Dual flush toilets use less water.
MediaCom (mediacomuk.com): Media agency	Encourages employees to walk or bike to work and to meetings. Provides shower and changing rooms for those who bike or walk to work. Turned central London office balconies into vegetable gardens. Challenged staff teams to grow the best-looking tomato.

Figure 10.4 Top UK Green HR Initiatives
Check out *The Sunday Times'* Best Green Companies: business.timesonline.co.uk.

ensure that there is absolutely no discrimination based on sex, race, age, heritage, background, or any other demographic quality.

Assess the diversity of your staff and stakeholders, and ask whether this matches the diversity of your region. Rarely will a staff population perfectly match the regional population, and this may be for innocent reasons. However, you may not be aware of hiring or contracting practices that exclude or discourage certain demographics. Are you giving disadvantaged groups an opportunity to apply for positions, or are these groups perhaps intimidated by your hiring practices?

If staff and stakeholders are predominantly of one majority demographic, in an otherwise widely diverse region, and no practical reasons for this can be deduced, you may wish to consider assessing your hiring and contracting practices. How might you encourage the rest of your regional population to apply for positions with your company? By taking part in this process, you may learn more about the regional population and culture, helping your business to better serve this area.

One tool to help chart your progress in this area is an *Equal Opportunities Monitoring Form.* Attached to all job or vendor applications, this voluntary form asks for ethnographic data such as race, sex, and age from the applicant. The form must be anonymous, and thus completely separated from the application form, but helps to track the diversity of applications received.

It is extremely important to be sensitive when communicating about equality on the workforce. Saying that you would like to hire a specific demographic can be just as insensitive and potentially offensive as saying that you would not like to hire this same demographic. Equality does not mean giving an advantage to one group; it means giving an equal opportunity to everyone.

Frank Supovitz, vice president of events for the National Football League (NFL), knows the importance of equality and fairness in hiring and contracting practices. This is why he asks key contractors to use the NFL's emerging business program database to qualify businesses owned by women and minorities for subcontracts. He noted that by communicating this sensitivity up front, the NFL can avoid future problems.

One additional aspect of equality is language. If your staff, stakeholders, and attendees speak languages other than English, consider translating your documents into these languages for them. Consider providing public documents and signage in the languages of your region.

Accessibility

According to the United States Census Bureau's 2002 Survey of Income and Program Participation (SIPP), there are 51.2 million Americans with disabilities, approximately 18 percent of the entire population. If your next meeting or event reflects the national average, one out of every six attendees may have a disability of some kind. Make sure that staff, stakeholders, and attendees with disabilities receive equal opportunities and accessible facilities before, during, and after the event experience.

Your first step toward accessibility is understanding the appropriate terminology to use in this sensitive area. Using sensitive, accurate, and consistent language can help to ensure that everyone feels welcome and no offense is taken. Although this terminology evolves over time, Figure 10.5 offers some basic guidelines.

Teach your staff the correct terminology for addressing persons with disabilities, and also engage them in sensitivity training. For instance, when talking to persons with disabilities, make sure not to raise your voice or talk as if speaking to a child. Do not interrupt a person with a speech impairment, trying to finish sentences for them. When addressing a person with a disability, speak clearly, at a normal volume, and directly to them, rather than to their friend or support worker. When addressing a person in a wheelchair, avoid standing above them for a prolonged period, sitting or crouching down so as to address them at eye level.

The *Americans with Disabilities Act (ADA)* is a federal civil rights law that prohibits discrimination against people with disabilities. The U.S. government provides guidance for businesses to comply with the ADA at www.ada.gov/business. The ADA requires that businesses modify policies and practices that discriminate against the disabled, comply with accessible design standards, and provide auxiliary aids and services when necessary. The federal government rewards businesses that comply with these standards through tax credits or deductions. Figure 10.6 outlines some basic ADA guidelines that you may apply to your next meeting or event.

Do Say	Description	Don't Say
Persons with disabilities	Persons with any impairments, activity limitations, or participation restrictions	The disabled, the handicapped
Mentally disabled	Persons with any cognitive, sensory, emotional, or developmental impairments, activity limitations, or participation restrictions	Retarded, slow, crazy
Persons with physical disabilities	Persons with any physical impairments, activity limitations, or participation restrictions	Handicapped, crippled
Visually impaired	Persons with partial or complete loss of sight	Blind
Hearing impaired	Persons with partial or complete hearing loss	Deaf
Person of short stature or little person	Any person significantly below the average height for a person of the same age and sex	Midget, dwarf
Wheelchair user	Any person using a wheelchair	Wheelchair bound

Figure 10.5 Dos and Don'ts of Accessibility Terminology

Clear all accessible walkways and parking spaces of snow, debris, gravel, and leaves.

Provide accessible pathways at least 3 feet wide.

Provide ramps for any elevated pathways.

Provide clear signage directing patrons toward accessible entrances and pathways.

Provide accessible countertops lowered to suit patrons using wheelchairs.

Ensure that all restrooms are fully accessible.

Ensure that all signs include Braille translation.

Provide Braille and large-print alternatives to all printed materials.

Provide audio enhancement devices.

Provide captioning services or audio description.

Inform all employees about accessibility services, appropriate behavior, and language.

Figure 10.6 Accessibility Guidelines from the Americans with Disabilities Act (ADA)

Consider implementing an *accessibility audit*, or an assessment of your meeting or event's accessibility for patrons of all abilities. Engage with disabled stakeholders to find ways to serve them better. Distribute an accessible survey in large print or Braille, or have a member of staff conduct survey research orally. Conduct on-site walkthroughs with disabled stakeholders, looking for any possible impediments to their experience.

Work together with persons with disabilities to ensure that your next meeting or event is completely accessible to all persons. Accessibility is a key aspect of social sustainability, and an accessible experience can ensure a lasting, positive impact on attendees. Kimberly Lewis believes that equality and accessibility are two of the best outcomes for sustainable events, saying, "Everybody has a hand in making the change, and that is my inspiration."

Local Roots

Locally produced foods are extremely popular at the moment, as customers increasingly want to support small, local providers. Customers demand products attached to a specific person or location, such as a local farmer or farm. Greener meeting and event pioneers can capitalize on this trend by sourcing not just goods but also services such as catering, decoration, and entertainment from local markets. Figure 10.7 provides a local shopping list, featuring fun ideas for local goods and services at greener meetings and events.

The Big Tent Festival in Fife, Scotland, is a fantastic example of how local goods, services, décor, and entertainment can improve an event. Attendees were thrilled with Pillars of Hercules's tent featuring local farm produce and hay bale furniture. Local Puddledub burgers were a hit, as was the smoked fish from Arbroath. Regional artisans showed their talent at the traditional craft of woodcarving, displaying amazing furniture and sculptures. Although the musical performances featured artists from as far afield as Brazil, the headline acts were King Creosote (www.kingcreosote.com), a major recording artist from Fife, and Roseanne Cash (www.rosannecash.com), daughter of Johnny Cash, whose ancestors came from Fife.

Although the local aspects of the Big Tent Festival wowed eco-conscious attendees and provided a truly unique experience, the actual benefits of local goods and services go far beyond that.

In addition to these benefits, local sourcing shows your commitment to a more sustainable society. Look for smaller food, service, decoration, and entertainment providers that are local to the region of your next meeting or event. Local roots make for stronger and more unique meetings and events.

Legacy

Like a musical performance or a ballet, a meeting or event is a temporary occurrence that exists in a specific time. However, viewed through the prism of sustainable development, greener meeting and event pioneers consider the effects that these temporary occurrences can have in the far future. In addition to negative impacts like pollution, meetings and events also have the potential to create positive impacts, or lasting legacies, for the

Category	Local Providers
Food and drink	Neighboring farms can provide fruits, vegetables, milk, and meat. Regional fisheries can provide fresh, local seafood. Local microbreweries and wineries can provide beer and wine.
Linens and decor	Support local linen hire businesses. If possible, use linens weaved by local artisans. Support local florists who use live, organic, regional plants. Team with local artists for design and decoration.
Sets and signage	Support local signage and production companies. Pursue reused materials from other local organizations. For larger signs, hire local artists, or, if appropriate, schoolchildren.
Handouts and prizes	Procure handouts with regional significance, such as seeds for local plants. Use regional crafts. Consider planting a tree or a garden in a local area in recognition of an honoree.
Entertainment	Hire local performers. Represent local music, such as Dixieland Jazz in New Orleans or Go-Go bands in Washington, DC. Consider hiring local amateur groups, such as school choirs, as support acts.

Figure 10.7 Local Shopping List

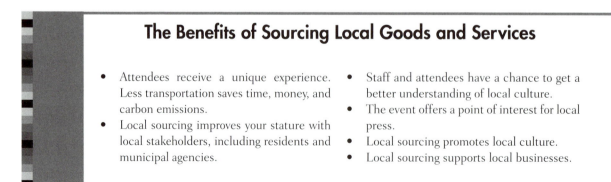

The Benefits of Sourcing Local Goods and Services

- Attendees receive a unique experience. Less transportation saves time, money, and carbon emissions.
- Local sourcing improves your stature with local stakeholders, including residents and municipal agencies.

- Staff and attendees have a chance to get a better understanding of local culture.
- The event offers a point of interest for local press.
- Local sourcing promotes local culture.
- Local sourcing supports local businesses.

regional or global environment and population. These legacies might include improved health, rebuilt ecosystems, and revitalized urban environments.

Health

One key aspect of a sustainable society is the health of the population. Poor eating habits and lack of exercise are common social problems that affect health, and meetings and events have the power to educate people and promote more healthy habits.

As a major sports organization, the National Football League (NFL) understands that regular exercise can empower people to do great things, and one of its key initiatives is to fight childhood obesity and encourage good nutrition. Supovitz explains that the NFL's Play 60 initiative encourages children to play for 60 minutes per day. "We'd like it to involve football, sure," he told me in May 2010, "but run around, play tag, play another sport, just get out there and be active. This promotes good health through a lifestyle change, and those effects can be life-long."

The NFL supports its Play 60 initiative through various events, including flag football games. "This provides kids with a way to enjoy a lower impact version of our game," says Supovitz. "Come to an event and you'll see flag football clinics, running games, passing games and kicking games." Supovitz believes that inspiring children to exercise at Play 60

A book exchange at the Edinburgh Festival Fringe allows performers and visitors to trade used books.

events is a powerful legacy for NFL: "It can be as exciting to participate in that kind of environment as it is to watch the best of the game show their stuff."

You can help attendees make healthy lifestyle choices by promoting healthy eating and exercise at meetings and events. Rather than provide extra-large portions of food on each plate, consider allowing attendees to choose their own serving sizes. Feature fruits and vegetables in catering menus, and avoid excessively unhealthy foods. Providing gourmet organic foods is a great way to get attendees excited about healthy eating options. Offer fun, interactive exercise activities such as a bicycle race or basketball tournament. Even light activities such as walking or stretching can promote exercise and break up a meeting or conference.

Ecosystem Rebuilding

London 2012 (www.london2012.com) is committed to delivering a truly sustainable Olympic Games. In addition to reducing waste, promoting inclusion, encouraging healthy living, and combating climate change, London 2012 views protecting and promoting regional biodiversity and ecology as a key part of the London 2012 legacy. Its approach includes minimizing and mitigating the impact of construction activity, developing new and enhanced water and land habitats, implementing the Olympic Park Biodiversity Action Plan, protecting sensitive habitats and species at other competition sites, and promoting awareness of the value of biodiversity and its links to sport and healthy living.

The Masterplan for the Olympic Park includes the creation of 45 hectares of new habitat and 102 hectares of open space, in an area currently deprived of green space. The new habitats include wetland, open river banks, and grassland. These will form part of one of the largest new urban parks that Europe has seen in the last 150 years. A process has been established to protect existing habitats during construction, and more than 5 km of waterways have been improved within the Olympic Park site, including removal of rubbish, dredging and repairing river walls. The first tree was planted on the Park by Her Majesty the Queen in November 2009. There will be a total of 4,000 trees planted around the Olympic Park and Olympic Village. To ensure the sustainability of the Olympic Park, an area the size of 10 soccer fields has been cleared of weeds, 675 bird and bat boxes will be installed, and more than 4,000 square meters of living roof will be created.

London 2012's plans represent one of the most ambitious and far-reaching plans for ecosystem rebuilding ever undertaken by an event, but your meeting or event can improve the environment in many ways as well. Gardening is a fun, inspirational activity that is accessible to all. Challenge your attendees to get down and dirty during their next breakout session and spend an hour of supervised gardening on the meeting or event grounds.

London 2012 has created various initiatives to encourage interest in biodiversity. These include inviting the public to design a Great British Garden for the Olympic Park and encouraging schoolchildren to design bug hotels as part of the EDF Energy education program (www.jointhepod.org/), as well as various tree-planting initiatives as part of the London 2012 Inspire Programme. You can challenge your attendees to envision a garden that reflects regional biodiversity and culture. Research the environmental issues of your ecosystem and discuss with attendees ways to protect and promote local plants and wildlife.

Pillars of Hercules serves organic food at The Big Tent.

Urban Regeneration

On an abandoned inner-city block on the gritty streets of Glasgow, Scotland, two urban youths disappear down a darkened alleyway to visit a derelict building site, where they deal with their business. Their business is gardening.

These youths are participating in SAGE (Sow And Grow Everywhere), an urban gardening project created by NVA (www.nva.org.uk), an innovative public arts company based in Glasgow. With the support of ERZ landscape architects, SAGE transforms vacant city blocks into vibrant gardens and allotments for city dwellers to grow their own food, thus supporting *urban regeneration*, or the improvement and revival of the urban environment and the quality of life for urban residents.

Kathy Speirs, project coordinator at NVA, explains that once these urban allotments are set up, they are managed by community groups. When I spoke with her in September 2010, she explained, "Just like any local project, the community has to take ownership. There has to be sustained support at the beginning, but at some point you have to leave, to allow them to get on with it." Speirs said that you can't just set up an urban garden and walk away. "You need community engagement to allow them to come together, and it's a tricky process."

As part of its commitment to urban regeneration, in August 2010, NVA produced Glasgow Harvest, a celebration of urban farming. Envisaging something similar to an event held at the Champs Elysee in Paris, NVA initially wanted to stage it in Glasgow's central plaza, George Square. While they may do this in the future, the first Glasgow

Harvest was instead hosted by the Hidden Gardens (www.thehiddengardens.org.uk), a former industrial wasteland behind the Tramway performing arts center (www.tramway .org), which NVA transformed into a community garden space in 2003.

Glasgow Harvest featured many elements, including a Jam Wall, a 3D interactive shelving unit to which attendees could add their own homegrown jars of jam. Lit from behind, the unit illuminated the multicolored jars of jam to produce a rainbow spectrum. Speirs says that the creator, artist Rachel Mimiec, wanted the participants to be the artists.

Attendees were encouraged to compete in the Creative Container Challenge, in which contestants grew plants in unusual reused or decorated items. "A container made

Greener Sports Event: The National Football League (NFL) Super Bowl

The 2010 Super Bowl XLIV, in which the New Orleans Saints triumphed over the Indianapolis Colts, was the most watched television program in history, beating the final episode of *M*A*S*H* with 153.8 million U.S. viewers. As America's top sporting event, everyone knows the Super Bowl, but few know the rigorous environmental policies that are annually implemented to keep this mega-event sustainable and responsible.

Vice president of events for the National Football League (NFL) Frank Supovitz explains that, after each Super Bowl, cardboard, wood products, office supplies, cloth, paper, office supplies, plastics and metals are recovered and recycled before they get into the waste stream. "We also recover used sports equipment through students in the host cities of Super Bowls," says Supovitz. "Not just football equipment, but bats, mitts, protective gear, anything that would go to waste because a kid has outgrown it, and we get them to families that may not be able to afford them. It's another way of doing good while reducing waste flow."

The NFL sees this commitment to waste reduction and redistribution as the right thing to do, rather than a marketing angle, which is why these initiatives are unpublicized, and many are surprised to hear about them. "We recover 90,000 pounds of unserved prepared foods left over," says Supovitz, "not only from NFL activities at the Super Bowl, but also from participating hotels, broadcasters, sponsors, and events not affiliated directly with the league, and get them to shelters and food distribution services."

This is in addition to the efforts of Hunger Related Events, Inc., the charity that runs "Taste of the NFL" in every Super Bowl city. "'Taste' involves restaurants representing NFL home team cities all over the country in an upscale tasting event on the night before the game," says Supovitz, "and it is the single most successful annual fundraising event of the weekend, generating between $400,000 and $700,000 annually for America's Second Harvest."

"We are also proud of our carbon mitigation efforts," says Supovitz. "Trees are planted to mitigate some of the emissions we will add to the environment during the time we're in town. For Super Bowl XLII in Arizona, our efforts helped repopulate an area of the Chadeski-Rodeo forest that had been hit with a forest fire before our arrival. In South Florida, trees were from toy building blocks won, but there were containers made from old television sets, a toaster, and even a guitar case," says Speirs.

27 Glasgow schools also participated in the Double Rubble Chip Challenge, in which students grew potatoes and brought them to Glasgow Harvest to be turned into one of Britain's favorite foods, chips (known as french fries in the United States). At Glasgow Harvest, children peeled and chopped potatoes as dinner ladies from their schools cooked the chips. Each school's chips were judged by the audience in a blind tasting, and the schools with the best chips won £100 to improve their school environment, which could include a garden or new furniture.

added to Florida Keys that lost foliage due to hurricanes."

As part of its commitment to leaving a positive legacy, the NFL builds a community youth center, called a Youth Education Town (YET), in every city that hosts a Super Bowl. "NFL YET Centers have been around for 15 years," says Supovitz. "They are brick-and-mortar facilities, most often run by the local Boys & Girls Club, that offer low-income and at-risk youth a safe, supportive environment that offers educational, recreational and life-skill growth opportunities.

Every year, the NFL donates $1 million toward a YET in the Super Bowl host town. "Some cities have more than one YET," says Supovitz, "like the Miami–Ft. Lauderdale and Tampa–St. Petersburg areas, but most often, we build one, and if we return, we donate the same amount to help refurbish or recapitalize an existing NFL YET."

"In 2009, the NFL opened its first YET Center in a non-Super Bowl region," says Supovitz. "In recognition of the state of Hawaii playing host to 30 years of the Pro Bowl, our annual all-star game, the NFL funded and built a YET Center in Nanakuli, a Hawaiian Homelands area on the island of Oahu." Supovitz is particularly proud of this center because, with solar panels installed on its roof, it is the first YET designed to be LEED certified by the U.S. Green Building Council (USGBC).

Supovitz's advice to green event pioneers is this:

> Do what's right for the right reason. It's easy to engage in environmental programs because you might think it would make people feel better about your event, company, or brand, but the public is getting increasingly hip to self-serving programs. If you're doing the right things because they are the right things to do, the public will see your efforts as real, genuine, and appreciated. Buying renewable energy credits is laudable, but it's too easy and leaves the work to someone else. Show the community you care enough to roll up your sleeves and actively improve the environment, or mitigate the ecological effects of your event on the region.
>
> —*Frank Supovitz, NFL, interview,*
> *May 2010*

By recovering and redistributing thousands of pounds of sports equipment, event materials, and foods, as well as making enormous contributions to environmental and social charities, the NFL shows a determination to roll up its sleeves and get the job done. Supovitz and his team make social and environmental responsibility an integral part of their high-profile business.

"We are getting children to grow potatoes and enjoy eating what they've made," says Speirs, who counts the Double Rubble Chip Challenge as one of the most successful events at Glasgow Harvest. "They really enjoyed it. Everyone loves chips in Glasgow."

Although chips are not always the healthiest of foods, the emphasis was on empowering children to grow and cook their own food. "Our emphasis is not on health, but health comes with it when you're cooking and growing your own food," says Speirs. "One of the major byproducts of home growing is that you eat less fast food." She believes that rather than preach, "It's important to maintain neutrality and not make villains out of fast food chains."

Speirs has seen projects similar to SAGE and Glasgow Harvest in the revitalization of New York and Chicago, which has given her hope for Glasgow. "As Glasgow was an industrial city, many tenements are not set up with green space," she says. "We want to inspire people to change their lifestyle and work to improve their environment."

Sustainable Communities

ASAE has already made achievements in creating guidelines for social responsibility, but president and CEO John Graham says that he looks forward to ASAE's continuing involvement as a facilitator of social responsibility discussion in the association and non-profit community. "Social responsibility is definitely a journey."

> I think every organization should adopt a social responsibility platform and work closely with staff, members and/or stakeholders to become more responsible with their actions and consider the long-term implications of their decisions not only on the environment, but also on the communities where we live and work. Obviously we can't do much alone, but even the smallest steps, like starting a recycling campaign or working with a local school, can have a tremendous impact on the greater community.
>
> —*John Graham, ASAE, interview, May 2010*

Greener meeting and event pioneers can use tools such as CSR, volunteerism, philanthropy, equality, and accessibility to create a legacy of social sustainability. We can work together to improve our communities and create enhanced standards of living.

Summary

A commitment to social sustainability can be just as important as environmental protection at greener meetings and events. Develop a CSR commitment to the community through volunteer, financial, in-kind support, or carbon offsetting. Conduct an audit of your human resources, equality, and accessibility policies to ensure that staff, stakeholders, and attendees are happy, healthy, and comfortable. Source goods and services locally to provide unique experiences and support the regional economy. Most importantly, consider ways in which to leave a positive legacy for your region—one that could include improved health, rebuilt ecosystems, or urban regeneration.

Key Terms and Definitions

- **Corporate social responsibility (CSR)**: a theory promoting ethical and charitable corporate behavior.
- **Philanthropy**: the act of charitable aid or responsibility.
- **Charity galas**: formal events featuring quality food and entertainment for guests who make donations to charitable causes.
- **In-kind support**: supporting a charity by donating goods and/or services, rather than funds.
- **Carbon credits**: the financial units in which carbon offsetting is measured.
- **Equal Opportunities Monitoring Form**: a form that requests ethnographic data from potential job applicants or contractors, in order to track the diversity of applicants. Forms must be submitted anonymously, and separated from the application form.
- **Americans with Disabilities Act (ADA)**: a federal civil rights law that prohibits discrimination against people with disabilities.
- **Accessibility audit**: an assessment of your meeting or event's accessibility for patrons of all abilities.
- **Ecosystem rebuilding**: preservation and promotion of regional biodiversity and ecology.
- **Urban regeneration**: the improvement and revival of the urban environment and the quality of life for urban residents.

Blue Sky Thinking

You are in charge of planning a major corporation's annual Employee Celebration Day, in which employees enjoy free food, drink, entertainment, and activities in celebration of their work. Plan activities that showcase the company's commitment to CSR and give employees an opportunity to improve their community or environment. How will you make sure that the day is accessible and welcoming to persons with disabilities?

Renewable Resources

Americans with Disabilities Act (www.ada.gov).

Hennigfeld, Judith, Manfred Pohl, and Nick Tolhurst (2006). *The ICCA Handbook on Corporate Social Responsibility.* Hoboken, NJ: John Wiley & Sons.

Llewellyn, A. Bronwyn (2008). *Green Jobs: A Guide to Eco-Friendly Employement.* Avon, MA: Adams Media.

London's Seventeen Events uses washable graffiti as sustainable signage to direct attendees to the hip, sustainable Ethical Awards.
Courtesy of Seventeen Events.

CHAPTER 11

Greener Meeting and Event Marketing

"Green marketing is mostly about making (breakthrough) green stuff seem normal—and not about making normal stuff seem green."

—*John Grant, in The Green Marketing Manifesto (2007)*

In this chapter, you will learn:

1. How to define features, benefits, and values to create an offer for your meeting or event

2. How various demographic segments perceive greener meetings and events

3. How to use online media and social networking to connect to attendees

4. How to write a blog or record a vlog

5. How to connect with attendees through grass roots efforts

6. How to use marketing tools strategically for each demographic segment

7. How to educate attendees on sustainability

8. How to secure appropriate sponsorship

9. How to achieve industry certification and recognition

10. How to avoid greenwash

As president and CEO of Meeting Professionals International (MPI) (www.mpiweb.org), Bruce MacMillan has seen many trends come and go. He believes that sustainability is here to stay. "The great news for our industry is that we've finally reached a tipping point where we are seeing mass engagement in sustainability and corporate social responsibility," he says. As sustainability increasingly becomes a core value of the meetings and events industry, MacMillan says that the way in which sustainable practices are communicated and marketed takes on new significance.

> The meetings industry is perhaps one of the unique industries that has such a global reach and touches so many different businesses and other industries. Our role is also very public and communicative, and therefore we have the possibility and maybe even a responsibility to be a role model for other industries in the inevitable, profitable and exciting journey towards a sustainable future.
> —Bruce MacMillan, Meeting Professionals International (MPI), interview, August 2010

As a highly visible industry that reaches across all sectors, meetings and events have a key role to play in communicating sustainability, and the way in which this is communicated can be just as important as the practices themselves.

The Green Offer

In order to formulate a comprehensive marketing plan for your next greener meeting or event, begin by defining what you have to offer. Gather your green team of staff and stakeholders for a session of blue sky thinking, and summarize the main features of the meeting or event you wish to market. Next, analyze the concrete benefits that these features bring to attendees, as well as the abstract values that these features promote. Figure 11.1 analyzes eight basic values of greener meetings and events, showing the benefits and values that these features promote.

A central selling point of any meeting or event should be a superior experience, which means both a smarter and a cleaner experience, both of which are deeply ingrained desires in the human mind. Ethics are important for greener attendees, which is why they seek the "feel-good" factor of reducing their personal carbon footprint. In addition to the critical business goal of efficiency and economy, there is also the basic desire to provide an outstanding, memorable event, which gives attendees the wow factor.

Your meeting or event may have some or all of these features in different proportion, or depending on its nature, may have altogether different qualities. Style is the most important criteria for a green fashion show, while social responsibility and equality are more important for a political convention.

In addition to these motivating forces that pull attendees toward the meeting or event, there are also antagonizing forces that can push attendees away. Ask your green team to think of some potential attitudes or perceptions, whether true or false, that could turn people away from the meeting or event. Figure 11.2 shows some common antagonists for sustainable practices and how to combat these negative attitudes.

Features: *What is it?*	Benefits: *What does it do for me?*	Values: *What does it mean to me?*
Superior experience	Provides seamless, unforgettable event experience	Teaches value of sustainability
Smarter event	Allows more efficient operation	Intelligence, business savvy
Cleaner event	Improves event atmosphere	Happier experience
Socially responsible	Makes a difference in society	Ethical backbone
Personal audit	Reduces individual carbon footprints	The "feel good" factor
Operating fairly	Creates equal, accessible experience	Equality
Economical (not wasteful)	Saves money and resources	Thrift
Stylish	Provides attractive event design	The wow factor

Figure 11.1   Motivating Forces behind Greener Meetings and Events

Antagonist	Solution
Skepticism of environmentalism	Frame green practices as stylish, economical, and efficient, rather than environmental
Perception that green practices hinder business as usual	Show how practices like going paper-less can make business operations more efficient
Dislike of change	Make gradual adjustments toward greener practices
Perception that green practices cost extra	Show how water and energy efficiency save funds
Disinterest in green practices	Do not overbroadcast or preach about your policies
Disinterest in social responsibility	Show how equality and accessibility improve the event experience, and how social responsibility attracts interest
Preference for luxury goods and services with negative environmental impacts	Provide luxury organic and ethical options

Figure 11.2   Potential Antagonists for Greener Meetings and Events

In marketing, bracing yourself for a negative response is just as important as planning for success. Be sure not to overpromise or preach about your sustainable practices, at the risk of exhausting attendees with too much information or setting their expectations too high. Avoid criticizing unsustainable practices; instead of talking about pollution and waste problems, talk about sustainable solutions. Kevin Danaher, executive co-producer of Green Festival (www.greenfestival.com), knows the importance of combating negative perceptions with positive ones. When we spoke in May 2010, he told me, "We liberals are often accused of being critical, so we want to provide solutions."

Look at the key features, benefits, values, and possible antagonists toward your meeting or event, and formulate your *offer*. Write a paragraph describing what unique, sustainable aspects your meeting or event has to offer attendees.

Sustainable Demographics

It is important to communicate to different sorts of attendees in different ways. Business-minded professionals will be interested in cost savings, while environmentalists will be more interested in carbon savings. There is now a wide spectrum of awareness about sustainability, and while many attendees at your next meeting or event may have no interest in or knowledge of sustainable practices, you may also find several highly aware and eco-savvy attendees.

Meeting or event attendees may exhibit a wide range of awareness and interest in sustainability, from environmental activists with expert knowledge, to skeptics who may dismiss any notion of sustainability. Somewhere in the middle are professionals with varying levels of commitment to environmental and social responsibility. Investigate these various *demographic segments*, or groups of persons with similar characteristics and behaviors, to assess the best ways to communicate your sustainable practices to them.

Environmentalists

Persons of any age, sex, race, or background who are firmly committed to improving the environment and actively attend greener meetings and events to increase their knowledge of sustainability and support sustainable causes can be described as environmentalists. These may include more extreme environmentalists, such as political activists, moderate environmentalists, or recreational environmentalists, such as nature enthusiasts.

Environmentalists can be the most rewarding demographic at any greener meeting or event, but they will also have the highest of expectations. Environmentalists want to do whatever is best for the planet, no matter the price. They will seek out greener meetings and events that have outstanding environmental and ethical policies, and will expect the most of them. They may choose to walk, cycle, or take public transportation to greener meetings and events to lower their footprint, and they will expect recycling facilities and organic food when they arrive. Environmentalists see these sustainable practices as a core reason to attend any meeting or event, rather than an additional benefit.

Meetings and events that are clearly labeled as environmental or sustainable are likely to attract environmentalists. To appease this demographic, plan a comprehensive sustainability program that touches each area of the meeting or event. You will impress environmentalists with a serious, far-reaching, hard-working campaign for sustainability, not with green gimmicks. Environmentalists will scrutinize events labeled as *carbon neutral* through the use of carbon offsetting, and they will expect an event to reduce its impact before offsetting it.

Danaher works hard to combat any potential skepticism from some of the more extreme environmental activist attendees. "Liberal people can confuse social enterprise with corporate domination," he explains. "For example, recently some people criticized our use of carbon offsets, and threatened to protest the Green Festival. Our solution was to give all the protesters free tickets, because we welcome that debate."

By allowing environmentalists to interact, discuss, and assist with the sustainable practices of your meeting or event, you can harness their knowledge and enthusiasm for a successful outcome. Welcome them into the debate, and allow their creative feedback.

Professionals

Corporate meetings, conferences, and events generally serve professionals, a demographic group that can be loosely defined as office workers aged between 21 and 65. This demographic may include a range of attitudes toward sustainability, from those who work explicitly for environmental causes to those completely uninterested. There also exists a broad spectrum of CSR commitments among professionals, from those with complex giving programs to those who support basic equality and accessibility standards.

All professionals should recognize the value of efficient business operations and cost-savings, two areas that can be emphasized when communicating sustainability to this group. Ethical professionals, or those with CSR commitments, will want to see their corporate values showcased in the event plan. They may make a priority of fair hiring practices, accessibility, support for local businesses, and ethical food sourcing. Professionals may require comprehensive and transparent sustainable policies that are managed and tracked over time.

Jeff Hall, executive chef at Savor . . . San Francisco, creates exquisite sustainable menus for many corporate events at the San Francisco Moscone Center. Hall says that attendee response has been very positive regarding sustainable foods. "Attendees are pleased to find out that much of the menu items are locally sourced and seasonal." He also reports that the professional attendees are becoming increasingly eco-conscious, requesting more advanced services.

> Creating menus that utilize sustainably produced product is greatly important for the future of the meetings and conventions industry. We are receiving more and more requests from our clients for food miles tracking, reporting on food donations, amount of product diverted from landfill and programs such as composting or recycling.
> —Jeff Hall, Savor. . . San Francisco, interview, August 2010

Professionals may not be as outspoken as environmentalists, but their needs for services that support their CSR commitments are increasingly advanced. Professionals will want to see sustainable practices managed, measured, and reported in a transparent manner.

Skeptics

When researching demographics, be sure to also research those groups that may *not* attend greener meetings or events, or those that may *not* show an interest in sustainable practices. Attendees may be indifferent, apathetic, or even skeptical of sustainable practices, depending on their background, education, and preconceived notions.

Those who are indifferent or apathetic toward sustainable practices may participate in greener meetings and events without even knowing it. Basic practices such as equality, accessibility, sustainable foods and water, and energy efficiency may be put in place with little notice. However, apathetic attendees may fail to appreciate greener activities requiring participation, from using public transportation to simply using recycling bins. It is your job to make these green practices as easy, normal, and pleasant as possible, so that attendees may participate in them without question.

There are always skeptics, so plan to face at least one opinionated attendee who may criticize your sustainable practices. Whether this person does not believe in the science of climate change, thinks recycling is a hoax, or prefers bottled water to filtered tap water, be prepared with answers to their criticism. Emphasize that these sustainable practices are in place to improve the meeting or event experience and to save resources and funds. Be sure to thank skeptics for their feedback, and then respond to their concerns. Figure 11.3 provides some useful talking points when responding to critical feedback.

Attendees of greener meetings and events may present a wide spectrum of different attitudes toward sustainability. Environmentalists will keenly appreciate detailed information on sustainability, seeking to participate in green practices, while skeptics may prove unreceptive. Figure 11.4 describes seven specific demographic segments that may attend greener meetings and events, as well as which style of communication each segment might be most receptive to.

Take a look at your original list of features, benefits, and values for greener meetings and events, and determine which of these qualities are most appropriate for each demographic segment. Ethical professionals, for instance, might be most interested in social responsibility, while indifferent professionals may be more interested in economy and style. Once you have assessed the qualities that each demographic segment expects from your greener meeting or event, you can design specific marketing tools to communicate these qualities.

> Marketing is the science and art of exploring, creating, and delivering value to satisfy the needs of a target market at a profit. Marketing identifies unfulfilled needs and desires. It defines, measures, and quantifies the size of the identified market and the profit potential. It pinpoints which segments the company is capable of serving best and it designs and promotes the appropriate products and services.
>
> —Dr. Philip Kotler, marketing expert (www.kotlermarketing.com)

Critical Feedback	Possible Response "Thank you for your feedback. . ."
Recycling is a waste of time and money.	"We reduce and reuse materials first, but for those materials that cannot be reused, we believe it is important to recycle them rather than increase our already over-full local landfill. We are working with industry-certified local recycling experts to ensure that our recycling stream is clean and efficient."
Why are we no longer serving foie gras? It is a delicious gourmet food.	"We are working to provide the most outstanding gourmet foods in our new sustainable menu, which sources rare local items and organic delicacies. Part of this commitment is to avoid unsustainably or unethically harvested foods, such as foie gras."
Why are you encouraging public transportation? It is filthy and unreliable.	"Our event is located directly next to a public transit station, in a central location convenient for many attendees. With several public transit services available, public transit is actually a faster and more convenient way of getting to and from our event, and reduces urban traffic congestion."
Your carbon offsetting program is a phony scam.	"We work hard to minimize our environmental impact as much as possible. Because renewable energy is not yet available in our area, we have chosen to offset our energy use by supporting local renewable energy projects through third-party verified, industry-certified renewable energy credits."
Why is bottled water not available at this meeting?	"Filtered tap water is available in all meeting rooms in refillable jugs with reusable glasses. While most attendees prefer glasses, if you prefer to use a plastic bottle, please feel free to bring one in and reuse it."
Climate change is a hoax.	"We are in the business of providing high-quality events that operate efficiently and provide excellent return on investment for our clients. No matter what you believe about climate change, our sustainable policies have saved money and resources for our clients and presented superior experiences for attendees."

Figure 11.3   Responding to Critical Feedback at Greener Meetings and Events

Sustainable Marketing Tools

As a consumer, you are no doubt familiar with the basic marketing tools that are used to sell goods and services. Advertising is the most widely recognized form of marketing, whether it is an ad in the newspaper, a banner ad on a Web site, a commercial on television or the radio, or a billboard on the highway. Other common forms of marketing include direct mail or telemarketing, where the consumer is contacted directly via mail or phone, and publicity, or press attention. Movie reviews, whether good or bad, are examples of publicity.

Demographic Segment	Description
Political activists	Strong-minded, fiercely individual persons, often aged either 15–25 or 45–65 (baby boomers), who expect to actively participate in extremely pro-environment activities
Strict environmentalists	Enthusiastic supporters of environmental policies who seek detailed information and the option to participate
Environmental professionals	Professionals, usually aged 21–65, with environmental business commitments who seek transparent sustainable policies, carefully managed, measured, and reported in professional style
Ethical professionals	Professionals, usually aged 21–65, with CSR commitments who seek socially responsible events with transparent CSR and sustainable policies, managed and measured professionally
Indifferent professionals	Professionals, usually aged 21–65, interested in quality meetings or events delivered in an efficient and economical fashion
Apathetic attendees	Persons not interested or unaware of sustainable policies, who may only participate if these policies are made easy, normal, and pleasant
Skeptics	Persons who may actively criticize sustainable policies because of preconceived notions or concerns about long-term ramifications of new technologies, or who require an explanation or justification for sustainable policies. Skeptics aren't always anti-green, as this otherwise indicates.

Figure 11.4 Demographic Segments for Greener Meetings and Events

There is a great deal of information available, in books and online, about these traditional marketing tools. In addition to these basic tools, greener meeting and event pioneers will pursue new and exciting marketing tools tailored for their sustainable outcomes. By using new technology and sustainable concepts, you can create powerful sustainable marketing tools.

Online Media and Social Networking

In the past ten years, no invention has changed our lives more than the Internet. Now widely available at work, at home, at cafes, on our televisions and on our phones, the Internet allows us to connect with people around the world in increasingly complex ways. Google (www.google.com) has been at the forefront of this revolution, creating Google Earth, Google Maps, and Google Streetview, which have effectively mapped out the entire public world and made it available to navigate online.

Perhaps just as influential is Facebook (www.facebook.com), which began life unassumingly as an online directory for undergraduate students at Harvard University and has grown exponentially to become the world's premier social networking site. Millions of users now log on to Facebook on a daily basis to connect with friends, share photographs, network, and, most important for our industry, plan events.

New Web sites appear every day offering new, interactive ways to connect with staff, stakeholders, and attendees of meetings or events. Many of these offer innovative new media, such as blogs, message boards, webcams, live chats, and streaming audio or video and podcasts. Figure 11.5 explains these new media tools, and shows how they can be used to promote greener meetings and events.

Setting up a blog or message board is free and easy, thanks to Web sites like Wordpress (www.wordpress.com), which offer free Web domains for this purpose. Webcams are

New Media Tool	Description	Green Ideas
Blogs	Online journals that allow a person or persons to post writings, and others to read and/or comment	Create a behind-the-scenes journal of the planning process for your environmental strategies.
Message boards	Discussion forums that allow groups of people to share messages on given topics	Allow attendees to post their ideas on how to make the next meeting more sustainable on your Web site's message board.
Webcams	Video cameras that post live video feeds straight to Web sites	Install a webcam in a garden of your office or meeting venue that you are revitalizing, showing viewers your planting progress.
Vlog	Video diary posted to the Internet where a person talks directly to the camera	Have your environmental champion post a vlog telling attendees about the environmental policies of your next meeting or event.
Live chats	Real-time discussion forums that allow persons to exchange messages live, over a set time period, often with a celebrity or person of interest responding to questions	Ask an eco-speaker for your next sustainable event to take part in a one-hour live chat, open to the public via your Web site, in promotion for the event,
Streaming media	Audio or video files, either pre-recorded or live, that can be experienced on a Web site	Set up a digital video recorder for the keynote speech of your next greener meeting and stream it live on the Web site for those unable to attend.
Podcasts	Prerecorded audio or video files, often radio programs, that can be downloaded to computers or portable entertainment devices	Make an audio recording of a panel discussion on sustainability and offer it for download as a free podcast.
Apps	Interactive computer applications for mobile devices, such as the iPod or iPad, which could do anything from locating the nearest library to teaching you how to speak Chinese	Create an app for meeting attendees that allows them to calculate their own carbon footprint, then offers them specific advice on how to reduce it.

Figure 11.5   New Online Media Tools

increasingly affordable, and Web sites such as YouTube (www.youtube.com) allow you to upload videos to the Internet for free. Streaming media from your Web site or creating podcasts or apps will require technical assistance and some investment, but are still a very low-cost marketing strategy for small businesses. Indeed, most social media Web sites are free to use, while others charge just a small subscriber fee. The biggest cost may be purchasing greater processing capacity, or *bandwidth*, in order to present and transmit large media files on your Web site. Figure 11.6 outlines how some of the top Web sites for social networking can be used to promote greener meetings and events.

In promoting Glasgow Harvest, a celebration of urban gardening, producers NVA (www.nva.org.uk) used social media and online viral marketing to bring together the urban gardening community. "There are many different styles of gardeners, depending on their experience, whether they are traditional or guerilla gardeners, and we are trying to connect them all," says Kathy Speirs, project coordinator, who I spoke with in September 2010.

Web Site	Description	Green Ideas
Facebook (www.facebook.com)	Users register basic details and interests in order to connect with friends, send messages, share pictures and links, and invite others to join groups or attend events.	Form a Facebook group for your next meeting or event and send members special updates and behind-the-scenes insight.
Twitter (www.twitter.com)	Users post 140-character status updates, called *tweets*, to tell the world what they are up to.	Have the person in charge of your environmental plan start a Twitter account to give a view into the details of his or her job.
Flickr (www.flickr.com)	Users can store and share digital pictures.	Start a Flickr account for an outdoor event and invite all attendees to post photos. Award a winner for the best nature photo.
YouTube (www.youtube.com)	Users can upload and share digital videos.	Have your CEO record a short vlog about sustainability and post it to YouTube, then send links to it via Facebook.
MySpace (www.myspace.com)	Social networking site, similar to Facebook, but more popular for promoting artists and brands	Create a MySpace account for your event and post video or audio files.

Figure 11.6 Top Social Networking Web Sites

NVA gave away free chard and courgette plants and encouraged people to document their growing processes on Flickr. It also organized a Jam Dating Agency, a discussion forum on Facebook for jam makers to trade fruits, recipes, and jams. "We wanted to connect to new audiences, and also the many allotment societies in Glasgow," says Speirs, "so we started using Twitter and Facebook. We are trying to develop our audience with new mediums."

This online media and social networking brought a lot of new people together at the event, according to Speirs. "There was a real mix of people at Glasgow Harvest, and that was one of the most satisfying things about it," she says. "We had brilliant feedback from the whole day. It hit a real nerve."

A lot of people pitched up who were just growing privately in window boxes or back courts, which was a real joy for us. One of our intentions was to galvanize the silent growing majority, to "out" these secret gardens. The more people that know this is happening, the better.
—*Kathy Speirs, NVA, interview, September 2010*

Glasgow Harvest successfully brought the traditions of gardening into the twenty-first century with new media and social networking. Greener meetings and events can find increasingly creative ways to mix blogs and vlogs, live chats and live streams, Facebook, and YouTube to present attendees with a robust package of interactive media experiences. New media are not only effective, they are also paperless, thus reducing paper waste. Carbonfund.org even offers a way to make your blog or Web site carbon neutral at www. carbonfund.org/carbonfreewebsite.

Sustainable Spectacles

Public spectacles, whether parades of elephants, ribbon-cutting ceremonies, or fireworks, are one of the most old-fashioned ways of promoting a meeting or event. New technology, however, can create innovative spectacles that show off sustainability and generate the wow factor. These sustainable spectacles can make lasting impressions on even the most apathetic of attendees.

At the 2010 Coachella Valley Music and Arts Festival (www.coachella.com) in California, arts group Crimson Collective (www.crimsonsociety.org/crimsoncollective .html) created an enormous structure resembling an origami crane that loomed above attendees, providing shade and making a striking sight. At night, low-energy lighting illuminated the crane, changing colors from white to blue to pink. This lighting was powered by large solar panels that collected sunlight during the day and stored it in batteries to be used at night.

Titled *Ascension*, this installation made a striking addition to the festival grounds, while teaching attendees about renewable energy. Nick Vida put together an impressive off-grid solar array, with the generous support of the REC Group and REC Solar Inc.

He explains, "The approach for *Ascension* was to create a power profile and lighting design that was very thoughtful and visibly solar powered, as a vehicle to showcase the technology in use and put it in front of the festival goers."

In October 2010, I spoke with Vida, as well as Brent Heyning, founder and chief engineer at Toyshoppe Systems (toyshoppesystems.com), and Ian Garrett, executive director of the Center for Sustainable Practice in the Arts (www.sustainablepractice.org) who served as lighting designers on *Ascension*. In order to create a full wash of light over the entire crane, using only solar power, they had to source low-energy lighting instruments. "Basically we had a power ceiling," Garrett says. As research, he ran photometrics and did computer modeled lighting studies based on instrument placement and type. "We didn't have too many options of what we could use that would combine the throw, punch, control and energy efficiency required," Garrett says.

Garrett knew that he would need LEDs, but had to decide which kind to use, with an early lighting proposal of solid state LEDs drawing too much power. He eventually settled on an architectural wash unit called a ColorReach (www.colorkinetics.com/ls/rgb/colorreach/), made by Color Kinetics and supplied by Kinetic Lighting in Sun Valley, California. "We had eight of those, which due to interchangeable lens, acted as 16 instruments," Garrett says. "We also put smaller ColorBlasts inside the truss structure to highlight the skeleton."

In the end, using only the solar power collected during the day, they were able to fully power the crane from around 6 p.m. to 8 a.m. and still have over 40 percent capacity in the batteries. Heyning explains, "Power usage and balancing for the project was split through the geometry of the structure in a way to minimize impact of any problems." Vida believes that solar energy offers many benefits over traditional diesel generators, saying, "The relief of a solar powered lighting rig, with no background noise and no slight carbon monoxide poisoning, greatly influenced the very successful programming the lighting crew pulled off."

During the day, both the crane and the solar PV panels, which had been outfitted with benches, provided much-needed shade for attendees. At night, the illuminated crane lit up the night sky. For these two reasons, *Ascension* was massively popular. "The crane was the biggest shade structure during the day, so it was constantly mobbed," says Garrett. "At night, with the lights, it was basically a dance floor, and the only source of light on the field, aside from the stage." As a powerful spectacle, *Ascension* united attendees and showed them the power of solar energy.

The Solar Pump and Guerilla Cinema, two renewable energy attractions discussed in Chapter 7, are examples of spectacles. The Solar Pump attracted huge buzz at South by Southwest (www.sxsw.com), where attendees were delighted with the opportunity to charge their mobile phones, and Guerilla Cinema (www.spanthatworld.com/guerilla-cinema), creates the magical experience of a pedal-powered movie. A tall wind turbine, or even an organic garden that has been theatrically cultivated and decorated, can infuse an event with a sense of spectacle, and these spectacles can impress attendees who might not normally be receptive toward sustainability.

Grass Roots

The opposite of large spectacles is small, grass roots connections, which can be more effective for targeting local and community groups. Because part of sustainability is local support and equality, greener meeting and event pioneers may find community groups very receptive to their message. Get in touch with local schools, universities, and community clubs, and consider face-to-face meetings, to create a meaningful grass roots connection. Disadvantaged groups, or those representing minorities or senior citizens, may take an interest in sustainability as an agent of social change. Meet with these groups to tell them about your meeting or event.

Kevin Danaher relies strongly on grass roots connections to drive attendance at Green Festival. He galvanizes local activist, environmental, spiritual, and socially responsible groups to bring them together. "Green Festival is rooted in community, and is enterprise-based, with all that attendant creativity and innovation from the community level," he says. "We want our show to be festive, a positive solution."

Carbon Commitments

Professionals and persons with expendable income are increasingly interested in reducing their carbon footprint. One popular way to connect to these groups is by giving them an opportunity make a structured commitment to this reduction. IMEX (www.imex-frankfurt.com) provides a facility for attendees to offset their travel to the show. Many travel agencies now provide an opportunity to offset the carbon emissions from transportation.

The Big Tent (www.bigtentfestival.co.uk), a music festival in Scotland, offered attendees discounted admission if they made a commitment to either the 10:10 campaign, which works to offset 10 percent of the UK's carbon emissions or the Falkland Centre for Stewardship, the estate that hosts the event. By inviting eco-conscious attendees to commit to a cause that your meeting or event supports, you can connect to them in a deeper way and create a feel-good experience for them.

Segmented Strategy

Once you have explored various sustainable marketing tools, assess which tools are most appropriate for each of your demographic segments. Large-scale spectacles will have the highest impact on attendees who otherwise may not be interested in sustainability, while professionals interested in CSR might be more receptive toward making a carbon commitment. Figure 11.7 shows which tools may have a high or moderate impact on which segment.

Creating a chart such as the one in Figure 11.7 can help you determine how much to invest in certain marketing tools. Events geared toward a younger generation of activists may invest in online media, while those that might attract indifferent adults can consider a flashy spectacle to generate attention.

Demographic Segment	Online Media	Spectacle	Grass Roots	Carbon Commitments
Environmental activists	H	m	H	m
Environmentalists	H	m	H	m
Environmental professionals		m		H
Ethical professionals		m		H
Indifferent professionals	m	H		
Apathetic attendees	m	H	m	
Skeptics		H		
Key: m signals that this marketing tool has a moderate impact on the demographic segment. H signals that this marketing tool has a high impact on the demographic segment. Blank box signals that this marketing tool has a low impact on the demographic segment.				

Figure 11.7   Marketing Tools For Demographic Segments

Certification

The Scottish Seabird Centre (www.seabird.org) is an outstanding attraction for wildlife viewing located in North Berwick, Scotland, where visitors may glimpse seabirds, puffins, dolphins, and seal pups in their natural habitat, thanks to an array of cameras that bring visitors right into the action. Dedicated to protecting wildlife and the environment, the Scottish Seabird Centre takes its sustainable policies seriously. Island cameras are powered by solar energy, and extended rail service has significantly reduced car transportation.

These achievements have earned the Scottish Seabird Centre several awards, including the Thistle Award for Sustainable Tourism, The Chamber of Commerce Environmental Award, and the Green Tourism Gold Award. In 2009, Her Royal Highness Queen Elizabeth visited the Centre to present it with The Queen's Award for Enterprise (Sustainable Development).

I met Tom Brock, OBE, chief executive of the Scottish Seabird Centre, at a VisitScotland Sustainable Tourism Seminar in October 2010, and he explained that the Scottish Seabird Centre's awards are a powerful force for communicating sustainability to those who might not otherwise take notice. "It generates excellent public relations, raising and enhancing our profile with potential visitors as well as with supporters and potential funders." In addition to visibility, this award also demonstrates credibility. "It demonstrates that we practice what we preach."

One of the most powerful ways to promote your brand is to get your sustainable practices certified or accredited by respected third-party organizations. There now exists a wide variety of certifications, accreditations, and awards that greener meeting and event pioneers may pursue. This outside recognition shows that your organizational practices meet industry standards. Figure 11.8 lists ten standards, certifications, and awards that a greener meeting or event may pursue.

Achievement	Type	Description
Green Seal (www.greenseal.org)	Certification	A nonprofit organization that uses science-based standards to accredit a variety of environmentally friendly products and services
Green Meetings Industry Council (www.greenmeetings.info)	Membership	The premier association for green meeting pioneers
IMEX Green Awards (www.imex-frankfurt.com/greenawards.html)	Award	Industry-leading awards for sustainable incentive travel, meetings, and events, presented at annual IMEX exhibition
SKAL International Ecotourism Awards (skalnet20.skal.org/sustainable)	Award	Sustainable tourism awards from the world's largest travel and tourism professional association
Green Globe (www.greenglobe.com)	Certification	Third-party, industry-recognized certification for sustainable business
Green Awards for Creativity in Sustainability (www.greenawards.co.uk)	Award	British awards recognizing creative work that communicates sustainability
Event Awards (www.eventawards.com)	Award	British awards, including The Green Award, for professionals in the events industry
Professional Convention Management Association (PCMA) Environmental Leadership Award (www.pcma.org/x2714.xml#Green)	Award	Award celebrating a person or organization that promotes sustainable environmental efforts
Meeting Professionals International (MPI) RISE Awards (www.mpiweb.org/Community/AwardsAndRecognition)	Award	Awards recognizing outstanding achievements in the global community
American Society of Association Executives (ASAE) Summit Awards (www.asaecenter.org/Advocacy)	Award	Awards recognizing associations that solve local and national crises, foster volunteerism and develop initiatives for the public good

Figure 11.8 Ten Standards, Certifications, and Awards for Greener Meetings and Events

In addition to those listed here, there are many more awards, certifications, standards, and membership organizations that you may apply for, all of which are listed in the appendices of this book. Decide which of these achievements are the most relevant and most significant for your organization, and create a long-term plan for attaining them. Contact the awarding organizations to learn their criteria, and discuss with your staff how you can meet these criteria.

If you are successful in attaining recognition, tell the world. Include the logo of your new award or certification in all relevant materials, and refer to it in future marketing communication. Third-party recognition provides credibility and shows the public that your sustainable practices can be trusted.

Education

One of the most important aspects of greener marketing is education. If your sustainable policies are legitimate and serious, tell your attendees about them. Rather than using catch-phrases or image-marketing, communicate to attendees with facts and figures, educating them about the environment and about the specific practices you have undertaken. Instead of creating a false image, tell a true story.

"The most outstanding initiatives we've seen are those that really commit to integrating sustainable thinking throughout the event and providing those extra initiatives that not only make taking part easy for delegates but tell the story eloquently," says MacMillan. Tell the true story of sustainability through signage, language, or audience interaction.

Signage and Wayfinding

Any meeting or event professional will know that the key to signage is to make it easy for attendees. Signage should be clear and well placed, helping to shape attendee movement and behavior without impediment. The best signs are the ones that attendees follow without even noticing. Educational signage at greener events is much the same: attendees should learn about sustainability without realizing that they are learning.

Chapter 5 discussed signage for waste receptacles, the most important aspect of attendee behavior to control. Receptacles should be well labeled, well positioned, and well maintained. In addition to clear signage, which may include photos of the objects to be disposed in each receptacle, consider deposit slots that only fit the intended objects. For instance, a paper recycling bin might feature a narrow rectangular slat that only paper can fit through. Another bin for aluminum may have a small circular hole that only fits aluminum cans.

Other aspects of behavior that educational signage might control include energy use, transportation, and smoking. Friendly, informative signs can instruct attendees to turn off lighting or heating when not in use, to consider using public transportation and not to idle in their vehicles, and to properly dispose of cigarette butts. Be sure that signage is clear, straightforward, and polite.

Reusable signage presents the schedule of food demonstration talks at The Big Tent.

Gauge the interest level of your attendees when posting signage. Eco-conscious attendees might appreciate extra sustainable information sign-posted throughout the event site, to further educate them on sustainability. More indifferent attendees may find too much educational signage annoying if it does not have a clear purpose.

Interaction

Different people learn in different ways, and while some people prefer reading or listening to educational information, others need active participation. In the case of waste receptacles, some people may need to be physically shown how to use them. Consider assigning environmental stewards to show attendees how to use the recycling, compost, and garbage bins correctly. "It's easy to organize recycling bins on the event floor, but it's not always easy to get people to use them and to understand why they should care," says MacMillan. "Those events that go the whole way have initiatives such as sustainability volunteers, who can assist people in using bins and explain the process."

Whether they are called sustainability volunteers, environmental stewards or the green team, having dedicated staff interact with attendees can go a long way toward teaching sustainability. The Scottish Seabird Centre has found interactive participation a great way to educate children about the environment. In addition to educational communication via its Web site, paper documents, and media publicity, the Centre also visits schools and brings school groups in for educational visits. At the Centre, school groups can participate in interactive, talks, films, and activities designed to teach them about wildlife through active participation.

Consider the ways in which your meeting or event can promote interactive learning. Make educational displays interactive, so that instead of just reading, attendees are asked to play a game or answer trivia questions about sustainability. Light physical activities are great for breakout sessions between meetings, and Figure 11.9 offers a few ways in which you can get attendees on their feet.

Brainstorm your own games to get attendees involved in sustainable practices. Consider inviting attendees to up-cycle waste materials into artworks. By inviting them to participate in these games, you are making sustainability fun and engaging.

Activity	Description
Interactive poll	Ask attendees a series of yes/no or true/false questions, and designate one side of the room as "yes" and the other as "no." Ask attendees to represent their answer to the questions by standing to either side, or somewhere in the middle.
Who am I?	Write topics or issues from the meeting or event on labels and stick them to attendees' backs. Ask attendees to mingle and give each other clues about what their topic or issue is.
Bravo!	In a smaller meeting, ask one attendee to leave the room, then ask the remaining attendees to suggest a simple action for the missing attendee to complete, such as picking up a pen or moving a chair. When the missing attendee returns, the other attendees will try to guide his or her actions only by applauding movements or actions in the right direction, finally cheering, "Bravo!" when they complete the task.
Accessibility simulation	To teach accessibility, allow attendees to simulate a disability and experience the meeting or event from this new point of view. For instance, put attendees in pairs, and ask one to close his or her eyes to simulate visual impairment. Teach the other attendee how to be a guide, and have the sighted partners guide their "disabled" attendees around the meeting room.
Waste warriors	Make recycling fun! Create an arcade-style bin for aluminum cans and challenge attendees to throw their cans into the bin basketball-style from a certain distance.

Figure 11.9 Light Physical Activities for Active Learning

Sponsorship

When a company donates funds or goods and services to your meeting or event in order to promote its brand, it is called *sponsorship*. Meetings and events may recognize sponsors by inserting their logos into marketing materials, including them in publicity, or allowing sponsors to contact attendees directly. Major sponsors may receive *naming opportunities*, where a certain event or venue is named after the sponsor, such as the X Brand Keynote Speech, the Y Brand Post-Show Party, or the Z Brand Arena.

Sponsorship is a great way to bring in additional funds, goods, or services to a meeting or event, and you should research and pursue a wide variety of potential sponsors. In addition to obvious sponsors that have an interest in your attendee demographic, consider other companies that may be interested in aligning their brand with yours. For instance, manufacturers of musical instruments would be obvious choices to sponsor a convention for musicians, but a company that insures musical instruments, or a Web site that promotes bands, presents further possibilities. If the musicians are touring, perhaps a car insurance company would be appropriate.

The best sponsors for greener meetings and events are companies that are either dedicated to sustainability or that have environmental sensibilities. Health food, renewable energy, and nonprofits dedicated to social or environmental causes are perfect green sponsors. If a sponsor is not currently known for being environmentally responsible, but is making huge strides toward sustainability, make sure that this change in direction is clearly communicated. For instance, a fast food chain needs to communicate a serious move toward sustainable purchasing if it is going to be taken seriously as a sponsor of an environmentalist conference.

Successful sponsors gain an enhanced audience, increase the visibility of their brand, and support the event in useful ways. As long as they have a serious commitment to sustainability, any company can be a successful sponsor for a greener meeting or event. However, certain industries may not be comfortable sponsoring certain events, and could meet with potential backlash. Although there are always exceptions to the rule, Figure 11.10 suggests the industries that may be expected to sponsor specific events, and those that may not work as well.

The inappropriate sponsors in Figure 11.10 are unlikely to improve, or benefit from, the events suggested, although all companies are different. A university will typically benefit more from sponsoring a scout meeting than a dance music festival. Although it is inappropriate for an alcohol distributor to sponsor a scout meeting, it is common practice for that industry to sponsor music festivals for adult attendees.

A successful sponsorship constitutes a mutually beneficial relationship between the sponsor and the meeting or event. Look for companies that share your vision, style, and ethics, and assess the potential attendee reaction. Be sure that companies are eager to sponsor your event in order to support sustainable values, not to mask their own lack of these same values. Sponsors with limited knowledge of sustainability might be encouraged to make sustainable commitments as part of their role as sponsor. These new commitments can make a great impression on event attendees.

Sample Event	Appropriate Sponsors	Inappropriate Sponsors
Breast Cancer Awareness Charity Gala	Health care, pharmaceuticals, lingerie	Alcohol, tobacco
Annual Convention of Ornithologists (Bird Watchers)	Binoculars, wildlife protection agencies, outdoor clothing/equipment	Nonenvironmental tourism, leather goods
Regional Boy Scout Club Meeting	Camping gear, schools/universities	Alcohol, tobacco
Miami Dance Music Festival	Beer, sun-tan lotion, hotels, designer clothes	Universities
Sustainable Business Summit	Renewable energy, public transportation, carbon offsets, sustainable food	Cars, airlines, oil companies, fast food
Little League Baseball Championship Game	Sports gear, television channel, sports drink	Alcohol, tobacco, fast food

Figure 11.10 Sample Sponsors for Greener Meetings and Events

Greenwash

Using the language of sustainability without undertaking any actual practices is known as *greenwash*, or misleading marketing that falsely portrays a meeting or event as more sustainable that it is. Because of the popularity of sustainability as a business trend, certain companies have been enticed into calling themselves "green" without first assessing what that truly means for them. These companies risk being accused of greenwash, which can damage their public image.

Examples of greenwash may include . . .

- Painting your office building green with environmentally toxic paint
- Changing your logo into a green flower without changing the way you do business
- Using the words "sustainable" or "environmental" in your new mission statement without incorporating these values into business operations
- Claiming to be "carbon neutral" or "carbon negative" for offsetting electricity use, but not staff or attendee travel

"Actions speak louder than words," says John Graham, president and CEO of the American Society of Association Executives (ASAE) (www.asae.org), "and one of the biggest challenges regarding the environment and social responsibility is for organizations to act as they preach." Although it may begin innocently, be careful not to claim more than you are doing. Root your marketing claims in real sustainable actions that have been measured and reported. Making real achievements in sustainability is more difficult than painting something green, but it is also more impressive and better received by attendees.

> It's easy to proclaim one's commitment to a cause. It's not as easy to revamp an entire strategy to actually act and operate new guidelines.
>
> —*John Graham, American Society of Association Executives (ASAE),*
> *interview, May 2010*

Graham suggests that greener meeting and event pioneers define their commitment to environmental and social responsibility with specific detail. "With so many ways these two terms can be understood, organizations need to be careful to remain committed to what they proclaim."

Charles Henderson, managing director of Climate Futures (www.climatefutures .co.uk), understands the difficult situation that festivals can put themselves in when communicating their carbon offsetting. When we spoke in April 2009, he explained that the language is important. "*Balancing* is much less scrutinized than *offsetting*. If you are just *balancing*, then you can support projects that you have a local affinity with. That might suit you better."

Kimberley Lewis, vice president of events for the U.S. Green Building Council (USGBC) (www.usgbc.org), says, "Don't create a platform that's not authentic. Everyone is questioning whether you are authentically green. There can be a backlash if you advertise your green credentials but can't back that up with data. Show them how you've been able to minimize, how you've been able to change behavior."

When we discussed marketing sustainability in May 2010, Lewis noted that showing is better than telling. This is especially important for an increasingly eco-conscious audience. "The consumer body has really begun to understand what sustainability means," she says. In addition to measuring and reporting real sustainable practices to impress knowledgeable attendees, Lewis also suggests simple, easy-to-understand language. "Sustainability is nothing new. It's a return back to the days of old. It's looking at human behavior."

Find the marketing tools that speak clearly and directly to the different demographics of your meeting or event. Use certification, education, sponsorship, and other marketing tools such as online media to reach your intended audience. If you can communicate the age-old concept of sustainability in a fresh way, you may find new and exciting ways of connecting with attendees.

Greener Event: Oracle OpenWorld

Oracle OpenWorld is the world's largest technology event, and with over 400 companies exhibiting and over 37,000 people attending, the potential for waste is huge. That is why the staff at Oracle, together with event consultants MeetGreen, have worked hard to make OpenWorld the cleanest, greenest technology exhibition in the world, and this work was recognized when IMEX awarded OpenWorld a Green Event Award in 2008.

When we spoke in May 2010, Paul Salinger, Oracle's vice president of marketing, recalled strategic discussions about OpenWorld in 2006, which centered on how big the conference had become and how much of an environmental impact it had. Salinger asked his staff, "Could we reduce the resources it takes to produce an event of this scale and make a statement about Oracle leading the way as a sustainable conference?" Having received an overwhelmingly positive response, Salinger concluded, "We could start to incorporate some green practices into the OpenWorld process, both to support the company brand and values, but also because we wanted to take some of our personal passion and put it to work to help the environment and reduce the footprint of the conference."

Having achieved product leadership in the technology sector, Oracle was ready for another kind of leadership, which Salinger explains as, "One where the practices we put in place, the engagements we encourage throughout our supply chain, and the way in which we communicate could make a shift in thinking and make sustainable events a standard practice." Salinger saw green meetings as an opportunity to engage not just customers but also the technology industry as a whole. "We wanted to use our buying power to provide some leadership," he says, "so that other companies and other events can come in behind us and take advantage of what we are doing to transform the event industry, using sustainable events as a platform for Oracle to engage others in the environmental and social discussion."

Oracle enlisted the help of MeetGreen to create a comprehensive sustainability program, and Project Manager Shawna McKinley describes the multiphased process. "The first phase was determining what their baseline was," she says. "They had had a one-year cycle of doing some basic green practices and grabbing the low-hanging fruit. In the second phase of policy and training, we put together a manual for the corporate event marketing department that handles OpenWorld, and created procurement tools for them that would take things to the next level, so that instead of doing voluntary, informal practices, sustainability actually became policy and got included right into the planning processes."

MeetGreen provided in-person training for the core event team, and virtual training for the entire staff, which provided guidance on how to build sustainability into the event management plan. It based its work on BS 8901, the British Standard for sustainable events, which meant creating a project management system that uses various organizational tools to measure sustainability. McKinley explains that Oracle was using standard contract language and RFP surveys that it revised to promote sustainable criteria on a more consistent basis.

This detailed system of managing and measuring specific green goals culminated in a series of industry-leading results that could be expressed in specific calculations. For instance, in 2009, ground shuttles were reduced by 30 percent of peak usage, saving 18,000 pounds of carbon dioxide emissions and 800 gallons of fuel. Alternative purchasing decisions conserved 1,146,130 Mj of electricity, or enough energy to power 12 American homes per year, and 120,073 pounds of carbon dioxide, or the annual emissions of 11 cars.

The third step in the process, McKinley says, was engaging stakeholders, vendors, and attendees in sustainable practice. She describes the tactful way in which Oracle engaged its stakeholders and vendors in the sustainability initiative, "They cast the invitation open to the vendor team to say, 'We want you involved in this as well. We know you're doing stuff, that's great. Thank you. What can you do in addition to that to take us to the next level?' They've been really successful in overcoming what can often be a challenge, which is vendor engagement."

Salinger says that the key to stakeholder involvement is joined-up thinking. "We decided that the best way of alleviating skepticism and making it a more collaborative effort was to get everyone involved early on and not to mandate things to them, but let them be a part of the process," he says. Salinger formed a Green Team for Oracle OpenWorld that helped to establish key performance indicators (KPIs) and make commitments on measurement and reporting of the data against those indicators, allowing Oracle to build on baselines and look for areas of improvement within the entire team.

"Now, all of our major suppliers and key stakeholders across our event supply chain are on board with our initiatives," says Salinger, "and actively taking part in not only our event, but pushing their own staffs and their other clients to be more responsible in their meeting practices."

Event attendees may need time and direction before adjusting to new sustainable practices. "When we first started, attendees were sometimes skeptical," Salinger recalls.

For instance, when we first completely eliminated bottled water and moved to a system of letting them fill their own bottles, we got some negative responses, because some people thought we were just doing it to save costs. We sometimes have to lead our attendees and show them the way, but, little by little, they are getting what we are trying to do and are becoming more conscious about environmental issues.

Thanks to the passion and determination of Salinger and his team at Oracle, as well as the organizational leadership of McKinley and Meet Green, Oracle OpenWorld continues to achieve industry-leading results. At the 2009 OpenWorld, held in San Francisco, 45 percent of signs were donated or recycled, and 62 percent of signs used recyclable or renewable substrates. Through purchasing, reduction, reuse, and recycling, they diverted approximately 140 tons of material away from landfill, enough to fill over 10 garbage trucks. Of the food items, 60 percent were sourced within a 100-mile radius of San Francisco.

With these well-managed and well-reported results, it is no wonder that Oracle OpenWorld continues to be recognized as a leader in greener events, with OpenWorld 2010 set to be one of the most sustainable technology conferences ever.

Some new initiatives include measuring overall energy usage and engaging the venue, our suppliers and our local utility provider in a conversation about energy management, reduction, and use of renewable energy; working to further reduce transportation from shuttle buses and encouraging more walking, bike travel and local transportation, as well as hybrid vehicles for executive transport; and working with our exhibitors to increase sustainable resources in their booths.

"We have a lot of ideas, but it will take us a few more years in this journey to put all of them in place," says Salinger. Having achieved so much already, it is this vision of sustainability as a journey toward continual improvement that makes Oracle OpenWorld truly a model greener event.

Summary

Assess the unique features, benefits, and values that your greener meeting or event offers to various demographics of attendees. Environmentalists may seek vast and transparent sustainability programs, while more indifferent attendees may appreciate style and economy. Use online media, social networking, large-scale spectacles, grass roots connections, and carbon commitments to reach various demographics. Consider certification and awards that add credibility, educational information and activities, and appropriate sponsorships. Be careful to avoid being accused of greenwash by only promising what you can deliver.

Key Terms and Definitions

- **Offer**: the unique features, benefits, and values of your meeting or event.
- **Demographic segments:** groups of persons with similar backgrounds and behaviors.
- **Blog**: online journal that allows a person or persons to post writings, and others to read and/or comment.
- **Vlog**: video diary posted to the Internet where a person talks directly to the camera.
- **Bandwidth**: Web site processing capacity, used to transmit media files.
- **Sponsorship**: when a company donates to a meeting or event in order to promote its brand.
- **Naming opportunities**: where a certain event or venue is named after a major sponsor.
- **Greenwash**: misleading marketing that portrays a meeting or event as more sustainable than it actually is.

Blue Sky Thinking

You are in charge of planning the African American Family Gardening Society's annual outdoor picnic and barbecue. This year's theme is urban gardening. What features, benefits, and values might this event offer attendees? Describe four demographic segments that might attend, and which features of the event each segment might appreciate the most. Describe four marketing tools that could be used to promote the event, and chart which tool may have the highest impact on which demographic segment.

Renewable Resources

Grant, John (2007). *The Green Marketing Manifesto.* London: John Wiley & Sons.

Skinner, Bruce and Rukavina, Valdimir (2002). *Event Sponsorship.* Hoboken: John Wiley & Sons.

TopRank Online Marketing Blog (www.toprankblog.com).

YouTube Marketing Tips & Online Video Marketing Tips! (www.youtube .com/watch?v=fd0DTiI6U9k).

Reusable signage welcomes artists like King Creosote and Rosanne Cash to The Big Tent.

CHAPTER 12

Greener Events in Practice

"Look abroad through Nature's range,
Nature's mighty law is change."

—*Robert Burns, Scottish Poet (1759–1796)*

In this chapter you will learn:

1. How to take the first step

2. How to turn challenges into opportunities

3. How to think globally and act locally

4. How to unite staff, stakeholders, suppliers, and attendees

5. How to tell your story

In the world of theater, reading a play on the page is very different from directing one on the stage. While a playwright can dictate the style, plot, and characters, it is up to the director to coordinate the actors, technicians, and artists who will make the play come alive in front of an audience.

Meetings and events are much like plays. We can discuss, plan, design, and risk manage every aspect, but ultimately we need the actual experience of working hands-on in the event environment. In order to reflect the practical, realistic aspects of greener meetings and events, this book has provided interviews with more than 50 professionals working in the tourism, hospitality, meetings, and events industries. Case studies at the end of each chapter have given insight into real meetings, conferences, festivals, and events. Readers are encouraged to contact these diverse organizations, where Web sites are provided, for more information and to seek professional opportunities.

In conversation with some of the greener meeting and event pioneers featured in this book, you will find a diversity of opinions, some of which might even contradict each other. Meeting and event professionals face a tremendous amount of pressure while on site, and they each find their own unique way to promote sustainability. I discovered this in 2009, when I conducted interviews with professionals at 12 festivals in order to better understand the unique challenges and opportunities they faced regarding sustainability. This academic report culminated in a list of Best Practices for Sustainable Festivals, shown here as Figure 12.1, which includes some surprising, nontraditional advice.

1. Create meaningful connections between internal mission statements and the ethics of environmentalism.

2. Delegate environmental responsibilities on a departmental level.

3. Employ caution when publicizing environmental initiatives or rebranding an organization as environmental; prepare contingency plans for allegations of greenwash.

4. Present sincere environmental policies to civic and funding bodies to gain increased influence.

5. Research and take advantage of reuse infrastructure, including renovation of neglected buildings or used building materials, to develop long-term cost savings.

6. Develop successful, interactive programs to attract environmentalists. Examples include an e-cycling swap, a book and music swap, or a convenient recycling point for local residents.

7. Make recycling bins extremely obvious and convenient for patrons to understand and use.

8. Consider financial incentives, such as a cup-deposit scheme, to alter patron psychology toward waste.

9. Thoroughly research emerging technology, such as LED lighting or solar power, before investing in it.

10. Provide patrons, staff, and stakeholders with comprehensive guidance on using public transit systems to travel to and from the festival. Partner with public transit authorities to reach out to this potential audience. If necessary, campaign to extend commuter rail lines.

11. Consider a centralized location near public transit to increase convenience of travel for patrons.

12. Develop logical and accessible systems of documentation for staff to monitor energy consumption, carbon emissions from travel or generators, waste, recycling, and other resource use. Prior to implementation, develop a strategy for how these data will be used, including reduction goals and useful points of comparison. Untrained staff will require initial guidance on a departmental level, and outside consultancy or research may be necessary.

Figure 12.1   Best Practice for Sustainable Festivals

Although many of these best practices are straightforward reflections of the values in this book, others are more unusual. Several arts festivals recommended caution when marketing sustainability, for fear of greenwash allegations. Others suggested cautious research before investing in new technology such as LED lighting or renewable energy, despite their great success with these technologies.

Look at the mission statement for your meeting or event, and create a meaningful connection to sustainability. Every meeting or event is different and will need to incorporate sustainability in a different way. This chapter offers diverse practical advice, straight from the professionals who have experienced the opportunities and challenges of implementing sustainable practices in the field.

We begin with a major international megaevent, for which the challenges and opportunities could not be greater. The London 2012 Olympics are set to be a major landmark in the field of sustainable events. With a comprehensive sustainability plan that includes far-reaching legacies to reach UK social and environmental goals, London 2012 is leading the way for today's greener meeting and event pioneers. David Stubbs, head of sustainability for London 2012, was kind enough to share his inside perspective on a Sustainable Olympic Games.

Take the First Step

Bruce MacMillan, president and CEO of Meeting Professionals International (MPI) (www.mpiweb.org), knows that it is considerably more daunting for smaller businesses to begin addressing sustainability. "It's okay to start small and it's okay to make mistakes. Sustainability is a step-by-step process, with true sustainability as an end goal. Communicate clearly and often about what you are doing well and not so well. No organization is perfect. Avoid greenwashing or making sustainability a one-off thing: it should be integrated into everything you do."

> Lastly, try to make sustainability appealing and fun—it's the only way to ensure people are engaged in it.
>
> —*Bruce MacMillan, Meeting Professionals International (MPI), interview, August 2010*

Move slowly and strategically, communicate transparently, and make it fun. This advice is echoed by Kimberly Lewis, vice president of Events, U.S. Green Building Council (USGBC) (www.usgbc.org), who recommends planning far in advance:

> Give yourself time. Don't be too over eager. Keep a diary, and take notes as you go. Be open, be innovative.
>
> —*Kimberly Lewis, USGBC, interview, May 2010*

Sustainable Games: London 2012

If everyone in the world used the same amount of resources as we do in the United Kingdom, we would need three planets' worth of resources to sustain us. That was the premise of the London 2012 bid to host the Olympic and Paralympic Games in 2012.

Sustainability has been embedded into the culture of London 2012 from the beginning. Our plans take a balanced approach to social, environmental, and economic issues, from building the Games, to during the Games, to the legacy of the Games. This is the first time a summer Games has considered this, let alone been well on the way on the way to delivering it.

The London 2012 Food Vision is a great example of how we are tackling sustainability opportunities. Food presents an excellent medium through which we can communicate ethical and environmentally responsible sourcing.

In fact, we see three key areas where visitors to the Games can best relate to our sustainability program: these are travel, food, and waste. Each of these is part of the Games experience—the mode of travel to and from venues; the choice and high-quality of food and beverages provided, and a simple, clearly communicated system for placing your waste, which for the most part will be food scraps and food packaging. If we can get these three elements to be visible demonstrations of our sustainability commitment, they will provide a powerful and accessible means of engaging large audiences.

Sustainability is not an easy term to explain or communicate. It can seem worthy but dull, or just for techies. We want to demystify this subject and find ways of portraying it in fresh and meaningful ways.

Our foundation has been to concentrate on the basics of putting in place a solid and comprehensive program and then having this independently assured by the Commission for a Sustainable London 2012. This gives us a platform upon which to build our story; it is the reason for people to believe we are serious. Now comes the vital challenge of making it real for people from all walks of life.

For the more technically minded, we have developed various documents, such as our LOCOG Sustainable Sourcing Code, Temporary Materials Guidelines, and the London 2012 Sustainability Guidelines for Events, to create sector-specific guidance on implementing sustainability.

London 2012 is a Games event for everyone. Everyone is invited to take part. Our work spans the whole of the United Kingdom to ensure that everyone has an opportunity to be part of it. The London 2012 Festival and the Torch Relay are testament to that, with the latter coming within a one-hour journey for 95 percent of the population.

We hope to inspire people to enjoy more sustainable lifestyles where physical activity, inclusion, and respect for the environment and other people are all part of everyday decisions.

Source: David Stubbs, head of sustainability for the London 2012 Organising Committee for the Olympic and Paralympic Games (www.london2012.com)

Kevin Hacke, executive director of the International Special Events Society (ISES) (www.ises.com), says this,

> So many green practices are easy to implement, and with a little planning, can go a long way toward furthering client social responsibility goals. Our members have a wealth of experience in providing outstanding event experiences for their clients, and green initiatives go hand in hand with delivering a completely seamless event experience with no details left unattended.
> —*Kevin Hacke, International Special Events Society, interview, October 2010*

John Graham, president and CEO of the American Society of Association Executives (ASAE) (www.asaecenter.com), understands the challenges that need to be overcome. "I can see how social responsibility and the whole greening movement might seem intimidating for some," says Graham. "But with all the support available both in the industry as well as in the community, a commitment to social responsibility can be a very rewarding and gratifying journey, not to mention the business benefits that derive from cost-saving tactics."

> It takes some courage to make the first step to be innovative, but don't be afraid to make the first move.
> —*John Graham, American Society of Association Executives (ASAE), interview, May 2010*

Think Globally, Act Locally

Keep abreast of global trends, and incorporate them into your local infrastructure. Bruce MacMillan, CEO of Meeting Professionals International, cites a recent McKinsey Global Survey of respondents whose companies are addressing sustainability, with more than half of executives reporting an improvement in operational efficiency, an increase in brand loyalty and access to new markets (Bonini 2010). The recent "Deloitte Hospitality Research 2015, Game Changers or Spectators" report warns businesses to keep pace with stakeholders' increasing demands for sustainability, saying, "Regulatory, economic and stakeholder pressure will drive changes in the industry that will see social and business norms change with surprising speed. Organizations that fail to keep pace will not only incur additional regulatory costs but, in the longer term, risk a 'missed generation' in terms of consumer recognition of sustainability performance" (Kyriakidis 2010, p. 3).

> The environment is a major issue for the entire world, and it's now clear due to overwhelming scientific evidence that we can't go on as we have in the past. Businesses also understand now that alongside the genuine need to address these issues there is a clear business rationale in avoiding waste, increasing efficiencies, and joining the effort.
> —*Bruce MacMillan, Meeting Professionals International, interview, August 2010*

The Edinburgh International Conference Centre (EICC)

(www.eicc.co.uk)

Since opening in 1995, the Edinburgh International Conference Centre (EICC) has hosted over 2,100 events, delivering approximately £280 million of economic benefit for Edinburgh. Led by Chief Executive Hans H. Rissmann, OBE, EICC is now set on a major expansion program.

EICC's Sustainable Events Programme was launched in 1998 to raise conference organizers' awareness of sustainability issues in designing an event, and includes Plan-It Green, EICC's own guide to greener meetings and events. When we met in December 2010, Reynaldo Guino-o, human resources and total quality management for EICC, said, "Plan-it Green is our unique system of managing sustainability."

EICC's extensive green policies are generated by the Green Team, a group that includes at least one employee from every department, from catering to cleaning to management. "You need the people to make it happen," says Guino-o, who sees his role as supporting and guiding the Green Team. "The Green Team assesses the situation and identifies the activities that impact the natural environment, the well-being of the community, and the financial progress of EICC."

New employees at EICC are inducted into not only HR policies and internal processes, but also sustainability. "Sustainability is part of employee induction, and that generates interest and enthusiasm," says Guino-o. "Staff often ask me if they can join the Green Team, and I say, 'You already are!' Every member of staff is part of the Green Team." Guino-o believes that communication is key, which is why he provides all staff with detailed information, such as how EICC recycles and diverts waste from landfill. "Staff need to be aware of where waste goes, and why."

Staff members also have the opportunity to volunteer for environmental causes, such as cleaning litter off the streets and planting trees in the Scottish Borders, experiences that can provide a level of personal satisfaction. Guino-o knows the importance of staff engagement: "Clients are happy if staff are happy."

EICC holds several distinguished certifications, including the Gold Award for the Green Tourism Business Scheme, ISO 14001 for Environmental Management Systems and Investors in People for excellent human resource management. Guino-o knows that the pursuit and achievement of these certifications inspire EICC employees toward continual

Kevin Hacke has seen a marked increase in awareness of and sensitivity toward green event practices:

ISES members are keenly aware of marketplace shifts, and are responding in kind to requests from clients to incorporate sustainable practices and conservation measures in every aspect of their events," he says. "Our members freely offer green event innovations to each other, and I cannot think of a single ISES member who has not incorporated a number of these new practices into their business models.

—*Kevin Hacke, International Special Events Society, interview, October 2010*

improvement. "Standards are very important," he says. "They are part of our culture."

These standards also reassure clients that EICC operates on a high level, giving them competitive advantage. "They give the client added value." "The sustainable meetings market is more competitive now, and the level of awareness is high, as opposed to ten years ago."

It is often especially important for government bodies to demonstrate sustainability through their events. "As leaders, they are keen to walk the talk, and it is our responsibility to keep in line with government targets," says Guino-o. "Scotland is playing an important role in the international market for sustainable events. We want EICC to be a leader as well, and we have the responsibility to lead."

EICC has achieved recognition and certification through careful and consistent measurement of sustainable initiatives. Careful management of event materials and asking clients to minimize resource use has reduced waste. Food waste has been reduced by ensuring exact requirements of clients are known—thus avoiding unnecessary production of food. The average waste produced per major event has declined from 7.5 to 3.4 UK tonnes per event.

Although their measurements are extensive, Guino-o describes that any meeting planner should be comfortable measuring things such as energy and water usage. These measurements are critical for reporting the success of the event to the client. "You want to tell them, 'This is what we achieved. If you come back next time, we can improve our results,'" says Guino-o.

Guino-o firmly believes that sustainability improves the event experience, even if clients do not necessarily take notice. "Clients are not necessarily looking for green events, they are looking for successful events," he says. "However, we can generate awareness and interest in sustainability." He sees sustainability as a competitive advantage in today's marketplace: "We offer sustainability as an innovative idea to clients, and innovation is necessary in this economy."

Along with measurements of energy and recycling, EICC also measures *client delight*. "If we work with the client and are able to delight them, we have made a successful event," explains Guino-o. "Our purpose is to generate economic impact, and successful events fulfill this purpose. We are in the business of running successful events. That is our main product."

To those venue managers who may be intimidated by the prospect of measuring carbon or implementing sustainability, Guino-o says, "A conference centre does not necessarily need to invest in solar panels or wind turbines to be green. We were not designed with these features, but we are being innovative in our internal processes and making the most out of our limited resources."

Greener meetings and events are a global phenomenon, and different parts of the world have vastly different attitudes about sustainability. Martin Sirk, CEO of the International Congress and Convention Association (ICCA) (www.iccaworld.com), however, believes that any meeting or event, no matter what country hosts it, has the ability to go green in today's globalized economy: "I don't think it makes sense to make a distinction at the level of continents."

What we're seeing instead is a very fractured and fragmented situation throughout the world. New venues are setting the standard, since they have sustainability built into their DNA, and many of the big developments in recent years have been in locations such as Asia-Pacific and the Middle East. They could argue that they are more sustainable than older facilities in established destinations in North America and Western Europe, where the challenge is how to retrofit improvements.

There's also a very mixed legal picture, with, for example, German venues having to adhere to much stricter legal standards for waste disposal, and other countries letting voluntary measures take precedence. One could argue that North America is setting the pace for designing standardized models for sustainable meetings, but there are plenty of examples of European destinations that are well ahead of what's being proposed.

Multinational clients are bringing their own sustainability policies and standards with them wherever they meet, breaking down national boundaries.

—*Martin Sirk, CEO, International Congress and Convention Association (ICCA),*
interview, September 2010

MacMillan foresees a growing focus on Scope 3 emissions, a category of indirect emissions that arise as a consequence of an organization's activities. "Events fall into this category, and organizations will increasingly need to report on the environmental impact of their events to keep up with legislation."

As a Category A liaison to the PC 250 committee creating the ISO20121 Sustainable Event Management Standard and a member of the Advisory Group for the Global Reporting Initiative Event Sector Supplement, MPI is helping to set industry standards for sustainability. "The challenge is that standards are often set in a particular language, and sustainability itself can get very complicated when you get into the minutia," says MacMillan. "To ensure mass adoption of these standards, the challenge is to translate these documents and language into something more accessible for our industry. Meeting professionals by their nature are not experts on sustainability, but we need to give them the tools and knowledge to be more sustainable and not be intimidated by new and complex terminology."

Turn Challenges into Opportunities

Producing greener meetings and events is not exactly as easy as a walk in the park. It is a challenging but rewarding practice that can provide immense opportunity for those pioneers with the ambition to turn challenges into opportunities.

Ben Challis, founder of A Greener Festival (www.agreenerfestival.com), knows that a new industry presents new challenges. When I met him in April 2009, he told me, "At the beginning of any period of change, clearly there are difficulties that have to be surmounted," he says. "With a lack of knowledge, with a lack of suppliers, and often high costs associated with change, many festivals find it difficult to adopt green policies."

Challis believes that it is important to retain the integrity of sustainable values as they become popular. "We are now seeing green entering the mainstream, and as more promoters adopt green methods, products, and priorities, there will be more suppliers and lower costs," he says. "But worries remain: Biofuels have a massive downside and also we are also seeing a rise in greenwash, schemes designed to look green when they are nothing of the sort."

Kimberley Lewis has also experienced the challenges of rapid growth. "The everyday person is starting to understand what sustainability means in his or her life," she says. "The challenge is when you don't know what the anticipated growth is going to be. How do you make sure that your goals and incentives match your growth?"

From 2006 to 2007, Greenbuild (www.greenbuildexpo.org), the annual convention and tradeshow of the USGBC, went from 13,000 to 24,000 attendees. "They just kept coming," recalls Lewis. "We doubled our tradeshow floor." This unprecedented growth strained Greenbuild's ability to meet sustainable demands.

"When you put a certain percentage rate for local and organic foods, and you need 10,000 more, that's really stressful for your local chef," she says. "If I put a distance barrier

Staff at the Edinburgh International Conference Centre spend a day volunteering for environmental causes.
Courtesy of the Edinburgh International Conference Centre.

Green New Orleans

Perhaps no city in America knows the meaning of turning challenges into opportunities better than New Orleans, the historic capital of the State of Louisiana. New Orleans was hugely devastated and depopulated by Hurricane Katrina in 2005, and the BP Oil Spill of 2010 further diminished tourism and the local economy. In recent years, Louisiana has become almost as famous for environmental disasters as it is for jazz music and spicy food.

The citizens of New Orleans are fighting back in a big way, from major rebuilding projects to small home improvements. One intriguing aspect of this revitalization is the burgeoning reuse infrastructure, as startup companies collect and redistribute used building materials to promote reuse and recycling.

The ReUse District (thereusedistrict. org) is a commercial zone encompassing the 7th Ward, Bywater, Marigny, St. Claude, and St. Roch neighborhoods, which promotes the reuse of building materials and increases access to them. Shops in this area include sellers of used books, vintage clothing, antique furniture, used building materials, bicycle repair shops like Rusted Up Beyond All Recognition Bikes (RUBARB) (rubarbike.com), and even up-cycled art galleries, like Dr. Bob's Folk Art (www.drbobart.net).

One of the stars of the ReUse District is The Green Project (www.thegreenproject.org),

for him, where I don't want him to go past the 100-mile perimeter of sourcing food, and we have an extra 10,000 folks show up on site—which is what happened in 2007—that's going to be a challenge. When we say we're not going to use disposables, we're going to use china service, and 10,000 extra people show up, they'd have to send trucks all across the nation to cover that." Although the challenge of rapid growth might intimidate some, it energizes Lewis and inspires her to improve practice year upon year.

> We want to make sure that we're not only doing the minimum, we're pushing the bar every year.
>
> —*Kimberly Lewis, (USGBC), interview, May 2010*

As recycling manager at San Francisco's Moscone Center (www.moscone.com), Kathleen Hennesey knows firsthand the many challenges that expositions and tradeshows present for sustainable concerns. "Foremost is the sheer scale of these events," she says. "Events may have 50,000 or more attendees, and bring in over a million pounds of freight per day," says Hennesey. "The meeting and convention industry is among the leading consumers of energy and generators of waste; they are reportedly second only to the construction and demolition industry in terms of the amount of waste generated for disposal." Hennesey lists exhibitor booths and their components, signage, product samples, handouts, metals, packing materials, crates, pallets, carpet padding, and containers from food and beverage services as just some of the many items disposed at conventions.

located in the Bywater-Marigny area. Featuring a warehouse, lumberyard, paint recycling center, art studio, electronic waste recycling facilities and educational programs, The Green Project is a one-stop shop for all your sustainable building needs.

The Trailer Trash Initiative (www.trailertrashinitiative.com) is not what it sounds like. Serving the French Quarter, Marigny, and Bywater, this nonprofit initiative transports recyclables to the appropriate facilities using bicycle trailers, thus cutting down on carbon emissions from cars.

Repurposing NOLA Piece by Peace (repurposingnola-piece-by-peace.com) is a boutique shop that transforms local used materials into fashionable clothing and home products. The shop has recently partnered with the National Football League (NFL) to repurpose stadium banners and fence wraps from the 2010 New Orleans Saints Super Bowl victory. This partnership has given a fantastic afterlife to the decorations used in the 2010 Super Bowl, as they have now been repurposed into holiday stockings, aprons, shower curtains, and doggie bed duvets, sales of which will benefit the New Orleans economy.

The repurposing of NFL Super Bowl banners was made possible in part by the 2013 New Orleans Super Bowl Host Committee (www.nolasuperbowl.com), who won the bid to bring the 2013 event to New Orleans, in part thanks to an impressive environmental program. Sustainable ventures such as The ReUse District and The Green Project are helping to rebuild New Orleans as a tourist destination and a world-class host for major international meetings and events.

Moscone Center manages to divert many of these materials away from landfill as part of its industry-leading recycling program, but Hennesey explains that it is not an easy process. "It entails coordination with a host of players, from show management to exposition service contractors and their labor, to individual exhibitors, attendees, and nonprofits, in addition to combating severe time and space limitations," she says. "Despite these challenges, the Moscone Center has made a long-standing commitment to sustainability and has been able to successfully implement many widely recognized environmental initiatives."

Hennesey firmly believes that sustainability is a team effort, and credits the Moscone Center's achievements to the dedication of staff and stakeholders. "Our success is due to the close collaboration of numerous players," she says, "including not only staff, but also show management, general and exhibitor-appointed contractors, attendees, exhibitors, the City and County of San Francisco, and a complicated multiemployer union labor workforce who have made these programs standard operating procedure."

Unite

Create a green team that includes staff, stakeholders, attendees, and other persons invested in the sustainability of your business. By bringing these groups together, you can form a comprehensive strategy for sustainability that touches each aspect of your meeting or event. Richard Aaron, president of BizBash Media (www.bizbash.com), has seen a tremendous growth in greener events, and believes that the most successful companies have a strong unifying plan. "Younger planners are adopting this issue as a serious platform in their event planning philosophy. Creating a company policy is number one."

> Sourcing local food and gathering sustainable resources are important, but creating a dialogue at the preevent planning meeting to suggest how to green the event process from the start is critical.
>
> —*Richard Aaron, BizBash Media, interview, October 2010*

Arlene Campbell is former chair of the Environmentally Responsible Exhibitions and Events Committee at the International Association of Exhibitions and Events (IAEE) (www.iaee.com). She believes that comprehensive sustainability programs begin in the boardroom and trickle down. In our August 2010 conversation, she said, "Interest in environmental trends comes from the strategic plan of the organization," she says. "Without support from the board, environmental policies for corporations and associations cannot be successful. The impetus for the board can be because of social responsibility or it can be business based, in that the client or attendee is demanding the environmental footprint be minimized."

Kevin Hacke says, "Business leaders are citizens of the world just like everyone else. We see waste and excess every day, and people do want to make a difference—regardless of how small—to do their share to be responsible citizens."

> I have never met a CEO who did not care about the public's perception of his or her company. From a personal, as well as corporate standpoint, sustainability is just a smart business strategy.
>
> —*Kevin Hacke, International Special Events Society (ISES), interview, October 2010*

Campbell believes that municipal and government stakeholders also have a critical role to play: "Events are great economic generators for cities and governments. One of the large environmental challenges for events is site selection. Cities and government need to invest in the required infrastructure to support environmental programs such as waste diversion, water conservation, or green energy programs."

Hacke has seen ISES members creating far-reaching change throughout the entire supply chain. "Many of our members are on the cutting edge of green event practices," he says, "and are requiring their business partners to assist them in implementing permanent changes in how events are planned, constructed and executed. This is not some passing fad—ISES members are implementing changes throughout the events they plan and produce that are permanent."

Campbell has also seen an increasing investment in sustainable practices at the supplier side to make these programs happen. "There is now a basic expectation of social responsibility at the supplier level and this translates into green practices now being accepted as part of the normal operating practice," she says. Richard Aaron has also seen vendors increasingly adopting sustainable policies, saying, "Suppliers are realizing that it can be a marketing advantage to have an ethically responsible platform."

Finally, attendees must be brought into the process, making it easy for them to participate in sustainability. Campbell said, "Awareness is key, whether it be choosing local foods for your menu selections, to green meeting space and hotel accommodation."

Understand what your attendee wants from an environmental perspective.
—*Arlene Campbell, Allstream Centre, interview, August 2010*

Meetings and events can be powerful forces for unity. Bring together your directors, government stakeholders, staff, suppliers, and attendees in order to create a stronger sustainability plan.

To Plant a Tree

Based in Austin, Texas, St. Edwards University (www.stedwards.edu) is an outstanding institution of higher education with a broad international outlook. When President George Martins and Thomas Evans, associate vice president for global initiatives, traveled to Jakarta, Indonesia, as part of the Institute of International Education (IIE) Presidential Delegation, Syarif Hidayatullah State Islamic University (UIN) held a tree-planting ceremony to commemorate the visit.

Evans was inspired by the sustainable aspect of planting a tree, rather than giving an award, as recognition: "We had a delegation from our partner university in Angers, France, coming the next week, and were so impressed by the ceremony that we called our marketing department following the event to ask them to create a similar one to commemorate our partnership."

Evans says that the trees planted in recognition of strategic partnerships symbolize the relationships that will grow stronger throughout the years. "Our ability and willingness to take care of the tree is symbolic of our desire to do the same with our partner institution," he says. "Also, we have specifically chosen not just any tree, but the oak tree. It is a strong tree and is adaptive to different environments—an oak can be found almost anywhere in the world."

Participants in a tree-planting ceremony are generally surprised and touched by the environmental honor. "Not only do they seem to like the symbolic elements," says Evans, "but they like the idea of something that can be visited each time they are on campus, to see the growth of something that is living and that needs nourishment—just like our partnership. Our partners ask about their trees frequently and fondly, and even want to water them sometimes!"

Consider planting a tree for your next honoree or important stakeholder. Living trees carry deep symbolic value, and show a true commitment to maintain a meaningful relationship. Honorees who have received other awards and trophies may be touched by the novelty of having a tree planted in their honor, and impressed by your commitment to permanently change your property's landscape.

Tell Your Story

"Environmental initiatives are another great example of how meetings can change the world," says Bruce MacMillan.

> The industry has experienced criticism during the economic downturn, and we've all become better at articulating the value of meetings. This is something MPI has been leading the industry in, alongside our other initiatives such as CSR. We have to articulate not just the return on investment of our meetings and events but also their environmental impact.
>
> —*Bruce MacMillan, Meeting Professionals International (MPI), interview,*
> *August 2010*

MPI launched a Sustainable Event Measurement Tool in July as a member benefit that addresses just this. "It's the only industry tool that goes beyond carbon calculation and gives a holistic view of an event's environmental and social impact," says MacMillan.

MacMillan says that consumer expectations have shifted toward sustainable commerce, CSR, and progressive thinking:

> With increasing interest and scrutiny on how organizations fulfill these commitments, companies realize that this commitment has to be evident in their meetings and events. There is increasing international and national regulation and focus on emissions, and many businesses are reporting on their operations."
>
> The meetings and conventions industry has a lot of potential, especially in terms of the way we're doing business with respect to social responsibility," says MacMillan. "And this is something many organizations that represent this industry have already implemented. Their commitment to social responsibility is portrayed in the increased number of greener meetings and events, for instance.
>
> —*Bruce MacMillan, Meeting Professionals International (MPI), interview,*
> *August 2010*

Arlene Campbell believes that self-regulation is the key to maintaining a healthy and vibrant meetings and event industry. "The power of the face to face interaction is what our industry is about," she says, "but meetings and events need to minimize their carbon footprints by taking proactive steps now."

> Write down your event's environmental strategy and then measure your success against that. Having a clear understanding of what you want to accomplish is the key to getting it done.
>
> —*Arlene Campbell, Allstream Centre, interview,*
> *August 2010*

Greener Event: Green Festival

Green Festival (www.greenfestivals.org) is America's premier conference and trade-show for the green economy. A joint project of Global Exchange and Green America, Green Festival annually travels to San Francisco, Seattle, Washington, DC, and Chicago to celebrate and promote these growing green economies.

When I phoned him in May 2010, Kevin Danaher, executive coproducer, told me that the timing was right for establishing a green economy tradeshow. "We did our first one in San Francisco and had about 13,000 people show up," he says. "It developed its own momentum. We're doing two a year now in San Francisco."

Because Green Festival attracts many environmental activists, it takes its greener event policies seriously. All Green Festivals are water-bottle-free events, with water jugs provided. All plates, silverware, and food accessories are 100 percent biodegradable and are composted. Event signs are designed with reuse in mind, and everything that can be recycled is recycled.

Green Festival even provides e-waste receptacles where attendees can deposit electronic devices to be recycled. "We subcontract e-waste in San Francisco to a company called Green Citizen," says Danaher, who explains that this company actually makes a good profit on their e-cycling business. "What people don't realize is that there's paladium, gold, and silver inside electronics. The main thing is making sure it doesn't get shipped to China."

Danaher believes that the phrase *zero waste* is misleading, because all events generate waste, although Green Festival has nearly reached this goal. "Zero waste is a goal you aim for, not necessarily an actual possibility," says Danaher. "At Green Festival, over 90 percent of waste gets diverted away from landfill into recycling and compost. We hit as high as 98 percent in San Francisco, and that's mostly with volunteer labor."

Results vary city to city. Similar to Meet Green's "Best Places to Meet Green" Guide, Green Festivals carefully chooses which cities to visit based on the maturity of the green movement in that area. Danaher notes that, while San Francisco, which has a strong environmental ethos, has a city waste diversion rate of 72 percent, Chicago's recycling division doesn't take all seven kinds of plastic, so Green Festival has to hire a private contractor to sort the remaining materials.

Danaher's biggest difficulty is getting large convention centers to understand the ethos and practices of Green Festival. He explains that Green Festival often has to pay a convention center a premium for them to close their food court, so that they can serve organic food. "You have to pay to make their hamburgers and hot dogs go away," he says, noting that he is reorganizing his venue contract in order to facilitate these discussions.

Staff engagement is just as important. "You want to do as much humble educating as possible with staff," says Danaher. "I find it useful to go out really early in the setup stage and talk to the union guys about who we are, and how we support union causes." This fosters a good working environment.

Attendees of Green Festival can expect a stalls from local green businesses, organic

(continued)

(continued)

foods, a kid's zone, a teen unity zone, yoga classes, as well as information on alternative energy, health and climate change. "We call it festival because we want it to be a fiesta, a party," says Danaher. "We look at the different roles anyone plays. You're a child of a parent, a parent of a child, a student, a worker, a consumer and a citizen. We try to be as comprehensive as possible. Nature's core principle is unity of diversity, and that's what we try to do."

Danaher hopes that Green Festival will teach others how to manage greener meetings and events. "We have specific conference themes of how to green an event," he says. "We don't approach this as a proprietary model. We want people to do green events. If we don't accelerate the transition to a green economy, our species is endangered. We want to proliferate the model."

A key element of the Green Festival waste minimization process is the Green Team, a group of volunteers who assist with the mammoth task of sorting waste streams. Danaher recalls two young people he met while sorting waste with the Green Team in Chicago a few years back. "It was midnight on Sunday," he says, "and we were breaking everything down and packing it up. The Green Team was out back, literally inside the big garbage containers, pulling out stuff that was contaminating the waste stream."

"We took a break and I started talking to two young Latino women, one a nurse, one a graduate student," Danaher remembers. "They had come all the way from California just to volunteer at the Chicago Green Festival sorting garbage. It turns out that they had volunteered sorting garbage at the San Francisco event and had had so much fun that they decided to travel to the Chicago event. I started to cry and had to turn away," he recalls. "I couldn't believe it."

It's that kind of change in people's lives that makes all the hard work worthwhile for Danaher. "That's where the rubber hits the road and where you start to feel the traction of a movement starting to build," he says.

Capstone Project

1. **For students, or those starting in the meetings and events industries**: Produce a greener meeting or event. Contact a local church, school, workplace, university, or community organization and ask if you can produce its next meeting or event. As part of the planning process, form a green team and create green strategies that address transportation, waste management, energy and water, cuisine and decor, venues, vendors, equality, and accessibility. Write a green mission statement, choose key performance indicators (KPIs) to measure and assess your risks. Create a marketing strategy and coordinate the meeting or event according to your plan. Afterward, measure your success based on the initial plans and create a report with suggestions for future improvements.

2. **For those already working in the meetings and events industries**: Gather a green team from staff and stakeholders and formulate a green mission statement

for your next meeting or event. Detail sustainable practices for transportation, waste management, energy and water, cuisine and decor, venues, vendors, equality and accessibility, and prioritize these strategies. Assess the risks and create SMART KPIs to measure the success of these strategies. Work to gradually and methodically introduce these strategies into your existing practice, beginning with simple strategies and graduating to more complex ones. Survey your attendees, staff, and stakeholders for feedback, and measure your success during the meeting or event. Create a report with suggestions for future improvements that will contribute to your company's sustainable triple bottom line.

APPENDICES

APPENDIX 1

References and Resources

Below is a list of all books, articles, speeches, websites, etc. that have been referenced in this work. Quotes used throughout from the 50 professionals are based on first-person interviews, which are referenced here first. This appendix also includes Further Resources, or extra sources of information that can be of great use to greener meeting and event pioneers.

■ Interviews

Aaron, Richard, interview by author, e-mail, October 2010.

Bauer, Carina, interview by author, phone, March 2010.

Brienza, Julianne, interview by author, Capital Fringe Festival, Washington, DC, July 2009.

Brock, Tom, interview by author, e-mail, October 2010.

Campbell, Arlene, interview by author, e-mail, August 2010.

Challis, Ben, interview by author, EventScotland, Edinburgh, UK, April 2009.

Danaher, Kevin, interview by author, phone, May 2010.

Dayboll, Sarah, interview by author, e-mail, September 2010.

Frankel, Joe, interview by author, phone, July 2010.

Garrett, Ian, interview by author, Radisson Hotel, Royal Mile, Edinburgh, UK, August 2009.

Graham, John, interview by author, e-mail, May 2010.

Grant, Matt, interview by author, phone, December 2008.

Griffin, Patricia, interview by author, e-mail, September 2010.

Guino-o, Reynaldo, interview by author, Edinburgh International Conference Centre, Edinburgh, UK, December 2010.

Hacke, Kevin, interview by author, e-mail, October 2010.

Hall, Jeff, interview by author, e-mail, August 2010.

Harry, Leigh, interview by author, e-mail, May 2010.

Henderson, Charles, interview by author, EventScotland, Edinburgh, UK, April 2009.

Hennesey, Kathleen, interview by author, e-mail, July 2010.

Heyning, Brent, interview by author, phone, October 2010.

Hill, Lori, interview by author, e-mail, March 2010.

Hudson, Dale, interview by author, phone, March 2010.

Jones, Terrence, interview by author, e-mail, July 2009.

Lewis, Kimberly, interview by author, phone, May 2010.

MacMillan, Bruce, interview by author, e-mail, August 2010.

Mainland, Kath, interview by author, EventScotland, Edinburgh, UK, April 2009.

McArthur, Eve, interview by author, Austin, TX, September 2009.

McArthur, Eve, interview by author, phone, May 2010.

McKinley, Shawna, interview by author, phone, May 2010.

Neff, Barbara, interview by author, Radisson Hotel, Royal Mile, Edinburgh UK, August 2009.

Randall, Richard, interview by author, e-mail, August 2010.

Raven, Bryan, interview by author, Fringe Central, Edinburgh, UK, August 2010.

Rawls, Thomas, interview by author, e-mail, September 2010.

Rush, Arlene, interview by author, e-mail, March 2010.

Salinger, Paul, interview by author, e-mail, May 2010.

Sexton, Deborah, interview by author, e-mail, July 2010.

Shea, Mike, interview by author, phone, May 2010.

Sirk, Martin, interview by author, e-mail, September 2010.

Speirs, Kathy, interview by author, phone, September 2010.

Supovitz, Frank, interview by author, e-mail, May 2010.

Vida, Nick, interview by author, e-mail, October 2010.

Williams, Andrew, interview by author, phone, May 2010.

Wright, Matthew, interview by author, The Big Tent Festival, Falkland Estate, Fife, UK, July 2010.

Zavada, Nancy (Wilson), interview by author, phone, May 2010.

■ References

Baragona, John (2007). *Event Solutions 2007 Annual Forecast: Forecasting the Events Industry.* Event Publishing LLC.

Barron, James (2008). "Coming Soon at Steinway, Solar Power." City Room, *The New York Times* (December 26). cityroom.blogs.nytimes.com [online] http://cityroom.blogs .nytimes.com/2008/12/26/steinway-by-barron-for-sat/?scp=11&sq=california%20 solar%20power%20fair&st=cse [Accessed February 2009].

"Best Green Companies" (2009). *The Sunday Times.* London, 2009. [online] Available from: http://business.timesonline.co.uk/tol/business/related_reports/best_green_ companies/tables/ [Accessed February 2011].

"Binge and Purge: Norway and the Environment." (2009) *The Economist* (January 22) [online]. Available from: http://www.economist.com/displaystory.cfm?story_id=12970769 [Accessed February 2009].

Bittman, Mark (2008). "Rethinking the Meat-Guzzler." *New York Times* (January 27). The World, Week in Review. [online] Available from: http://www.nytimes.com/2008/01/27/ weekinreview/27bittman.html?_r=1.

Bonini, Sheila, Stephan Görner, and Alissa Jones (2010). "How Companies Manage Sustainability: McKinsey Global Survey Results." *McKinsey Quarterly* (February). Available from: http://www.mckinseyquarterly.com [Accessed February 2011].

British Standards Institute (BSI) (2007). "BS 8901: Specification for a Sustainable Event Management System with Guidance for Use." *London: BSI British Standards* (November 30). Technical Committee SDS/1. pp. 1, 8–9, 10, 13, 19, 24.

BS 8901 "Case Studies: EC&O, Lord's Cricket Ground, Manchester International Festival, and Live Nation." [online] Available from: http://www.bsi-global.com/en/Standards-and-Publications/Industry-Sectors/Environment/BS-8901-case-studies/ [Accessed August 2009].

Columbus, Gene (2010). *The Complete Guide to Careers in Special Events.* Hoboken, NJ: John Wiley & Sons.

Crail, Bonnie (2009). "Something Green: A New Wedding Experience at the Ritz-Carlton, San Francisco." [online] Available from: http://corporate.ritzcarlton.com/en/Press/Properties/SanFrancisco/Releases/something_green_a_new_wedding_experience.htm.

Elkington, John (1998). *Cannibals with Forks: The Triple Bottom Line of the 21st Century Business.* Stony Creek, CT: New Society Publishers.

Fairtrade Foundation (2008). [online] Available from: http://www.fairtrade.org [Accessed December 2008].

Fennell, David A. (2007). *Ecotourism.* London: Routledge.

"Five Reasons to Choose Organic" (2011). UK Soil Association. [online] Available from: http://www.soilassociation.org/Whyorganic/Whatisorganic/Fivereasonstochooseorganic/tabid/334/Default.aspx [Accessed February 2011].

Friedman, Thomas (2008). *Hot, Flat, and Crowded.* London: Allen Lane.

Grant, John (2007). *The Green Marketing Manifesto.* London: John Wiley & Sons.

Green Events (2009). *Special Events.* [online] Available from: http://SpecialEvents.com/green_events [Accessed: January 2009].

Green Meeting Industry Council (2009). [online] Available from: http://www.GreenMeetings.info [Accessed: January 2009].

Green Music, Green Screen and Green Theatre (2009). Mayor of London. Available from: http://www.london.gov.uk (search: "green music," "green screen," "green theatre")

Hamilton, Craig M. (2009). *The Global Economy, Ecology and Interactions with the Environment in Quintana Roo and the Sian Ka'an Biosphere Reserve, Mexico.* Edinburgh Napier University.

Hayes, Nicole (2009). "NBTA Enhances CSR Toolkit with Emerging Concepts, New Look." [online] Available from: http://www.hospitalitynet.org/news/4042980.search?query=green+globe+nbta+environment.

Jones, Meegan (2009). *Sustainable Event Management.* London: EarthScan.

Keep America Beautiful (2010). [online] Available from: http://www.kab.org [Accessed February 2011].

Kotler, Dr. Philip (2011). "Dr. Philip Kotler Answers Your Questions on Marketing." [online] Available from: http://www.kotlermarketing.com/phil_questions.shtml [Accessed February 2011].

Kyriakidis, Alex (2010). *Hospitality 2015: Game Changers or Spectators?* London: Deloitte. Available from: http://www.deloitte.co.uk/hospitality2015 [Accessed February 2011] (p. 3).

Live Earth (2009). [online] Available from: http://www.LiveEarth.org [Accessed January 2009].

Live Earth (2009). *Green Event Guidelines.* [online] Available from: http://liveearth.org/docs/greenguidelines.pdf [Accessed February 2011].

London 2012 Inspire Programme (2011). [online] Available from: http://www.london2012.com/get-involved/inspire-programme/index.php [Accessed February 2011].

Manfredi, Katherine (2010). "Clean the World." *one+* (January). [online] Available from: http://www.mpiweb.org/Magazine/Archive/US/January2010/CleanTheWorld.aspx [Accessed June 2010].

Markham, Adam (1994). *A Brief History of Pollution.* Earthscan.

Mark Lynas, (2007). *Carbon Calculator.* London: Collins.

Meeting Professionals International. *2008 Corporate Social Responsibility Survey Summary.* 2008. Available from: http://www.mpiweb.org.

Meeting Professionals International. *EventView 2009 North America.* MPI, Event Marketing Institute and George P. Johnson. Available from: http://www.mpifoundation.org.

Monck, Geoff. *A Greener Festival.* Available from: http://www.agreenerfestival.com.

Natural Resources Defense Council (2008). [online]. Accessed August 2010. Available from: http://www.nrdc.org/water/drinking/qbw.asp.

Oceana North America (http://www.na.oceana.org).

Salt River Project (2008). "Super Bowl XLII in Glendale gets clean, green energy from SRP." [online] Available from: http://www.srpnet.com/environment/earthwise/greensuperbowl.aspx [Accessed February 2011].

San Francisco Bay Area State of the Urban Forest Final Report (2007). Center for Urban Forest Research (December) (www.fs.fed.us/psw/programs/cufr/).

Tarlow, Peter (2002). *Event Risk Management and Safety.* Hoboken, NJ: John Wiley & Sons.

UK Soil Association (http://www.soilassociation.org).

United Nations (1987). *Report of the World Commission on Environment and Development: Our Common Future.* UN Documents Cooperation Circle. NGO Committee on Education [online] (March 20). Available from: http://www.un-documents.net/wced-ocf.htm [Accessed February 2009].

U.S. Department of Agriculture (1990). *Organic Foods Production Act.* Title 7, Part 205, Code of Federal Regulations. Available from: http://www.ams.usda.gov/AMSv1.0/nop.

U.S. Department of Labor (2011). "Green to Gold" [online] Available from: http://www.dol.gov/dol/green/greengoldsafe.htm [Accessed February 2011].

U.S. Environmental Protection Agency (2009). "Green Meetings." [online] Available from: http://www.epa.gov/oppt/greenmeetings [Accessed: January 2009].

U.S. Green Building Council (2008). "A Grand Slam for Washington, DC: Nationals Stadium Earns LEED Silver Rating." Projects and Case Studies. [online] Available from: http://www.usgbc.org/ShowFile.aspx?DocumentID=5108 [Accessed February 2011].

The White House Office of the First Lady (2009). Discussion with The First Lady, Social Secretary Desiree Rogers, Executive Chef Chris Comerford, Pastry Chef Bill Yosses, and students from L'Academie De Cuisine (February 22). Available from: http://www.whitehouse.gov/the_press_office/Discussion-with-the-First-Lady-Desiree-Rogers-Cris-Comerford-Bill-Yosses-and-Students-from-Lacademie-de-Cuisine/ .

Widdicombe (2008). "Born Green." The New Yorker (May 19), p. 31.

World Health Organization (http://www.euro.who.int/noise).

■ Further Resources

Americans with Disabilities Act Business Guide (http://www.ada.gov/business).

"ASAE Global Principles for Socially Responsible Associations & Nonprofits" (http://www .asaecenter.org/Forms/SocialResponsibilityPrinciples).

"Best Places to MeetGreen" (http://www.bestplacestomeetgreen.com).

Eat the Seasons (http://www.eattheseasons.com): seasonal food encyclopedia.

Fish Online (http://www.fishonline.org): guide to sustainable seafood.

Goldblatt, Joe (2010). *Special Events: A New Generation and the Next Frontier.* Hoboken, NJ: John Wiley & Sons.

National Recycling Coalition (http://www.nrc-recycle.org).

Natural Resources Defense Council (http://www.nrdc.org).

Special Events magazine: Greener Events (http://specialevents.com/green_events).

The Theatres Trust Carbon Calculator (http://www.theatrestrust.org.uk/events/ green-theatre) (UK).

Treehugger (http://www.treehugger.com): green lifestyle and consumer guide.

UK Soil Association (http://www.soilassociation.org).

U.S. Department of Agriculture (http://www.usda.gov).

U.S. Department of Energy. Renewable Energy Supplier Directory (http://apps3.eere .energy.gov/greenpower/buying/buying_power.shtml).

U.S. Department of Energy. Database of State Initiatives for Renewables & Efficiency (DSIRE) (http://www.dsireusa.org).

U.S. Department of Energy. Building Technologies Program (http://www1.eere.energy .gov/buildings).

U.S. Department of Energy. Energy Savers (http://www.energysavers.gov): guide to energy efficiency

U.S. Department of Energy. Energy Star (http://www.energystar.gov): energy efficiency certification.

U.S. Department of Labor, Green to Gold (http://www.dol.gov/dol/green/greengoldsafe.htm).

U.S. Environmental Protection Agency, National Drinking Water Database (http://www .ewg.org/tap-water/welcome).

U.S. Environmental Protection Agency. Guide to biofuels (http://www.epa.gov/otaq/fuels.htm).

U.S. Environmental Protection Agency. Guide to e-cycling (http://www.epa.gov/osw/ conserve/materials/ecycling).

U.S. Environmental Protection Agency. Guide to greener meetings and events (http:// www.epa.gov/oppt/greenmeetings/).

U.S. Environmental Protection Agency. Guide to safe drinking water (http://www.epa .gov/safewater), or 1-800-426-4791.

U.S. Environmental Protection Agency. "Green Vehicle Guide" (http://www.epa.gov/ greenvehicles).

U.S. Environmental Protection Agency. "Landfill Methane Outreach Program" (http://www .epa.gov/lmop).

U.S. Environmental Protection Agency. "Managing Wet Weather with Green Infrastructure" (http://cfpub.epa.gov/npdes/greeninfrastructure/technology.cfm).

U.S. Environmental Protection Agency. "Water Sense" (http://www.epa.gov/owm/ water-efficiency).

Model Greener Events, Venues, Organizations, and Associations

This book is inspired by the outstanding work of those leaders at the forefront of the green meeting and event industries. These leaders include the professionals working within specific greener events, sustainable venues, pioneering organizations, and responsible associations that are putting sustainable practices forward. Here is a list of these model greener events, venues, organizations, and associations.

■ Model Greener Events

All Points West (www.apwfestival.com): Coachella's sister-festival in New York

Austin Marathon (www.youraustinmarathon.com)

The Big Tent (www.bigtentfestival.co.uk): environmental arts and music festival in Scotland

Capital Fringe Festival (www.capitalfringe.org): Washington, DC's wild and crazy festival of the performing arts

Coachella Music Festival (www.coachella.com): pop music festival in California desert

Edinburgh Festival Fringe (www.edfringe.com): world's largest performing arts festival in Scotland

Edinburgh International Book Festival (EIBF) (www.edbookfest.org.uk): UK book festival with extensive environmental plan

Fuji Rock Festival (www.smash-uk.com): Japanese music festival

IMEX (www.imex-frankfurt.com): international convention for meeting and incentive travel industries

Glastonbury (www.glastonburyfestivals.co.uk): famous UK music festival

GreenBuild (www.greenbuildexpo.org): annual conference for the U.S. Green Building Council (USGBC) (www.usgbc.org)

Green Festival (www.greenfestival.com): green economy convention

Live Earth (liveearth.org): major music events for environmental causes

London 2012 Olympic and Paralympic Games (www.london2012.com)

Manchester International Festival (MIF) (www.mif.co.uk): BS 8901-certified UK arts festival of new work

Peats Ridge Sustainable Arts and Music Festival (www.peatsridgefestival.com.au): Australian environmental festival

Roskilde (www.roskilde-festival.dk): Danish music festival

Sailfest (sailfest.org): summertime public festival in New London, Connecticut

Solar Power International (SPI) (www.solarpowerinternational.com): major convention

South by Southwest (SXSW) (www.sxsw.com): music, film and interactive festival and convention

Sundance Film Festival (festival.sundance.org): premiere showcase for independent films

Super Bowl (www.superbowl.com): America's favorite sporting event

■ Model Greener Venues

Allstream Centre (allstreamcentre.com)

Arcola Theatre (www.arcolatheatre.com)

Colorado Convention Center (www.denverconvention.com)

Edinburgh International Conference Centre (www.eicc.co.uk)

Greenspun Hall at the University of Nevada, Las Vegas (urbanaffairs.unlv.edu/about/greenspun-hall.html)

The John Hope Gateway, Royal Botanic Garden Edinburgh (www.rbge.org.uk)

National Theatre (www.nationaltheatre.org.uk) (London, UK)

Melbourne Convention and Exhibition Centre (www.mcec.com.au)

Messe Frankfurt (www.messefrankfurt.com)

Moscone Center (www.moscone.com)

Portland Center Stage (PCS) (www.pcs.org)

The Premises (www.premisesstudios.com)

Scottish Seabird Centre (www.seabird.org)

Wolf Trap (www.wolftrap.org): America's National Park for the Arts

■ Model Greener Organizations

A Greener Festival (www.agreenerfestival.com): UK advocates for environmentalism at festivals

Arcola Energy (www.arcolaenergy.com) The Center for Sustainable Practice in the Arts (CSPA) (www.sustainablepractice.org): advocates for and consultants to sustainability in the visual and performing arts, as well as news source for environmental art

Broadway Green Alliance (www.broadwaygreen.com)

Climate Futures (www.climatefutures.co.uk)

Doubletree Hotels (www.doubletree.com)

EventScotland (www.eventscotland.org)

Fairmont Hotels (www.fairmont.com)

Green Globe Productions (www.greenglobeproductions.net)

International Centre for the Study of Planned Events (www.qmu.ac.uk/be/research/ICSPE)

Julie's Bicycle (www.juliesbicycle.com)

Lori Hill Event Productions (lorihillevents.com)

MeetGreen (www.meetgreen.com): industry-leading producers of sustainable meetings

National Football League (NFL) (www.nfl.com)

NVA (www.nva.org.uk)

Oracle (www.oracle.com): international company that has incorporated sustainability planning for all meetings and events

Savor . . . San Francisco (www.cateringbysmg.com): sustainable catering for the Moscone Center

Seventeen Events (www.seventeenevents.co.uk): leading London producers of stylish, sustainable events

■ Model Greener Associations

American Hotel and Lodging Association (AH&LA) (www.ahla.com)

American Society of Association Executives (ASAE) (www.asae.org): promoting CSR for association meetings and conventions

Convention Industry Council (www.conventionindustry.org)

Convene Green Alliance (www.convenegreen.com)

Fairtrade Foundation (www.fairtrade.org)

Forest Stewardship Council (FSC) (www.fsc.org)

"Green" Hotels Association® (www.greenhotels.com)

Green Keys (www.greenkeyglobal.com)

Green Leaf Program (greenleaf.auduboninternational.org): from Audubon International

Green Meetings Industry Council (www.greenmeetings.info)

International Association of Exhibitions and Events (IAEE) (www.iaee.com)

International Congress and Convention Association (ICCA) (www.iccaworld.com)

International Festivals and Events Association (www.ifea.com)

International Special Events Society (ISES) (www.ises.com)

Meeting Professionals International (MPI) (www.mpiweb.org)

Professional Convention Management Association (PCMA) (www.pcma.org)

Sustainable Catering Association (www.sustainablecateringassociation.org)

APPENDIX 3

Greener Supplier Directory

More and more sustainable goods and services are available to meeting and event professionals every day. In addition to sourcing products with ethical, social, and environmental responsibility, remember to shop locally as often as possible. Work with small local suppliers to help them go green and provide superior products. The following is not a list of preferred traders, but rather, represents those green businesses that have arisen through research. Want to be featured in the Greener Supplier Directory? E-mail GreenerEvent@ Gmail.com.

◼ Arts and Entertainment

The Center for Sustainable Practice in the Arts (www.sustainablepractice.org)
Crimson Collective (www.crimsonsociety.org/crimsoncollective.html)
EcoSpeakers (www.ecospeakers.com)
Guerilla Cinema (www.spanthatworld.com/guerilla-cinema)
Reverend Billy and the Church of Life After Shopping (www.revbilly.com)
Sustainable Dance Club (www.sustainabledanceclub.com)
Sustainable Living Roadshow (www.sustainablelivingroadshow.org)

◼ Carbon Calculators

Doubletree Portland (www.doubletreegreen.com/calculator/)
Meet Green Calculator (calculator.meetgreen.com)
MPI (mpi.sustainableeventtool.com)
U.S. Environmental Protection Agency (EPA) (www.epa.gov/climatechange/emissions/ind_calculator.html)

◼ Carbon Offsetting

Carbonfund.org (http://www.carbonfund.org)
The Carbon Neutral Company (http://www.carbonneutral.com)
Choose Renewables (http://www.chooserenewables.com)
Climate Care (http://www.jpmorganclimatecare.com)
Earth Era (http://www.earthera.com)
*Native*Energy (http://www.nativeenergy.com)
TerraPass (http://www.terrapass.com)

■ Catering

Affairs to Remember (www.affairs.com)
Back to Earth Organic Catering (www.organiccatering.com/)
Black Isle Brewery (www.blackislebrewery.com)
Brita Water Filter (www.brita.com)
Cairn O'Mohr Fruit Wines (cairnomohr.homestead.com)
Culinary Capers (www.culinarycapers.com/)
Fancy Girl Catering (www.fancygirlcatering.com/)
Green Planet Catering (www.greenplanetcatering.com)
The Green Table (www.thegreentable.net/)
Kate Dwyer Catering (www.katedwyer.com)
Prestige Scotland (www.prestigescotland.co.uk)
Trojan UV Water Filter (www.trojanuv.com)
Vegware (www.vegware.com): compostable, bioplastic food packaging and accessories
Windows Catering Company (www.catering.com)

■ Energy

Aerostar Wind Turbines (www.aerostarwind.com): wind
Bergey Windpower (www.bergey.com)
Canyon Hydro (www.canyonhydro.com)
Current Cost (www.currentcost.com): energy metering
Firefly Solar (www.fireflysolar.co.uk): solar
Focus Solar (www.focussolar.de) (Germany)
Magnificent Revolution (www.magnificentrevolution.org): pedal power
Mobile Solar Power (www.mobilesolarpower.net)
People Powered Machines (www.peoplepoweredmachines.com): human power
Solar Home (www.solarhome.com)
SolarPump (www.soldesignlab.com)
Solio (www.solio.com): handheld generators
Utility Free (www.utilityfree.com): hydropower
Vegawatt (www.vegawatt.com): generator which recovers waste vegetable oil
Windstream Power (www.windstreampower.com)
Wholesale Solar (www.wholesalesolar.com)

■ Decor and Linens

Caterers Linen Supply (www.catererslinen.co.uk)
Ecoparti (www.ecoparti.com): confetti
Gossypium (www.gossypium.co.uk)
Laundry Environmental Stewardship Program (www.laundryesp.com)
White Bio Dove (www.joylantern.com/pshow.asp?ps_id=6): balloons

■ Furniture

Design Public (www.designpublic.com/shop/sustainable-design)
Knú (www.getknu.com/)
Plushpod Eco Friendly Furniture (www.plushpod.com/catalog/Eco_Friendly-84-1.html)
Steelcase (store.steelcase.com)
VivaTerra (www.vivaterra.com)

■ Giveaways and Prizes

Rivanna Natural Designs (www.rivannadesigns.com): awards
Simon Lee Guitars (www.simonleeguitars.com): guitars made from recycled plastics
Saffron Winds (www.saffronwinds.com): bags made from used mosquito netting
Green Toys (www.greentoys.com): toys made from recycled plastic milk jugs
Green Guru (www.greengurugear.com)
TerraCycle (www.terracycle.net)

■ Maintenance

BioBag (www.biobagusa.com): bioplastic bags
Ecolab (www.ecolab.com): maintenance solutions
Ecover (www.ecover.com): cleaning products

■ Office Products

Biobadge (www.biobadge.com): name badges, mugs, golf tees, luggage tags and pens
Ecocard (www.eco-card.co.uk): business cards
Eco Green Office (www.ecogreenoffice.com)
Green Promotions (www.greenpromotionsltd.com): conference supplies
Pilot b2p (www.pilot-b2p.com): pens made from recycled water bottles
Remarkable (www.remarkable.co.uk/): pencils and office supplies
Weisenbach Recycled Products (www.recycledproducts.com): pens, bags, and many other accessories made from recycled materials

■ Reused Materials

16th Century Salvage Yard (www.reclaimedbuildingmaterial.com)
Artefacts (artefacts.ca)
Building Materials Reuse Association (www.bmra.org)
Community Forklift (www.communityforklift.com)
The Door Store (thedoorstore.ca)
Earthwise Architectural Salvage (earthwise-salvage.com)
The Freecycle Network (www.freecycle.org)
The RE Store (www.re-store.org)

The ReUse Center (www.thereusecenter.com)
The ReUse People (thereusepeople.org)
Second Use (www.seconduse.com)

■ Sound, Lighting, and Technical Production

Access Lighting (www.accesslighting.com)
Philips Color Kinetics (www.colorkinetics.com)
Philips Lumileds LED Lighting (www.philipslumileds.com)
White Light (www.whitelight.ltd.uk) (UK)

■ Technology

GoTo Meeting (www.gotomeeting.com)
Skype (www.skype.com)
TelePresence by Cisco (www.cisco.com)

■ Tents and Outdoors

Ascot Structures Bamboo Tents (www.bambootents.com)
ShadePlex (www.shadeplex.com)
Smart Solar (www.smartsolar.com)

■ Transportation

Main Street Pedicabs (www.pedicab.com)
Manhattan Rickshaw Company (www.manhattanrickshaw.com)
Pedal Bike Tours (www.pedalbiketours.com)
Revolution Rickshaws (www.revolutionrickshaws.com)

■ Waste Management

Bokashi Composting Australia (www.bokashi.com.au)
Boodi (www.boodi.co.uk)
Envirolet (www.envirolet.com)
M.J.Church (www.event-waste-management.com)
Mobiles2Recycle (www.mobiles2recycle.com)
Natural Event (www.naturalevent.com.au)
NatureMill (www.naturemill.com)
Recology (www.recology.com)

APPENDIX 4

Sustainable Menu

This *sustainable menu*, featuring delicious ingredients that are local, ethical, natural, and seasonal, is provided by Jeff Hall, executive chef of Savor . . . San Francisco at The Moscone Center. When he showed me this menu in August 2010, Hall explained: "Toy box tomatoes are small, assorted sizes and come in a variety of colors. Chicken under a brick is an Italian technique of cooking a chicken. We employ that technique to cook the chicken quickly, evenly brown and to give a better plate presentation."

■ **Buffet Menu for a Charity Event for 500**

Season: Summer
Location: San Francisco

Summer Squash Carpaccio, Arugula, Fiscalini Farms Cheese, Pine Nut Vinaigrette

Heirloom Melon and Anise Hyssop with California Olive Oil and Crisp Prosciutto

Warm Grilled Bread Salad, Heirloom Tomatoes, Basil, and Cucumber

Boneless Free Range Chicken "Under a Brick," Lemon and Herbs

Brentwood Corn with Toy Box Tomatoes and Spicy Peppers

Sustainably Harvested Black Cod, Yellow Pepper-Rhubarb Agrodolce, Chive Oil

Charred Meyers Ranch Strip Loin, Porcini Jus, Summer Savory, Fried Onions

Creamy Polenta with Rosemary and Crescenza Cheese

Grilled Peaches with Mint Syrup, Pistachios

Buttermilk Panna Cotta, Strawberry Marmalade, Almond Tuille

APPENDIX 5

Greener Artist Rider

Many artists have ethical considerations and would prefer to perform at events that are environmentally and socially responsible. Artists can share their ethics with the events that host them by submitting a Greener Artist Rider, an attachment to their contract that outlines sustainable event practices that are either required or suggested. Ben Challis, founder of A Greener Festival (http://www.agreenerfestival.com) and lawyer for UK music festival Glastonbury (http://www.glastonburyfestivals.co.uk), has seen both major and minor artists help events go greener. Below is his Greener Artist Rider.

■ Sustainability

It is a fundamental term of this Agreement that the Promoter of the event or events to which this contract rider applies (the "Event") has considered the environmental impact of the event and taken all steps reasonably practicable to reduce greenhouse gas emissions from the Event. Without limitation to the generality of the foregoing, the Artist will only perform at event(s) that comply with the following conditions 1 to 7 inclusive. The Artist reserves the right to withdraw from the Event without notice and/or cancel any performance without any liability on our part whatsoever where the following conditions are not met.

1. The Promoter shall ensure that it has a policy and implemented strategy in place for the Event to minimize greenhouse gas emissions and waste in its office. This would include a "turn off and save policy," the use of so-called green energy, paper recycling, and promoting public transport. The Artist agrees to accept evidence of compliance with the Julie's Bicycle Benchmark standards on Offices as compliance with this condition.
2. The Promoter shall ensure that it has a policy and implemented strategy in place for the Event to minimize greenhouse gas emissions from the Event. The Artist agrees to accept evidence of compliance with either the Julie's Bicycle benchmark standards on Venues or the Julie's Bicycle benchmark standards on Outdoor Events as compliance with this condition.
3. The Promoter must have in place a coherent transport and/or traffic policy which *as a minimum* must promote all public transport routes and services to the Event and the Promoter will ensure that members of the public are properly made aware of all modes of public transport available to them to attend the Event. As a minimum, the Promoter must provide a public facing website setting out public

transport services and details of public transport options should be featured in all paid advertising connected to the Event.

4. The Promoter must ensure that the venue hosting the Event has a bona fide strategy and implemented system for recycling paper and glass and where appropriate plastics, metals, and food. The use of disposable plastic containers for either food or drink is not acceptable to the Artist. All and any food and drinks served should be served in either reusable containers or in paper/card receptacles that can be recycled. All cutlery and utensils provided to the public must be recyclable or biodegradable.

5. The Promoter must ensure that recycling points are provided at the venue hosting the Event and where practicable these should be provided for different waste streams allowing for separate recycling (glass, paper, plastic, cans and metals, foodstuff). All goods left to be recycled must be in arranged with a recognized recycling organization. In the United Kingdom, local authorities would be considered a recognized recycling organization.

6. We reserve the right in our absolute discretion to approve any carbon neutral scheme or similar carbon offsetting scheme that might be connected to or offered with the Event. Any such scheme MUST be provided by a registered charity or a not-for-profit organization. A carbon neutral scheme may *not* be provided by a commercial company or entity or by a for-profit organization. Please notify us at least ten days in advance of the first performance date of any carbon neutral scheme you might wish to be associated with for our approval.

7. The waste of water should be minimized wherever practicable. The Promoter must himself or must ensure that any venue hosting the Event encourages visitors to minimize water wastage. Promoters must ensure all caterers, bars, and traders use only eco-friendly cleaning products.

■ Our Ethical Policy

The Artist tries to maintain an ethical stance, and there are certain industries (along with companies and organizations servicing those industries) we will not deal with. We will not deal with those involved the production, sale, or distribution of arms and ammunition. We will not deal with those who are involved in the exploitation of nonsustainable resources in forestry and in the agricultural, mining, and fuel industries. We will not deal with those who exploit the individual and/or who do not respect those basic human rights enshrined in the European Convention for Human Rights. It is a fundamental term of this Agreement that we will **not** appear under any banners, posters, logos, or advertising, or appear at any event sponsored, endorsed or supported by any company or organization that does not comply with our ethical policy.

■ Our Aspirations

We support fair trade and an environmentally efficient approach. Let's all try and make poverty history.

For practical advice and tips, see www.juliesbicycle.com and www.agreenerfestival.com.

INDEX